TRACING YOUR
LIVERPOOL
ANCESTORS

FAMILY HISTORY FROM PEN & SWORD

Tracing Your Yorkshire Ancestors
Rachel Bellerby

Tracing Your Royal Marine Ancestors
Richard Brooks and Matthew Little

Tracing Your Pauper Ancestors
Robert Burlison

Tracing Your Army Ancestors
Simon Fowler

A Guide to Military History on the Internet
Simon Fowler

Tracing Your Northern Ancestors
Keith Gregson

Your Irish Ancestors
Ian Maxwell

Tracing Your Air Force Ancestors
Phil Tomaselli

Tracing Your Secret Service Ancestors
Phil Tomaselli

Tracing Your Police Ancestors
Stephen Wade

Tracing Your Jewish Ancestors
Rosemary Wenzerul

Fishing and Fishermen
Martin Wilcox

TRACING YOUR LIVERPOOL ANCESTORS

A Guide for Family Historians

M i k e   R o y d e n

Pen & Sword
FAMILY HISTORY

First published in Great Britain in 2010 by
PEN & SWORD FAMILY HISTORY
an imprint of
Pen & Sword Books Ltd
47 Church Street
Barnsley
South Yorkshire
S70 2AS

ISBN 978 1 84415 990 1

A CIP catalogue record for this book is
available from the British Library.

Typeset in Palatino and Optima by
Phoenix Typesetting, Auldgirth, Dumfriesshire

Printed and bound in England by
CPI UK

Pen & Sword Books Ltd incorporates the Imprints of
Pen & Sword Aviation, Pen & Sword Maritime, Pen & Sword Military,
Wharncliffe Local History, Pen & Sword Select, Pen & Sword Military
Classics and Leo Cooper.

For a complete list of Pen & Sword titles please contact
PEN & SWORD BOOKS LIMITED
47 Church Street, Barnsley, South Yorkshire, S70 2AS, England
E-mail: enquiries@pen-and-sword.co.uk
Website: www.pen-and-sword.co.uk

CONTENTS

Dedication
For Lewis and Liam

ACKNOWLEDGEMENTS

I have been fortunate to have been educated and encouraged by many well-known historians and archaeologists at work in the Liverpool area. Paul Booth and Dr Jenny Kermode of the University of Liverpool gave me much encouragement, both before and during my degree. Paul also invited me to lecture in Continuing Education at the University of Liverpool, which began my career in teaching. Dr Dorothy O'Hanlon, both as a friend in the Merseyside Archaeological Society, and as my tutor in teacher training, was a great influence (did you know her father placed Hess under citizen's arrest when he landed on his Scottish farm in 1941? . . . now there's a story I never tire of hearing). Dr Janet Hollinshead, Dr O'Hanlon's colleague at St Katherine's College, Liverpool Institute of Higher Education (now Hope University) gave me much guidance on local history research. Dr Rob Philpott and Ron Cowell, Field Archaeologists in National Museums on Merseyside, have given me a great deal of help in discussing research, attending excavations and guidance regarding document research. I thank them all.

Many thanks to the staff of Liverpool Record Office, past and present, who have helped me over the years, especially Roger Hull, who continues to guide the occasional enquiry my way, including the one he received regarding this volume, and Kay Parrott, who was always very patient and helpful and is now enjoying life carrying out her own writing and publishing.

Thanks to staff at Merseyside Maritime Museum Library and Cheshire Record Office.

Thanks to members of the various local and family history societies who have helped with my research over the years, and have given me regular invitations to lecture at their meetings.

Grateful thanks also to students of my university Continuing Education classes, many of whom contributed to the student articles on my local history pages website. Many are still active, producing their own publications on Port Cities, street names and underground Liverpool, and have helped in the reopening of Williamson Tunnels. Others went on to form the successful Liverpool History Society.

Special thanks are due to Harold and Joyce Culling, founder members of Liverpool & SW Lancs Family History Society back in May 1976, who have continued to hold office to the present day. They gave me help and guidance on numerous occasions and it was a pleasure, at their invitation, to give the opening lecture at the Society's 20th Annual Conference at Liverpool Cathedral in 2008.

Thanks also to my mother, Hazel Royden, a silver surfer and still a world traveller in her late seventies, who has been a great source of oral history.

Finally, thanks to my teenage sons Lewis and Liam, who kept me supplied with cups of tea, occasionally cooked the dinner, and designed and built the garden during our house move. It has been a busy year. Right, let's go sailing.

INTRODUCTION

'I am the English sea-queen; I am she
Who made the English wealthy by the sea
The street of this my city is the tide
Where the world's ships, that bring my glory, ride'
A Masque of Liverpool (1930) by John Masefield

It is always something intriguing that first ignites your interest – reading about an ancestor or relative in a newspaper, your surname appearing on a passenger list for the *Titanic*, watching a celebrity have their tree traced for them on television. In my case it was quite ordinary. As a child I wanted to know why there was a Royden Street in the Dingle in Liverpool, an area where generations of my father's family had lived. It was, and still is, a rare name, so surely there was a connection? And so it proved. After a period of research I discovered it was named after Sir Thomas Bland Royden, a local shipbuilder, MP for West Toxteth and Mayor of Liverpool in 1878. And we were related. However, even before that research had been forced upon me when, as a fourteen-year-old in the Third Year (Year 9 in new money) I was given History homework: 'trace your family tree for next lesson'. That was in 1970 – and it must be the longest homework assignment on record. I am still working on it.

In those days of course there was no internet, so trips to record offices were frequent. Even the Liverpool Family History Society, which has given help and guidance to many thousands of researchers since the mid-1970s, did not exist back then. Occasional trips to London were necessary, to visit the Public Record Office (PRO), or St Katherine's House to consult the Birth, Marriages and Deaths indexes in order to obtain the corresponding certificates. And now all this is available with a few mouse clicks. Nevertheless, knowing how to carry out your research is still just as important and before you start it is essential to be aware of the most commonly used sources. The good news is that a great deal is now on the internet and much more will be there in the future, and although I sometimes complain about the cost of documents online or paying to gain access to certain archive pages, it is still much cheaper than travel and accommodation. I do still think, however, that it is more fun to go into a record office and consult the original archives when possible.

There have been many publications of a specialist nature about the history of Liverpool and booklets about where to find particular records, but none to combine the two and provide a handbook for family and local historians. I hope this work will fill that gap and you will find it useful.

Section One

WORK AND ECONOMY

Chapter One

THE RISE OF THE PORT

The early port – the fishing village

When looking at the quaintly peaceful illustrations of the Pool, where water gently lapped around sailing ships tied up below the castle, it is hard to imagine that this seventeenth-century sheltered fishing hamlet would become one of the greatest ports in the world. It just needed a kick start to get it going.

There had been little growth in the town from the time of the borough foundation down to the mid-seventeenth century. Liverpool, like its surrounding townships, was too dependant on agriculture and its products for its livelihood, though there was always fishing and some maritime trade. The same seven streets continued to appear in the taxation lists and, even as late as 1660, there were only around 190 houses covering these main routes. Throughout much of the fifteenth and sixteenth centuries Liverpool was in a state of economic hardship, even decay. The population was ravaged by disease in the 1540s and 1550s, and a storm did serious damage to the haven in 1561. By 1571 Rauff Sekerston MP petitioned Elizabeth from the 'decayed town of Liverpoole', stating:

> Liverpole is your owne towne. Your majestie hath a castell and two chauntries . . . the fee fermes of the towne, the ferrie boot, twoe wynd-mylnes, the custome of the duchie, the new custome off tonnage and pondage which was never paid in Liverpole before your tyme, you have a gud haven, and all the hole towne and the comoditie thereoff is your majesties. For your own sake suffre us not utterlie to be caste awaye in your graces tyme but relief us like a mother.
> (*Liverpool Town Books* Vol.1, fol.157r, Liverpool Record Office)

Little help was forthcoming and Elizabeth continued to refuse a new charter. Yet towards the end of the century she did grant letters of marque and privateering statutes to Liverpool sailors which, despite being licensed piracy, brought a great improvement to the local economy. A key

An impression of Liverpool in the 1680s by Herdman, showing the Tower, the third Customs House and the Castle.

development came in 1647 when Liverpool was made a free and independent port, no longer subject to the Port of Chester.

Rapid expansion was encouraged and in the 1660s and 1670s the principal landowners laid out several new streets, including Lord Street, Moor Street, Fenwick Street, Red Cross Street and St James's Street. The town's growing status was reflected in many of the new buildings constructed during the period, such as the Town Hall (1673–4), Bluecoat School (1721), the Custom House (1721), St Peter's (1704) and St George's Church (1734). Such growth was matched by the sweeping away of many of the buildings that had served the town since the medieval period, notably the Castle, the Crosse Hall, the Townsend Mill and the old Tithebarn. The ancient chapel of St Mary del Quay lasted until 1814 and the Tower of Liverpool was demolished four years later.

The old Pool, which had acted as a magnet to King John's advisors, the early settlers, and generations of merchants and seafarers (not forgetting a mythical bird), was being reclaimed by the end of the seventeenth century, although not totally, as it would provide the site for the town's first wet dock, designed by Thomas Steers, which opened in 1715. The Pool, now known as the 'Common Sewer', had become an eyesore. It was in need of dredging to make it fully navigable and was probably empty at low water. A programme of draining and dumping of earth and rubbish was mounted to create valuable building land on the site.

The opportunity to develop the area had been hastened in 1671 when the Corporation secured rights to the foreshore of the Pool and other privileges from the Lord of the Borough, Lord Molyneux. In return, he was granted freedom to build a bridge across the Pool from Liverpool Heath to his new street in Castle Hey ('Lord' Street).

Industry

Industry in Liverpool was relatively minor until the late seventeenth century. Various medieval and post-medieval documents mention brewers, goldsmiths, weavers and smiths, but these were mainly essential crafts to support the local community, as was milling, probably the largest of the industries. A respectable trade in pottery manufactured from local clays continued throughout the post-medieval period. Certain industries expanded as a result of growing trading links with Ireland and the colonies, from which the latter led to the establishment of a sugar refinery in Tarleton's Field in around 1670. By the eighteenth century glass manufacture, iron-working, clock-making and rope manufacture were all well established industries. In the registers of St Nicholas, twelve watchmakers are recorded in Liverpool in the 1670s, the first clear evidence that watch cases and springs were being made in the town.

In the rural townships, as in the town, most industries were those which were necessary to the economy and support of the township alone and were almost exclusively agriculturally related. In fact, many of these activities were secondary occupations to supplement farmers' incomes, especially through the winter. Farm buildings generally encompassed other outbuildings necessary for the additional trades, such as tanning, milling, iron-working or brewing, but later many farmsteads became more specialised, such as Tanhouse Farm and Court House Brewery in Halewood. Most townships had their own quarries, but again this was to satisfy a localised demand, as was the extraction of clay for brick-making. The materials for the eighteenth-century brick-built farms were often locally fired, and the sites of this are often betrayed by field names such as 'Kiln Croft' on nineteenth-century tithe maps.

Watch-making had spread to several townships during the seventeenth century, but these were often outworkers supplying tools and parts to the centre of the industry in Liverpool and Prescot. One of the earliest watchmakers in Britain was a 'Mr Aspinwell', who was described as 'an ingenious workman'. He was most likely Thomas Aspinwall, one of the new Puritan settlers in Toxteth Park, who died in 1624. There are other references to watchmakers in Aigburth, Halewood, Childwall, Huyton and West Derby. During the early 1980s a workshop was discovered in Paradise Row in Gateacre during renovations. The cottage is of late seventeenth or early eighteenth-century construction. Documentary research has revealed the names of at least a dozen inhabitants of Much and Little Woolton involved in the watch-making business between 1694 and 1851.

During the medieval and post-medieval period there was a thriving fishing industry in the waterside coves and inlets of the Mersey. In the late seventeenth century, the fisheries had become so extensive that they had become a hindrance to navigation. In 1697 Thomas Patten of Warrington, wishing to make the Mersey navigable to Manchester, believed the river to be over-fished and proposed to suppress the offenders. He wrote to Richard Norris of Speke Hall to complain about the fisheries between his land and Garston Dale:

> You very well know the mischiefs that are done in the River Mercy, or at least have frequently heard what vast numbers of salmon trouts are taken, so as to supply all the country and market townes for twenty miles around; and when the country is cloyed, or when they cannot get sale for them, they give them to their swine. Your brother did formerly take three or four salmon a week at a fishing, in or near Speke; but of late hath taken very few or none, of which he hath complained to me, and he imputes this loss to the destruction of the fry.

How difficult today to imagine that there were once so many salmon at Garston that they were fed to pigs.

Salt Trade – 'the Nursing Mother'

The discovery of rock salt in William Marbury's Cheshire estate in 1670 was to be the catalyst for the development and improvement in communications from the Cheshire salt fields and the Lancashire coalfields to the River Mersey and Liverpool. The Liverpool hinterland was opened up and the rise of the port swiftly followed. Salt has always been a necessity of life, not only for seasoning, but also as a preservative for meat and fish. As the population increased, the growing demand for the commodity made its preparation on a large scale essential. A few miles upstream on the Mersey, near the small hamlets of Oglet and Speke, a small refinery was constructed at Dungeon, where the remains of a small harbour can still be clearly seen. A few cottages lined Dungeon Lane, which housed the salt workers, with two Customs and Excise cottages (still standing) close by. The economic importance of salt had quickly been recognised by Liverpool merchants. According to the Liverpool antiquarian John Holt: 'The Salt Trade is generally acknowledged to have been the Nursing Mother and to have contributed more to the first rise, gradual increase, and present flourishing state of the Town of Liverpool, than any other article of commerce'.

Before this discovery of rock salt, brine had to be purified on site, but it was now a simple matter to transport the raw material to more economically sited factories where it could be refined. Three refineries sprouted on or near the Mersey: at Frodsham Bridge (1690–4), Liverpool (1696) and Dungeon (1697), all attempting to benefit from a closer proximity to the Lancashire coalfields.

Regular supplies of both salt and coal to the refineries continued to be problematic, and this was the motivation for developing the lines of communication into the salt fields of Cheshire and the coalfields of south-west Lancashire. In 1694 an Act of Parliament was passed to make the

River Mersey navigable to Warrington, while the Weaver Navigation, constructed to bypass the River Weaver where it proved un-navigable, was completed in 1733. By the early 1700s salt had become the major export product of the port of Liverpool. It was, for example, an essential commodity of the Newfoundland cod fisheries, from where the salted fish was taken to the West Indies and sold or exchanged for sugar, coffee or fruit. In the coastal trade it was of great importance: it was taken to Cornwall, from where in return came china clay for the pottery industries of Staffordshire and Liverpool. It was also necessary in other Liverpool industries such as metal and glass-working, where it was used as a flux, and later it became integral to the basic growth of the local chemical industry, as an ingredient in the manufacture of soda. By the 1750s, the Weaver Navigation supply route into the salt fields was complemented by a similar operation to that of the Lancashire coalfields with the opening of the Sankey Brook Canal. Much of the support had come from the merchants and industrialists of Liverpool and the proprietors of the salt works of Northwich and Winsford. The chief agitators from Liverpool were John Blackburne, owner of the Liverpool Salthouse Dock refinery, and John Ashton, now the owner of Dungeon. Ashton, in fact, provided just under half of the capital, owning 51 of the 120 shares in the Navigation, and the completion of the project was mainly down to him. The canal opened in November 1757 and its effect on the production of salt was quite remarkable: 14,000 tons in 1752 had become 40,000 by 1783, 100,000 by 1796 and 186,000 in 1820.

When the Dungeon works was inherited by Nicholas Ashton after the death of John Ashton in August 1759, he was quick to secure a regular and economic supply of coal by leasing coalmines at Parr, near St Helens. In fact, by the early 1830s every coal proprietor in and around St Helens owned salt-works in Cheshire. In 1772 Ashton purchased Woolton Hall, having previously resided at Hanover Street (where he was a neighbour of

The harbour wall at Dungeon.

John Blackburne) and Clayton Square in Liverpool. Ashton was still only 30 years old and had already held the office of High Sheriff of Lancashire. However, although the refinery was again passed down from father to son it was no longer a going concern by the mid-1800s, and may not have been able to compete any longer with Blackburne's refinery.

The salt trade is frequently ignored when assessing the factors that contributed to the rapid expansion of the port, yet this was a sizeable trade and quickly gave Liverpool a boost to surge past the declining port of Chester. It provided a solid infrastructure to be exploited by those who were to follow.

Further research

Ascott, Diana E., Fiona Lewis and Michael Power, *Liverpool, 1660–1750: People, Prosperity and Power* (Liverpool University Press, 2006). This is a modern and significant detailed study of the social and political structure of the town during this crucial period, using parish registers, probate material and town government records to consider the characteristics of a fast-growing and mobile population, the occupational structure, family lives and connections of workers in the town, and the political structures and struggles of the period.

The Liverpool area was the most important watch-making area in the world in the late eighteenth and early nineteenth centuries – local research and an exhibition can be found at the Prescot Museum (www.knowsley.gov.uk/leisure/museum). A local school website is also useful: www.watchmakinginvictorianprescot.co.uk. Prescot Museum has also published research in **Moore, Dennis**, *British Clockmakers and Watchmakers Apprentice Records 1710-1810*.

A good starting point for looking at the salt and coal trade would be **Barker, T.C.** *Lancashire Coal, Cheshire Salt and the Rise of Liverpool*, THSLC, Vol.103, 1951, while the question of salt and the rise of Liverpool, with emphasis on the role played by the Dungeon works, can be found within Mike Royden's Local History Pages at www.roydenhistory.co.uk. Further afield is the Salt Museum in Northwich (www.saltmuseum.org.uk).

The Slave Trade

By the end of the eighteenth century Liverpool had become a port of international renown, built largely on the profits of the slave trade and ranked after London as Britain's second port. A hundred years earlier the town's position had been rather different. The port of Liverpool at this time was only just rising to greater prominence than ever before and the new wet dock provided the impetus for spirited enterprise in a fast-growing mercantile area. The building of more docks soon followed, and, together

Burdett's View of the Custom House taken from Trafford's Wyent, *1770. There were several versions of this engraving and this is a later, sanitised, version. See the extract from an earlier copy on page 21 showing what is thought to be the earliest view of two black men (probably sailors) in Liverpool. They are missing from the above version.*

with the buoying of the channel approaches, new roads to Prescot and Warrington and the first canal in England (the Sankey Canal, which linked the Mersey to the coalfields of St Helens), Liverpool was elevated to its new status.

In the town, Church Street and Ranelagh Street were now well built up. Fine houses stood in both Duke Street and Hanover Street, and Mount Pleasant was lined with houses with large gardens. To the north building had extended as far as the new canal basin, with a much larger mass of housing in the south. However, overcrowding was already becoming a problem. The 1700 population of 5,000 had increased to 25,000 by 1760.

Part of the increase was due to the rise of new industries. Ship-building yards lined the north and south shore and rope yards were numerous, as were windmills. The watch-making industry was enjoying a good reputation, while the local potteries were still at their height. One of the main pottery-making areas was Shaws Brow, later renamed William Brown Street. Improved communications to the salt fields of Cheshire were well established, and the refineries, with their ancillary industries, provided further employment for the local inhabitants.

The overriding factor affecting the increase in population was the growth in worldwide trade. In 1700 there were around 70 port-owned vessels employing about 800 seamen. By 1751 these figures had increased to 220 vessels and 3,319 seamen. Trade was quite diverse in character. The bulk of the Irish trade now moved through Liverpool, due initially to the silting up of the Dee (although packet boats still sailed to Ireland from Parkgate), and now that Scotland and Wales were also commercially dependent on Liverpool the town was established as Britain's central port. Liverpool was even beginning to compete with Hull for the Baltic trade.

It was trade with the New World that brought most prosperity to the expanding port, although trade with the Americas was still fairly small-scale. For Liverpool, the West Indies were far more important. Not only did they supply the main staples of Liverpool trade (sugar, tobacco and cotton), but they were also the centre of the lucrative smuggling trade with Spanish Central and South America. At the beginning of the eighteenth century Bristol had the greatest share of this traffic, but by the middle of the century Liverpool was well to the fore, bringing in an annual profit of around £250,000. Growing industrialization in Manchester played a signif-icant role too, providing merchants with commodities that were much in demand in Africa, such as coarse woollens and cottons, thus giving the mills greater commercial incentives.

The first British slave-trading expedition was that of Sir John Hawkins in 1562. He sailed for Hispaniola with 300 Africans, returning with pearls, hides, sugar and ginger and a handsome profit. His later journeys were funded by Queen Elizabeth. Over the next two centuries trading continued on a sporadic basis as the Americas were colonized, but it was not until the late eighteenth century that Britain could make the shameful claim of being the leading slave-trading nation in the world. The story of this increase is mainly the story of the rise of Liverpool. Once the monopoly of the London-based Royal African Company was quashed in 1698, the trade was opened up to any Englishman who could comply with the new duty regu-lations of 10 per cent on all goods apart from gold, silver and slaves, imported in or out of Africa. The first recorded sailing of a Liverpool vessel took place two years later when the *Liverpool Merchant* transported 220 slaves from Africa to Barbados in September 1700. A month later the *Blessing* entered the triangular trade – a now infamous itinerary clearly reflected in the orders to her captain:

> Make the best of your way to the coast of Guinea... where dispose of what the cargo is most proper, and purchase what slaves you can... When you have disposed of your cargo and slaved your ship, make the best of your way to the West Indies. If you find the markets reasonably good, sell there; if dull, go down leeward to such island as you shall see convenient, where dispose of your Negroes to our best advantage, and with the produce load your ship with sugar cottons and ginger.

A second voyage was made by the *Blessing* in 1701 and again in 1703, when she was joined by the *Rebecca*.

As trade increased, so did the associated businesses inextricably linked to the expanding market. Chandlers, grocers, rope-makers, carpenters, joiners, ironmongers, painters, riggers, plumbers, gunsmiths, sail-makers, drapers, tool-makers, carters and so on supplied the growth in the markets and benefitted likewise. Between 1788 and 1793 it is known that 98 per cent of slaving vessels using the port were locally owned, and by the turn of the century there were over one hundred Liverpool vessels involved in the slave trade on a regular basis. The leading slavers were far from social outcasts – most came from the more affluent and powerful sections of society, and many held high office, such as councillors, bailiffs, MPs and mayors of the town. In fact all twenty mayors from 1787 to 1807 were involved in the trade. This elite often kept a tight grip on the trade by co-operation in planned expeditions. Their names regularly appear in the founding of institutions such the Bluecoat School, Heywoods Bank and Martins Bank, and are frequently remembered in local street names. This is an anathema to many, but thoroughfares such as Penny Lane have become a part of the character of the town as names, rather than because of their mostly forgotten connotations. For those wishing to read more about this, Steven Horton's *Street Names of the City of Liverpool* is recommended.

Prior to the 1780s, Liverpool merchants felt little need to justify their involvement in such lucrative trade. Yet by this time opposition was increasing and pressure was even coming from some quarters within the town. Although culturally and artistically Liverpool was still what Ramsay Muir termed a 'Philistine town', the period saw increased attempts by enthusiastic, intelligent men to improve the conditions of all members of society. Most of the credit for this can undoubtedly be centred on the radical Liberal factions who, with their frequently unpopular politics, tended to be looked upon with scorn and suspicion by fellow citizens. Vigorous advocates of political and social reform, their opposition to the slave trade, on which the port's wealth and prosperity was largely based, frequently earned a hostile reception from the mercantile ranks.

Among these reformers were such notable local men as William Rathbone (the fourth, 1758–1809), James Currie (a Scottish doctor, bi-ographer of Burns, author of several political pamphlets and the man largely responsible for the efficient administration of the Poor Law), Doctor Traill (a founder of the Royal Institution), the Reverend William Shepherd (Unitarian minister of Renshaw Street), and a man who is frequently alluded to as being one of Liverpool's greatest citizens, William Roscoe.

Born in 1753, Roscoe was the son of an innkeeper of Mount Pleasant and was articled to a Liverpool solicitor in 1769. A man of high intellect and wide reputation, he was nationally famous for his poetry and verses set to music. At the age of only 19, several years before the abolition move-ment commenced, he dared to publish his views in verse. Later, in 1787, once the movement had been established, he produced a long work enti-tled the *Wrongs of Africa*, following it up a year later with *A General View of the African Slave Traffic*. Throughout his life he was to continue this approach and he frequently spoke out about the injustices and corruption that he saw around him, especially those in his home town. In a similar literary exposé, Roscoe was supported by a friend, Edward Rushton, a blind poet and former sailor on slave ships who spoke from personal experience. He wrote his *West Indian Eclogues* in 1787, which although not regarded as great poetry, certainly drove home his hatred of oppression and love of liberty.

Public opinion regarding the slave trade began to change in England around this time, especially after the abolition movement had been established in London. Naturally, there was little turnaround in Liverpool, where the movement was received with much hostility. The Corporation even went to the trouble of paying a Jesuit, Reverend Raymond Harris, £100 for his pamphlet, which confirmed the scriptural approval of the slave trade, assuring 'its conformity with the principles of natural and revealed religion delineated in the sacred writings of the Word of God'.

Harris's work did not go unanswered in Liverpool, as a direct attack came from the Reverend Henry Dannett, incumbent of St John's, who published a reply in 1788 entitled *A Particular Examination of Mr. Harris's Scriptural Researches on the Licitness of the Slave Trade.*

Although there were only two Liverpool members of the London-based abolition movement, William Rathbone and Doctor Jonathan Binns, there were other sympathisers living in the town who did not wish to openly declare their beliefs for fear of reprisals. Most of these men were already friends and associates and had come together in the various societies formed in the previous two decades.

Societies engaged in various collective pursuits were being formed in late eighteenth-century Liverpool and were frequently political in nature. The Conversation Club had been formed as early as 1768, meeting at George's Coffee House, and debated such radical topics as voting by ballot. However, it was the French Revolution and the subsequent suppressive policy of Pitt's government that was to arouse the most widespread debating in Liverpool. Societies were formed with both conservative and radical foundations. In support of the government, for example, were the Association for King and Constitution, which met at the Buck and Vine in Hackins Hey, and the Friends to the King and Constitution, which met at the Eagle and Child in Redcross Street. Far more formidable was the fellowship formed by Dr James Currie and William Roscoe in 1795, the Debating Society, which met weekly in the Long Room, Marble Street, attracting large audiences. Inevitably, it was forced to dissolve itself in 1797, due to its contravention of the Seditious Meetings Act of December 1795.

A variety of letters and pamphlets appeared from both sides, with the trade's defenders frequently claiming slavery was the natural order of things and that the African was well treated on his Atlantic passage. More outlandish were the claims that his newly acquired benefits in the New World far outweighed the 'backward existence' he had endured in his homeland. Further justification was found in the upholding of economic advantages that were being derived by the Empire; to see slavery abolished would be the ruin of all.

Here lay the key to the dogged perseverance of these Liverpool men, desperate to hold on to all vestiges of trading rights that had brought them such abundant prosperity. Liverpool politicians petitioned London again and again in defence of the trade between 1788 and 1807, a total of sixty-four times, during a period when the government was being flooded with contrary petitions from towns all over the country. Not one petition in opposition came from Liverpool.

After the abolition of 1807, many who would be affected by the revision in the law in Liverpool found such a restriction to their livelihood hard to swallow. General Banastre Tarleton, for example, who had long supported the trade, promised in the elections held in the town after the abolition that he would restore the trade if elected. It may astonish us now, but this was still a town where he could send out two black boys on the campaign trail carrying a banner 'The African Trade Restored' as he continued under his slogan 'The Church and the Slave Trade for Ever!'. At least such action was condemned in the local press, however.

After the abolition there were no riots and no attacks, but there was a dip in tonnage clearing the port in the first year. However, many vessels carried on the trade illegally, although even this petered out by the 1820s. Most operators had realised the abolition was inevitable and had begun to reassign vessels to other routes and trades from the 1790s. Consequently, the port did not go into decline as most had expected. Nevertheless, alternative profits were found in the refitting of slavers from elsewhere, notably Portugal, while all manner of slave-trading goods, such as fetters and manacles, continued to be crafted in Liverpool and shipped to the Americas well into the mid-century.

Relatively few Africans made it as far as Liverpool during the period of the slave trade, but this has done nothing to dispel the frequently quoted urban myth that they were kept captive in the cellars beneath the buildings along the Goree and Strand while awaiting transhipment. To add credence the 'original shackles' can still be seen. This, however, is not true. The few Africans who were brought to Liverpool came as domestic servants, as it was considered fashionable among the upper classes to have a black servant. Some did come as seamen – records in the Maritime Museum (the Davenport Collection) feature wage books listing Africans as crew members. According to the Museum the 'shackles', which do exist in several waterfront cellars, are actually simple metal rings. The quickest and easiest way to lower cask goods into a shallow basement was by the technique known as 'parbuckling'. Two ropes secured to rings in the basement wall are passed over the top of the cask, which is then rolled down the wall under control by a man on each of the ropes. When you consider the variety of goods that used to be packed in casks you can understand why there were lots of these 'slave rings' in Liverpool cellars.

Further Research

Due to the inconsistent record keeping during the eighteenth and nineteenth centuries, tracing black ancestors can be a daunting business. The standard of literacy in the records can also hamper progress. Nevertheless, core resources such as census, slave registers and other specialized records do exist and are increasingly appearing online. The advent of the internet has arguably benefitted this field of family history research more than any other, due to the dispersal of descendants and the inaccessibility of records.

As with any family research, the start point has to be with immediate relatives to discover anything that is known about movements, family documents, names, places – keep notes of anything that could be relevant. It is always advisable not to discard anything – it could prove to be valuable in later research. Secondly, carry out a search of UK records, to obtain birth, marriage or death certificates and census records for any relatives living in the UK prior to 1901. If relatives came to Britain after 1901, UK immigration records are available at the National Archives in London. These records include information such as name and age, last address in their home country, occupation, and also the names of other family members with whom they may have been travelling. Thirdly, when there is a firm idea of where a particular ancestor came from, local records in that particular area can then be concentrated on. These may indicate when they came to that area, if they were slaves and possibly a date of freedom. It must be remembered that surnames did not always correspond to the owner's surname. Also, use occupation and address, age and birthplace (if listed) in searches.

Searches of post-1834 records, if they are available, should also be undertaken, including censuses, parish records and birth, marriage and death records. If the slave owner can be discovered it is clearly worth searching their records too, as slaves were property bought and sold and may appear as such in their records.

Comprehensive lists of additional sources are now being carried by websites such as Ancestry (www.ancestry.co.uk/slavery), which also offers DNA testing as a way to make links with relatives around the world. Of course, this may not provide answers to a myriad of questions about ancestry, but it may provide some satisfaction where records simply do not exist. For example, Arifa Akbar reported in *The Independent* about Beaula McCalla, a youth worker from Bristol, who travelled to the island of Bioko, in Equatorial Guinea, after scientists traced her ancestry through her maternal DNA. There Ms McCalla, whose parents were born in Jamaica, met her distant relative Beatriz, from the indigenous Bubi tribe. After a two-day trek across the island to meet more relatives, she was given African names by her family and underwent a ritual to mark womanhood. Beaula said she always had a yearning to discover her lineage: 'My eyes were flooded with tears and my heart was pounding as the plane descended. I remember seeing the Atlantic. I have memories of the Atlantic as somewhere my ancestors were lying at the bottom of,' she said. On meeting Beatriz, she said: 'I felt like a daughter returning. It was like blood touching blood.' The reaction of Beatriz to the meeting was one of excitement, and relief at what Ms McCalla might be able to offer. 'Maybe she can help me,' she said. Ms McCalla was content to return to Britain. But she felt the experience helped her reconcile her British nationality with her ancestral past. 'If I know where my home is, I can go back whenever . . . I don't need to shout from the rooftops that I am an African woman. I know and that's enough,' she said. (*The Independent*, Wednesday 5 February 2003).

DNA evidence does bring to light another unsavoury aspect of slavery. Dr Peter Forster, a geneticist from the University of East Anglia, has declared that it is very common to find genetic material characteristic of white Europeans in samples provided by black British people. All the evidence shows that this is the result of white slave owners having sexual relations with their female black slaves. 'I'd say that for every Afro-Caribbean living in the UK, there's a 25 per cent chance that their Y (male) chromosome DNA will have come from a slave owner,' he says. Such an emotional discovery was made in front of millions by TV Chef Ainsley Harriott in the BBC's *Who Do You Think You Are?* series, where he discovered not one, but two white ancestors with direct involvement in the plantations and the abuse of slave girls.

Further Reading

The manner in which Liverpool's involvement in the slave trade has been written about by Liverpool historians over the last 150 years has been inconsistent to say the least. This was clearly epitomized in Chandler's City Council sponsored *Liverpool*, published in 1957 to celebrate the 750th anniversary of the borough. The trade merited two paragraphs within its 450 pages. The old adage of 'history being written from a perspective of the present' has to be borne in mind and applied time and again.

In recent years there have been attempts to come to terms with the past across the cultural spectrum, plus an 'official apology' along the way from Liverpool City Council in 1999. From the historian's point of view there have been many useful works over the last 30 years. **Anstey, P. and Hair, P.E.H.** 'Liverpool, the African Slave Trade and Abolition', *Historical Society of Lancashire and Cheshire*, 1976, arguably kicked off a fresh approach with a pioneering volume of essays collected to illustrate the latest research by the mid-1970s. The volume sparked some controversy, especially over the question of the profits made from slave trading. Many of the papers have stood the test of time, however, and the volume was reprinted with additional material in 1989. A short but useful historiography of writings by Liverpool historians is contained in **Cameron, G. and Cooke, S.** *Liverpool – Capital of the Slave Trade*, Picton Press, 1992. A conference held at the Maritime Museum in 2005 produced a new volume of essays reflecting the current state of research in the field, updating the Anstey and Hair collection for a new generation. See **Richardson, D., Schwarz, S. and Tibbles, A. (Eds)**, *Liverpool and Transatlantic Slavery*, 2007. A detailed analysis of Liverpool's role in the trade can also be found in **Howley, Frank**, *Slavers, Traders and Privateers: Liverpool, the African Trade and Revolution, 1773–1808*, Countyvise, Birkenhead, 2008. The recent volume *Liverpool 800* has sections devoted to the history of the trade and the role of the port, while the Maritime Archives and Library, Merseyside Maritime Museum, has a list of books and articles held in its own collections on slavery and the slave trade, and an information guide.

Liverpool History

Sanderson, F.E. 'Liverpool and the slave trade: A guide to sources', *Transactions of the Historic Society of Lancashire and Cheshire 124*, 1972, pp.154–76.

'Dicky Sam', *Liverpool and slavery: An historical account of the Liverpool-African slave trade*, Liverpool, 1884.

Williams, Gomer, *History of the Liverpool privateers and letters of marque: With an account of the Liverpool slave trade, 1744–1812*, 1897, reprinted by Liverpool University Press, 2004. Gomer Williams worked as a journalist for the *Liverpool Mercury* and drew on newspapers, private correspondence and first-hand accounts of the slave trade to produce this work in 1897. At that time he lamented the fact that Africans were still being threatened by the commercial interests of Europeans. By 1783 London, Bristol and Liverpool accounted for over sixty per cent of privateering commissions. This book is still considered to be the best source of information on privateering from Liverpool or any other port. The appendix lists all the Liverpool vessels bound for Africa from the beginning of the trade until abolition.

Mackenzie-Grieve, Averil *The last years of the English slave trade: Liverpool 1750–1807*, London, 1941. This brings together extensive eighteenth and early nineteenth-century writing in an eccentric style.

Parkinson, C.N. *The rise of the port of Liverpool*, Liverpool, 1952.

Costello, Ray, *Black Liverpool – The early history of Britain's oldest black community 1730–1918*, Picton Press, 2001.

Schwarz, Suzanne *Slave captain: The career of James Irving in the Liverpool slave trade*, Wrexham, 1995, revised edition Liverpool, 2007. Edited journal and letters with introduction and notes.

Tibbles, A. (Ed.) *Transatlantic slavery: Against human dignity*, 2nd edition, Liverpool, 2005. Reprint of essays collected at the opening of the gallery in 1994, with two additional commentaries on museums and remembrance. Includes several short papers on Liverpool's role in the slave trade.

Howley, Frank, *Slavers, Traders and Privateers: Liverpool, the African Trade and Revolution, 1773–1808*, Countyvise, Birkenhead, 2008.

Tracing Ancestors

Blockson, Charles L. and Fry, R., *Black Genealogy*, Black Classic, 1991.
Grannum, Guy *Tracing your West Indian Ancestors*, Public Record Office, 2002.
Kershaw, Roger and Pearsall, Mark *Immigrants and Aliens: a guide to sources on UK immigration and citizenship*, Public Record Office, 2000.
Porter, S.D. (compiler), *Jamaican records: a two part guide to genealogical and historical research using repositories in Jamaica and England*, Stephen D. Porter Publications, 1999.
Crooks, Paul, *A Tree Without Roots: The Guide to Tracing African, Anglo and Asian Caribbean Ancestry*, Blackamber, 2008.
O'Sullivan-Sirjue, Jennifer and Patsy Robinson, *Researching Your Jamaican Family*, Arawak Publications, 2007.

On the net

There is now a plethora of information on the web, but the researcher would do well to start at the enlightening International Slavery Museum. The Museum explores both the historical and contemporary aspects of slavery, addressing the many legacies of the slave trade and telling stories of bravery and rebellion among the enslaved people. These are stories which have been largely untold. For further information about the slave trade and Liverpool's involvement see the International Slavery Museum website at www.liverpoolmuseums.org.uk/ism.

AfriGeneas: www.afrigeneas.com

A site devoted to African American genealogy, to researching African ancestry in the Americas in particular and to genealogical research and resources in general.

BBC History Abolition of the Slave Trade: www.bbc.co.uk/abolition

Includes references to individuals involved in the fight against the slave trade and information on people who have researched their own family history back to slavery (e.g. local author Victor Okrafo-Smart).

Caribbean Roots: Caribbean ancestry and heritage
www.caribbeanroots.co.uk

Caribbean Roots was launched in 2007 to encourage and promote research into Caribbean genealogy, identity and heritage. Its aim is to signpost resources and to inform visitors about new events, books, websites and software to help with research.

Every Generation: www.everygeneration.co.uk

An online resource for the Black community in the UK, designed: 'to facilitate the personal development and empowerment of young people and to bridge the gap with the older generation through history, family genealogy and heritage'. Useful family history and genealogy pages.

Tracing Ancestors in Barbados: www.barbadosancestors.com

Website based on the book *Tracing Ancestors in Barbados: A Practical Guide* by Geraldine Lane, with additional links and useful advice.

Moving Here: www.movinghere.org.uk

Moving Here explores, records and illustrates why people came to Britain over the last 200 years and what their experiences were and continue to be. It offers free access to an online catalogue of versions of original material related to migration history from local, regional and national archives, libraries and museums.

Paul Crooks: www.netcomuk.co.uk/~prcrooks/index.html

A website devoted to the story of Paul Crooks's own experiences tracing his family from Africa to the Caribbean and Britain.

Slave Database of Mauritius: http://vcampus.uom.ac.mu/slavemap

Produced by the Nelson Mandela Centre for African Culture's Family History Unit, this is a database containing the names of all Mauritian slaves freed in 1835. It is part of an ongoing project listing all people included on the Slave Registers held by the National Archives in London.

Events

Slavery Remembrance Day: www.liverpoolmuseums.org.uk/ism/srd.

A commemoration and celebration of the end of slavery, held in Liverpool on 23 August each year.

Liverpool Black History Month Group: www.liverpoolblackhistory.co.uk

Events and activities in Liverpool for Black History Month, held every October in Britain.

Africa Oyé: www.africaoye.com.
The UK's largest free African music festival, held in Liverpool each June.

Abolition 200: www.abolition200.org.uk/index.html.
The bicentenary of the abolition of slavery in 2007.

Freedom Schooner Amistad: *www.amistadamerica.org.*
A re-creation of the famous slave ship which visited Liverpool from 20 to 26 August 2007 as part of a transatlantic voyage retracing the slave triangle.

This shows what is thought to be the earliest view of two black men (probably sailors) in Liverpool. They are missing from the version shown on page 11.

Chapter Two

SHIPBUILDING

During the era of the sailing ship, the River Mersey had an active shipbuilding industry along the shoreline. Building wooden ships was the job of skilled craftsmen, usually working in small yards with minimal capital and equipment. With the transition to iron and then steel, the trade began to shift its centre to the north-east of England and the Clyde. Liverpool shipbuilding also faced a local threat from the early nineteenth century onward with the expansion of the commercial dock system. This use of the waterfront was much more lucrative, and successive port

Launch of steamships at the yard of Jones, Quiggin, half a mile south of the Albert Dock. (from the Illustrated London News, *1865)*

authorities pushed the town's shipbuilders out to the edges of the dock system, kept them on short leases, and eventually removed them from the Liverpool waterfront altogether.

During the eighteenth century, Liverpool was not only rising to prominence as a commercial port, but also as a centre for shipbuilding. One of the earliest men to become involved in the industry was John Okill (1687–1773). Little is known about his early life, although by the time he had reached fifty he was a successful timber merchant as well as a shipbuilder, and was also a leading citizen of the town. His yard was on the south side of the Salthouse Dock and, in partnership with William Marsh, he built many coasting brigantines and sloops. His reputation travelled so far that he was commissioned by the Royal Navy to construct the first naval vessel to be built on the Mersey in 1739. This was the *Hastings*, a ship of 44 guns weighing 682 tons. He would build another eight ships for the navy between 1740 and 1758. Meanwhile, Okill became a member of the Company of Merchants trading to Africa. Yet his own company was the only firm to take no part in the slave traffic, instead trading in ivory. In 1773 he started work on a mansion house in Woolton called Lee Hall. He did not live to see it finished as he died later that same year, with work on the building completed by his heir and nephew, James Okill. James and his inheritors, the Dutton family, helped to plan and lay out what would become Gateacre. The Okills are also remembered in local street names, such as those in Halewood. (John Okill's commercial Day Book for 1752–1753, listing the daily transactions relating to his shipbuilding business, can be found in Liverpool Record Office).

Most of the shipbuilding yards were situated along the foreshore to the south of the town in rather cramped conditions. Although the yards were paying dues to the Town Council, they were taking up space that many thought could be better utilised within the dock expansion programme. As a consequence, leases tended to be short, offering little stability in security of tenure. High rents were the norm given the geographical position, and shipbuilders were moved about without compensation. When the shipyard sites they occupied were finally required for dock extension, the tenants were turned out without compunction by the Town Council, often resulting in the closure of businesses.

Before the construction of the Albert Dock, opened in 1846, there were shipyards on the site, west of the Salthouse Dock (Trentham Street). Some of the yards had at one time been occupied by shipbuilders in the eighteenth century. After these sites were requisitioned for the purpose of building the Albert Dock, the Shipbuilders' Association drew the attention of the Dock Trustees to the 'inconveniences, restrictions and disadvantages' under which the trade laboured. They asked for more space, lower rates and long leases. They also urged that private graving docks be attached to the shipyards.

In 1850 the shipyards on the Liverpool side of the Mersey were situated to the west of Queen's Dock (Baffin Street), southwards to Aetna Street and

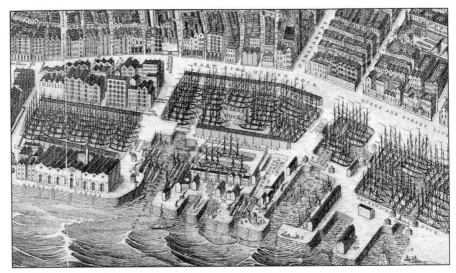

Detail from Ackermann's View of Liverpool from the South West, 1847, featuring the Baffin Street shipyard and slipways of Thomas Royden (centre foreground).

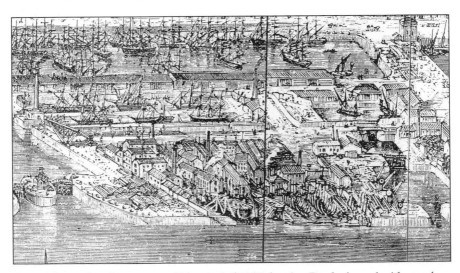

Extract from a broad panorama of Liverpool of 1865 showing Royden's yard with vessel under construction.

The 304-ton Ranger *built by Royden's yard for Lawrence Heyworth, Liverpool, in 1834.*

also to the west of the Brunswick Graving Docks and southwards to the Brunswick half-tide dock. The four principal shipyards in the Baffin Street area were, from north to south, Thomas Royden, Joseph Steel & Co., T. & R. Clarke and P. Chaloner & Son. Clarkes' yard had no river frontage and had no alternative but to launch vessels into the nearby dock basin, creating difficulties and dangers for those concerned.

By the mid-nineteenth century there were fifty-five shipbuilders listed in the port. Only sixteen appeared to have the capacity to actually build ships, while ten were 'boat-builders' and the rest ship repairers. In 1849 only six of the sixteen yards built ships. Ocean-going cargo vessels numbered five, one a sail pilot cutter, and six were paddle steamers.

Two of those vessels in that year originated from the yard of Thomas Royden and sons. As a youngster Thomas Royden had learned carpentry, working with his father back home in West Kirkby in the late 1700s, trying to bring in extra money with an additional trade to their farming liveli-hood, as was common at that time. However, attracted by opportunities for young craftsmen in the expanding port of Liverpool, he crossed the Mersey in 1808. After completing his apprenticeship in the local shipyards, he opened his own yard (initially in partnership) in 1818. Rising on the social ladder, he married the daughter of the head of an established and respected shipbuilding family and entered politics, while systematically purchasing parcels of land formerly farmed by his family in Frankby and West Kirby. When his estate was complete he erected Frankby Hall and sent his sons to Liverpool College. His eldest son, Thomas Jnr, would later become Mayor of Liverpool and a baronet in recognition of his concerns for marine insurance and the safety of ships at sea (he later agitated for the introduction of the Plimsoll Line). The social change in the family was well established when Royden's grandson (also named Thomas) was packed off to Winchester College and later Magdalen College, Oxford. This grandson Thomas would later head Cunard Line as its chairman and become a baron in his own right in 1944. Business interests diversified among the family's offspring, many of them moving south, although the Royden shipping line (the Indra Line) operated in Liverpool until 1952. Thomas Royden Snr was typical of the entrepreneurial class of his day. Similar examples of such a rise (and demise) can be found in numerous Liverpool merchant families during the period.

By the 1830s Royden's yard was rated as one of the leading builders on the Mersey. In common with other yards, it was situated in the South Docks at the waterfront Baffin Street site, directly below the town boundary of Parliament Street. By the mid-nineteenth century, decline in local shipbuilding had already set in and in 1850 the Liverpool Shipbuilding Inquiry was formed to investigate the root causes. Not un-expectedly, it determined that local shipbuilders were unable to fight outside competition due to high rents, lack of space, lack of tenure and high wage costs. In the evidence it was also stated that one of the principal causes for shipbuilding moving out of Liverpool was the fact that there was a lack of control over the workforce, as the employers were restricted to using public graving docks. Furthermore, Thomas Royden declared in evidence that it was not possible to build more than two ships at a time in his yard due to want of space. This lack of space, he said, necessitated timber being piled six or eight feet high, and when a particular piece was wanted from the pile, they were often obliged to get the men to remove the whole stack. With adequate space, timber could be spread out. Rents and taxes, he said, were very high and the mode of moving shipbuilders at six months notice was so disheartening that they could not consider renting a yard. Robert Clarke said in his evidence that he had been moved from his premises three times, and the removals had cost him £3,000. Michael Humble (of Humble & Grayson), another witness, said that their shipyard was at Trentham Street, until the Corporation required the land for the Albert Dock, when they moved to Barrack Street near where the Fort was to have been. They finally gave up shipbuilding because of the great loss and damage sustained by being turned out of their building yard. He told the enquiry that the Corporation had shown him the orig-inal plans for the Albert Dock and his yard was not to be interfered with in any way. Furthermore, he had received personal assurance from the Deputy Chairman of the Dock Trustees. On that basis they accepted further orders and began to construct a new vessel, which normally took ten or twelve months to build, employing apprentices only. After they had bought the materials to build the vessel, they received notice to quit at the end of six months, the Dock Committee having altered the plan for the new dock. He said he was obliged to complete the vessel in just under six months and was forced to take on extra journeymen labour. They had 120 apprentices employed in building the vessel and had to pay out £420 to journeymen, and when the ship was finished they had the apprentices on their hands with nothing to do. In his opinion he also stated that public graving docks were driving the shipbuilding trade out of Liverpool. The Chairman of the Dock Trustees actually admitted that this was correct, and added that the plans were just a means to secure the Act of Parliament, after which the *actual* plans would be drawn up. Despite many of the drawbacks raised at the inquiry being recorded in the report of the Special Committee, little was acted upon and shipbuilding gradually declined. Nevertheless, Royden and Sons decided to battle on in the face of insurmountable odds, surprisingly lasting until the end of the century. Meanwhile, in 1842 Thomas Royden was elected to the Town Council for Great George Ward and also to the Dock Committee in the same year. In 1851 he was elected for North Toxteth Ward. *(Here is the answer to the question raised in the introduction which aroused my interest in family history – both Thomas and his son represented Toxteth in politics – hence the reason for Royden Street being so named).*

In 1863 the yard launched its first iron ship, the *Silvia*, but the acceptance of the order by Thomas's eldest son, Thomas Bland Royden, caused Thomas senior to leave the yard and retire to Frankby. Clearly a traditionalist who had spent his whole life working with timber, he could not face the major transition the yard would have to go through, and felt it was a timely moment to hand over the reins to his two sons. Thomas and Joseph Royden had already begun to expand the yard in 1854 when they acquired the lease of an adjoining yard belonging to Peter Chaloner & Son. This effectively doubled their yard space and gave them two additional slipways, which could take vessels up to 420 feet in length. Production soon increased as a result. Until 1866 the highest number of vessels constructed in any one year was six, by 1867 it had increased to ten and by 1868 to fourteen, which, with twelve in 1869, amounted to thirty-six ships in three years. Their list of patrons included Thomas Ismay, Frederick Leyland, Alfred Holt, the African Steam Ship Company, the West India and Pacific Line and even the Emperor of Brazil. There is no doubt, however, that Thomas B. Royden was less than confident about the longevity of the shipbuilding trade, as they had also gone into ship ownership and management.

Other shipyards did try to make inroads in the market. Jones, Quiggin & Co. was founded in 1855 and built composite and iron ships, including sailing vessels, paddle and screw steamers. Much work was for customers abroad and included commissions for the Confederate Government, arranged through Fraser, Trenholm & Co. Ships built at this time include five blockade runners, one of which, the *Banshee*, became the first steel ship to cross the Atlantic in 1863.

However, towards the end of the nineteenth century the only shipyards remaining on the east side of the Mersey were Thomas Royden & Sons, R. & J. Evans & Co., W.H. Potter & Sons and John Jones & Sons. In 1893 Roydens launched their last vessel, the steel barque *Prince Robert* (2,846 tons), the 262nd vessel to be built at the yard. Their activities had started in the era of sails and wooden ships, and moved on into iron and steel steamships. Thus ended a shipbuilding firm well known and highly respected throughout the country.

The end of the Liverpool shipbuilding industry was not far off. In 1895 the steel barque *Lynton* (2,351 tons) was the final vessel launched by R. & J. Evans, and in 1899 John Jones & Sons vacated their shipyard. The same year Her Majesty's Gunboat *Britomart* left the slipways from the Queen's Dock yard of Potter & Sons, the last vessel to be built or launched from the Liverpool side of the Mersey. The shipbuilding trade, so far as Liverpool was concerned, then became extinct.

In stark contrast to Liverpool, where shipbuilders were relatively unwelcome, the story was much different over the water. In 1824 William Laird's ironworks and shipyard was founded in Birkenhead and rose to become the town's biggest industry and one of the world's best-known firms, pioneering ironclad warships and going on to build some of the best-known vessels of the twentieth century. Here, for example, Lairds constructed both the 1938 and 1955 versions of the iconic aircraft-carrier *Ark Royal*.

Despite their close proximity, there is not a lot of evidence to suggest that there was a close commercial alliance between the Birkenhead ship-builders and the Liverpool shipowners. Liverpool's shipowners mostly ordered their vessels from the Clyde, Belfast and the North East, where they had a wide choice of yards with experience of building large cargo and passenger vessels in great numbers.

Cammell Laird originated as a boiler works in 1824 before growing and diversifying to become one of a small number of companies worldwide

Bustling activity at Cammell Laird.

which could build, armour and arm the largest warships from the operations of a single company group. The firm merged with Charles Cammell of Sheffield in 1903 to become Cammell Laird. After the First World War, it was reconstructed as a naval and mercantile shipbuilder with important financial interests in steel and rolling stock manufacture. Booming activity during the Second World War and continuing prosperity until the late 1950s was followed by increasing competition and deepening problems. By the 1980s the firm's remaining steel interests had failed and in 1993 the once-great Birkenhead shipyard closed. One local company, however, McTay Marine of Bromborough, Wirral, is still building vessels of up to 500 tons.

Further Research

Considering the extent of the industry and the number of companies involved, there is a surprising dearth of primary material, and little surviving in the way of business records. Consequently there has been much to hamper researchers, and studies in this field are still rather sparse.

Early views and maps of the shoreline should be consulted at an early stage when researching any type of history of the port. Liverpool has been well documented in both formats. S. & N. Buck's *View of Liverpool* (1728), on display in the Merseyside Maritime Museum, shows the first dock in Liverpool and wooden ships can be seen under construction on the banks of the Mersey. During the mid-nineteenth century aerial illustrations of the town were made from a tethered balloon and working shipyards can be picked out.

Stewart Brown's *Liverpool Ships in the 18th Century* (Liverpool, 1932), is useful for a detailed account of the numbers of vessels produced, as well as biographies of individual shipbuilders. It also covers the early nineteenth century, ending with the great shipbuilding enquiry of 1850.

Business records of individual firms (with one exception) are very few. This is due to the fact that most of them went out of business at the end of the nineteenth century. The initial notes of A.C. Wardle, who planned a seven-volume history of British shipbuilding, are held in the archives of the Liverpool Nautical Research Society (D/LNRS) and preserved in the Maritime Archives and Library. The Maritime Archives and Library also holds an auction sale catalogue for equipment belonging to Lawrence & Co. (MDHB Legal H44), the specification of the Liverpool Shipbuilding Co. of 1855–1856 (formerly Jones, Quiggin & Co.) and a small quantity of items from R. & J. Evans. There are printed company histories of Graysons, Roydens and the Liverpool shipbuilding firm of Potters in John Masefield's *The Wanderer* (Macmillan, 1930), which is an account of their most famous vessel. Levels of production are covered by Frank Neal's paper, published in Research in Progress, Vol. 4. Local newspapers held at Liverpool City Record Office also carry reports of launching ceremonies.

From the mid-1850s, Liverpool builders converted rapidly to iron shipbuilding. It is possible to trace the details of individual ships built in Liverpool at this period, either through Lloyd's Registers, which have a particularly useful appendix from 1876 for the production of individual shipbuilders, or through the Liverpool Registers of Merchant Ships (C/EX/L/1-9). Royden's history has a complete listing of the vessels constructed in the yard.

A visit to the Maritime Museum is a must if a greater understanding of this aspect of Liverpool's history is to be gained. There are numerous models of Liverpool-built ships on display, including the 50-gun HMS *Grampus*, which was launched at John Fisher's shipyard in 1782. This superbly detailed model shows the three-master with three huge lanterns at the stern.

The *Jhelum* (1849) was one of the last Mersey-built wooden ships and was employed in the guano trade, shipping bird droppings for fertilizer. Her beached hulk still lies in Port Stanley, Falkland Islands. Mike Stammers of the Merseyside Maritime Museum has visited her and has published his findings, especially on what the present remains can tell us about shipbuilding techniques on the Mersey in the nineteenth century. Alongside a small model of *Jhelum* are a number of artefacts from the hulk including nails and copper sheathing. More on shipbuilding on the Mersey and related documents in the collections of the Maritime Museum can be found in the Maritime Archives section on their website. A new Maritime Tale, written by museum press officer Stephen Guy, appears every Saturday in the *Liverpool Echo*. Extracts can be found on his blog page, also on the Museum site: http://blog.liverpoolmuseums.org.uk/default.aspx (select Stephen's blogs).

Census records should be used in conjunction with detailed maps showing the streets stretching from the Strand to Parliament Street and further as the town expanded. This was a centre for the local workforce engaged in the shipbuilding industry. Among the regular dockers are recorded shipwrights, ropemakers (numerous roperies lay adjacent to the Salthouse and Queen's Docks), sailmakers, toolmakers, and all manner of occupations connected with the trade. The Maritime Archives and Library has also been able to collect records from many trades, despite the widespread loss of such records, including sailmakers, hatch manufacturers, nautical telegraph and instrument makers, marine engineers, rope-makers, ships' brass founders and cleaners, as well as a number of ship repairers.

Occasionally, works do surface on the stories of some of the vessels constructed in the Liverpool yards. Zoologist and diving instructor Henry Alexander came across the wreck of the *Dryad* on one of his regular dives off the South Devon coast thirty years ago. He then began a long journey of discovery, finding out where the vessel was constructed and how it came to lie off Start Point. Built in 1874, the *Dryad* was an iron barque and was travelling from the Tyne to Valparaiso carrying coal, coke and mining equipment when she slammed into the cliffs off Start Point during the infamous blizzard and storm of 9 March 1891, with the loss of all her twenty-one crew members. Alexander's obsession drove him to track down the great-grand-daughter of the *Dryad*'s builder (after this author put him in touch with a direct descendant of the shipbuilder). He also studied the life of Captain William Thomas and found his great-grand-daughter. Over the years Alexander raised hundreds of items, including the captain's watch, revolver and spare magazine. The full story is very well illustrated and documented in *The Life and Death of the Liverpool Barque Dryad 1874–91*(Aunemouth Books). The 1,069-ton fully rigged vessel had been built at the Liverpool yard of Thomas Royden and Sons, and Alexander's research provides a valuable link with rare physical remains of one of the more well-known Liverpool shipbuilders from the nineteenth century.

The *Wavertree* was built by the Liverpool shipbuilders Oswald Mordaunt & Co. in 1885. She shipped cargo all over the world until she was laid up and her mast removed. New York City's South Street Seaport Museum later acquired and restored her and today she is still there – docked at Pier 17 among other historic craft. The museum produced a book in 1969 – *The Wavertree: An Ocean Wanderer*, which highlighted Captain George Spiers' personal account of his trip in 1907–08 on the *Wavertree* as it sailed from Port Townsend in Washington to Chile to Portland, Oregon and home to Runcorn.

Maritime Museum Archive Library Sources

Some of the archive records relating to Liverpool shipbuilding held are:
A.C. Wardle's Research Files, D/LNRS/1/1–15 and D/LNRS/3/1–8.
Captain Beard's Collection, D/LNRS/4/2/1–19 (sailing ship histories)
Cochrane Collection (steamship histories)
The Cammell Laird Magazine, 1957–1965.
Liverpool Register of Shipping, 1835.
Liverpool National Register of Shipping, 1845.
Lloyd's Register, 1764 to date.
Marwood's Shipping Register, 1854.
Shipbuilding and Shipping Record, 1915, 1919–1922, 1933, 1936–1938, 1940–1964, 1968–1973.
The Shipbuilder, 1911–1912.
Mersey Docks and Harbour Board (MDHB) Estate Records.
Cammel Laird – the bulk of its archives are held by the Wirral Museum and Archive Service, Birkenhead.

Further Reading

Local

Stammers, M.K. and Kearon, J. *The Jhelum – a Victorian Merchant Ship*, National Museums Liverpool, 1992.

Stammers, M.K. 'Jhelum and Liverpool Shipbuilders' from **Burton, V.** *Liverpool Shipping, Trade & Industry*, 1989, National Museums and Galleries on Merseyside, p.85.

Royden, M.W. 'The Roydens of Frankby' in *The Wirral Journal*, Vol.3 No.3, August 1986, pp.24–27, plus unpublished family research.

Neal, F. 'Liverpool Shipping in the Early Nineteenth Century' in **Harris, J.R. (Ed.)** *Liverpool and Merseyside: Essays in the Economic and Social of the Port and its Hinterland*, Cass, 1969, p.169.

Royden, E.B. *Thomas Royden and Sons, Shipbuilders*, privately published, 1952.

Chris, Michael *Lelia*, Countyvise, 2004.

Hollett, D. *Men of Iron: Story of Cammell Laird Shipbuilders, 1828–1991*, Countyvise.

Brown, R.S. *Liverpool Ships in the Eighteenth Century*, Liverpool, 1932.

Burstall, A.R. *Shipbuilding in Liverpool, Sea Breezes*, Vol. XX, April–May 1936.

Warren, Kenneth *Steel, Ships and Men: Cammell Laird and Company 1824–1993*, 1998, Liverpool University Press. The major study of the firm.

Roberts, David *Life at Lairds: Memories of working shipyard men*, Wirral, 1992. Oral history and testimony from the workforce.

Collard, Ian *Cammell Lairds*, The History Press, 2004.

On the net

Cammell Laird: Shipbuilders to the World by Alex Naughton, www.ahoy.tk-jk.net/macslog/CammellLairdShipbuildersat.html.

Chapter Three

SHIPPING LINES
AND SEAMEN

Liverpool today is a city that has been shaped by its historic dependence on ships and maritime trade to an extent that is unique in Britain. There is a noticeable feel about the character that is distinctive and socially different from anywhere else in England. For over two hundred years Liverpool was one of the world's greatest seaports. Today it remains Britain's largest west coast port and continues to offer shipping services to many parts of the world. The earliest known view of the port is that by the Dutch artist Magenis – a view of the late seventeenth century which pre-dates the slave trade, but shows the foreshore was already well developed and dominated by its principal buildings – the St Nicholas Church (with the Town Hall to the rear), the Tower of Liverpool, the third Customs House and the Castle. The port at this time was a Crown source for sailors for the navy, while on land the porters – forerunners of the dockers – were competing with freemen of the borough for the right to work on the quay-side vessels. The local activities of the press-gangs were becoming notorious and men were often taken without pay, as this letter home from a dejected tar on the *Royal James* in 1666 testifies:

> Most dear and loving wife my kind love remembered unto you and our children hoping to the lord that you are in good health... I trust that we shall put an end to these wars... If it shall please God to spare my life and health I will see you the next winter whether I get any pay or none... I received two months pay which is all I have received since I departed from you which was from the 1st June to the 1st August.

As the volume of goods increased during the Industrial Revolution, so Liverpool shipping expanded as cargo became more generalised. This broadening of trade enabled Liverpool to become the second port to London by the late nineteenth century. Consequently, trade in the Atlantic routes was still maintained even after the abolition. During the early years of the nineteenth century other routes were developed to countries such as India and China, and South America was also opened up following the War of Independence. Liverpool tonnage doubled during 1815 to 1830 and again by 1845. This was still the period of sail and, due to the dominance of American shipowners, Liverpool-owned lines would not come to the fore until later in the century.

As the steamship began to play an increased role out of the port, Liverpool came to dominate, becoming the leading liner port in the world from the 1860s to the early twentieth century. The opening of the Suez Canal in 1869 was exploited by Alfred Holt, whose Ocean Steamship Company was trading in Asia, but it was the vacuum left by American companies following the Civil War of 1861–65 that enabled Liverpool lines to move in and fill the gap and dominate the Atlantic trade in the years that followed. According to Gordon Milne, three economic booms followed which had a considerable effect on the port. Firstly, the role of the textile industry continued to expand as markets developed worldwide. By the outbreak of the First World War cotton imports were at 30 per cent, while exports of cotton goods were 42 per cent. The second factor was the mass migration from Europe to the Americas, where unprecedented numbers travelled through Liverpool. Thirdly, Liverpool became a centre for the trading and processing of food supplies, especially sugar and grain.

Shipping companies

Liverpool's shipping companies had some of the best-known names of the nineteenth and twentieth centuries. Cunard, White Star and Blue Funnel were recognised worldwide, even by people who had never been to sea. Many local youngsters grew up fascinated by the shipping on the river and learned to recognise the various funnels and flags of the vessels as they sailed past. After 1945 academics began to pay serious attention to the economic and business history of shipping firms, especially following the work of Francis Hyde. As Professor of Economic History at Liverpool University, he built up a productive group of historians working on the subject, and research into the business history of shipping companies continues to be an active field today. Studies are not confined to the major lines, and brokers and agents are becoming increasingly researched. Interest in the history of shipping is very popular in the area and new publications covering ships, companies and the dock estate appear every year. A summary of brief histories of several key shipping companies operating out of Liverpool can be found on www.roydenhistory.co.uk (select Mike Royden's Local History Pages).

Further Research

Maritime Archives and Library at the Merseyside Maritime Museum
www.liverpoolmuseums.org.uk/maritime

This should be the first port of call for any researcher into Liverpool's maritime past. The museum holds one of the finest collections of merchant shipping records in the UK from the early eighteenth century onwards. Its website provides excellent coverage and gives plenty of advice and information about its collections. Information sheets are available which will ensure you are well prepared before your visit. There is a large selection, covering all aspects of Liverpool's maritime past and general maritime history.

Tracing seamen in the Merchant Navy

Information Sheet No.43 is recommended. Tracing Merchant Navy seamen can be extremely difficult since their occupation entailed them being away at sea for long periods. They were often absent from their homes when population censuses were taken. However, many forms of records, dating mainly from the mid-nineteenth century onwards, are available to the family historian, although they can take perseverance to track down. Many records are not kept in the Maritime Archives and Library. For example, they do not hold official lists of passengers or emigrants or official records of seamen. They can, however, advise on where you might find them. (See the chapter on Emigration for further advice). The archive does contain certain career papers of individual seafarers.

Records of Merchant Navy service

From 1835 onwards, central government started to take an interest in merchant seamen, both from a desire to improve their conditions and to help man the Navy in time of war. As a consequence, many more records have become available that allow the researcher to trace details of individual seamen. The main sources of information are the records compiled by the Registrar General of Shipping & Seamen, the majority of which are now held at the National Archives (TNA).

Merchant Navy training ships

The Maritime Museum also holds the records of HMS *Conway* and the TS *Indefatigable*, both training ships moored on the Mersey in the latter half of the nineteenth century. These were founded to give sea training to poor boys with a view to progressing into the Merchant Navy. Both of these collections contain records of the cadets who trained on them. See Information Sheet No.9.

Tracing Vessels

A useful start point would be the Lloyd's Register. This is an annual alpha-betical list of vessels giving details current at the time of publication. Until 1890 it was almost exclusively limited to British-registered vessels, although some foreign vessels that regularly traded with the UK were included. Copies are held in the Maritime Archives. Library copies are also to be found in other archives and libraries with maritime collections. Further information is held on the Maritime Museum website (see Information Sheet No.47).

Lloyd's Register will provide you with the name of the owner and the port at which the ship was registered. If it belonged to the Port of Liverpool you will be able to find out more from the Registers of Merchant Ships (1739–1988). The Maritime Museum may also have records of the shipping company who owned the ship.

The Maritime Archives and Library holds many records of major ship-ping companies operating from Liverpool. These include Ocean Transport & Trading, which incorporated Blue Funnel, Elder Dempster, Bibby Line, T. & J. Brocklebank and the Pacific Steam Navigation Company.

Images

It may be possible to obtain a photograph or plan of the ship your ancestor sailed on from the Maritime Archives. It is helpful to know when your ancestor served on the vessel as companies frequently had several vessels of the same name over time. Contact the Photography Department, National Museums Liverpool, PO Box 33, 127 Dale Street, Liverpool L69 3LA. Tel: 0151 478 4657. Fax: 0151 478 4028. Email: photography@liverpool-museums.org.uk. Website: www.liverpoolmuseums.org.uk.

Other sources for images:
Imperial War Museum, Lambeth Road, London, SE1 6HZ, Tel: 020 7416 522/1/2/6 Fax: 020 7416 5374. Email: docs@iwm.org.uk. Website: www. iwm.org.uk.
National Maritime Museum, Romney Road, Greenwich, London, SE10 9NF. Tel: 020 8312 8600 (Photographic Enquiries). Email: plansand-photos@nmm.ac.uk. Website: www.nmm.ac.uk.
Royal Naval Museum, Curator of Manuscripts, HM Naval Base, Portsmouth, Hampshire PO1 3NH. Tel: 023 9272 7577. Email: matthew.sheldon@royalnavalmuseum.org.uk. Website: www.royalnaval-museum.org.uk.
Ulster Folk & Transport Museum (For ships built by Harland & Wolff), Cultra, Holywood, County Down, BT18 0EU, Northern Ireland. Tel: 02890 428428. Email: ustm@talk21.com. Website: www.uftm.org.uk/collections-and-research.

Ship photographs can also be researched by contacting the yard where a ship was built. If the yard is no longer in existence, then a further search could be made to find out if the records from the shipbuilding yard have been transferred to an archive. A useful publication as a source for locating shipbuilding archives is:

Ritchie, L.A. (Ed.) *The Shipbuilding Industry – A Guide to Historical Records, Studies in British Business Archives*, Manchester University Press, 1992.

Adverts are often carried in *Sea Breezes* and *Ships Monthly*, which are useful for sourcing images. *Sea Breezes*, Units 28–30, Spring Valley Industrial Estate, Braddan, Isle of Man, IM2 2QS. Tel: 01624 626018. Email: seabreezes@manninmedia.co.im. Website: www.manninmedia.co.im.

Ships Monthly, IPC Country and Leisure Media Ltd, Marine Division, 222 Branston Road, Burton-on-Trent, DE14 3BT. Tel: 01283 542721. Email: shipsmonthly@ipcmedia.com.

Further Reading

General work on the shipping industry, including Liverpool material

Kirkaldy, A.W., *British shipping: Its history, organisation and importance*, London, 1914.

Sturmey, S.G., *British shipping and world competition*, London, 1962.

Hyde, F.E., *Liverpool and the Mersey: An economic history of a port, 1700–1970*, Newton Abbot, 1971.

Boyce, Gordon H., *Information, mediation and institutional development: The rise of large-scale enterprise in British shipping, 1870–1919*, Manchester, 1995.

Lane, Tony *Liverpool: City of the Sea*, 1997. This book is a second fully revised and updated edition of Tony Lane's *Liverpool: Gateway of Empire*, Lawrence and Wishart, 1987.

Milne, Graeme J. *Trade and Traders in Mid-Victorian Liverpool: Mercantile Business and the Making of a World Port*, 2000. Focuses on ship owners and their business connections during the period of transition from sail to steam.

Burton, V. (Ed.), *Liverpool Shipping Trade & Industry*, National Museums & Galleries on Merseyside, 1989 – a booklet containing several useful essays.

Stammers, M. *Liverpool Sailing Ships*, The History Press, 2008.

Older work on Liverpool steamship fleets

Willox, J., *The steam fleet of Liverpool*, 1865.

Kennedy, J., *History of steam navigation*, 1903. Contains accounts of Liverpool companies and pictures of house flags.

Coward, E. *Steamship lines of the Mersey*, 1880. Includes flags and funnels.

Fry, H. *The history of North Atlantic steam navigation*, 1896.

House flags and funnels of the English and foreign steamship companies (In the Record Office collection, no date).

Carter, C.J.M. *Ships of the Mersey*, 1966. With gramophone discs of liner whistles.

Liverpool's *Journal of Commerce* periodically published a flag sheet identifying the port's shipping companies and their fleets.

Collard, I. *Liverpool's Shipping Groups*, Tempus.

Fleet histories and listings

These books have detailed profiles of shipping companies and their fleets, and often an outline of the business history of the firms. They are important works of reference.

Bonsor, N.R.P. *North Atlantic seaway*, 5 vols, Jersey, 1975–80.

—— *South Atlantic seaway*, Jersey, 1983.

Chandler, George, *Liverpool shipping: A short history*, London, 1960.

Haws, Duncan *The Burma Boats: Henderson & Bibby*, Uckfield, 1995. This is just one of a long series of detailed fleet histories by Haws, each dealing with a particular shipping company.

Hollett, Duncan *Fast passage to Australia*, London, 1986. Has detailed listings of ships in the Australia trade in the mid-nineteenth century.

Fenton, Roy, *Mersey Rovers: The coastal tramp ship owners of Liverpool and the Mersey*, Gravesend, 1997. Detailed histories of coastal operators and their fleets.

Whale, Derek, *The Liners of Liverpool*, 3 vols, Birkenhead, 1986–88. Thoroughly researched histories of a large number of important ships, with excellent accounts of life and work on board.

Histories of individual companies

There are many histories of particular shipping and shipping-related companies. These can readily be found in the catalogue using the name of the firm.

Gibson, John, *Brocklebanks, 1770–1950*, 2 vols, Liverpool, 1953.

Davies, P.N. *The trade makers: Elder Dempster in West Africa, 1852–1972*, London, 1973.

Davies, P.N. *Henry Tyrer: A Liverpool shipping agent and his enterprise*, London, 1979.

Hyde, F.E., *Blue Funnel: A history of Alfred Holt & Co. of Liverpool, 1865–1914*, Liverpool, 1957.

—— *Cunard and the North Atlantic, 1840–1973: A history of shipping and financial management*, London, 1975.

Marriner, Sheila, *Rathbones of Liverpool, 1845–73*, Liverpool, 1961.

Haws, Duncan *Merchant Fleets Vol.19: The White Star Line*

On the net

Mersey Gateway www.mersey-gateway.org – an online history of the port and its people.

Liverpolitan liverpolitan.im/main/livships.htm – excellent list of ships associated with Liverpool (within a larger website on the History of Liverpool).

The Liverpool Nautical Research Society www.lnrs.co.uk/index.htm – a society and website dedicated to preserving and promoting interest in the history of shipping and all nautical subjects through research using the resources of the Merseyside Maritime Museum Archives and Library and other appropriate organisations. The society undertakes historical surveys of ships, their builders, owners, masters, crews and other nautical technical matters, particularly of local interest. They also assist in projects of the Merseyside Maritime Museum Archive, and offer advice and research to any organisations with nautical interests. In addition they offer, wherever possible, assistance with the range of appropriate enquiries that are received from the general public and outside bodies, without charge. A society journal *The Bulletin* is published quarterly and lectures are given at regular meetings.

Merchant Navy Association www.red-duster.co.uk – an excellent site containing a wealth of information about fleet histories, individual vessels and images and the early days of sail, as well as being a current site for the present-day activities of merchant shipping.

The Ships List www.theshipslist.com – maintained since 1999 by S. Swiggum and M. Kohli, the site is highly recommended. The site holds ships' passenger lists, immigration reports, newspaper records, shipwreck information, ship pictures, ship descriptions, shipping-line fleet lists and more; as well as hundreds of passenger lists to Canada, the US, Australia and even some for South Africa.

Ocean Liner Museum www.oceanlinermuseum.co.uk – a useful site detailing histories of shipping lines and ocean travel.

Chapter Four

ESTATE AND AGRICULTURE

By the first half of the nineteenth century the boundary of the town of Liverpool had still only extended as far as Parliament Street in the south and Kirkdale in the north, little more than a mile radius from the Town Hall. Only in the last hundred years or so has the landscape surrounding this early urbanisation become absorbed into the expanding city. Clearly, when studying the urban area of the city there is little regard for ownership of landed estate or agriculture, but of course, as research moves back through the nineteenth century and beyond and ancestors are discovered in rural surroundings, the history of the these hinterlands gains greater significance.

The medieval landscape

Parishes and Townships

By the eleventh century all of England south of the River Tees had been organised into shires with a capital town as the major centre of local government. The shire was subdivided into smaller units, the hundreds, to make the collection of local taxes and the administration of law and order easier. At the time of Domesday, South Lancashire was attached to Cheshire and did not develop a county structure until the reign of Henry II. However, West Derby Hundred was in existence by 1086 and its organisation was probably rooted in the pre-Conquest period. The mother church of the Hundred was Walton-on-the-Hill, while Childwall, where there was a priest in 1086, was probably a dependent church. The parishes in this area were much larger than those in the Midlands and south, probably due to the dispersed and sparser population. Consequently, it became necessary to divide the parishes into smaller, more manageable units called townships, which were largely self-sufficient territories providing the natural resources for exploitation by the community.

Conveniently, much of the district we are concerned with falls into the old parishes of Walton and Childwall. The parish of Walton-on-the-Hill

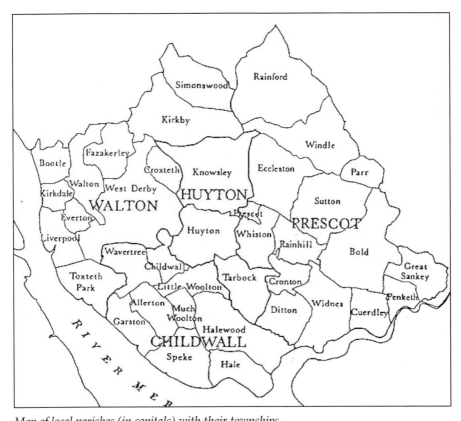

Map of local parishes (in capitals) with their townships.

consists of the townships of Walton, Everton, West Derby, Fazakerley, Kirkdale, Bootle, Toxteth Park, Liverpool, Kirkby and Simmondswood, while Childwall became the mother church for the townships of Childwall, Wavertree, Thingwall, Much Woolton, Little Woolton, Garston, Allerton, Speke, Hale and Halewood.

The Manor

The manorial system was superimposed on the township organisation and did not always relate to its boundaries. In basic terms it was the landed estate of the lord, which consisted of his own farmland (usually known as the home farm) and land leased to his tenants. Researchers may find that such holdings often overlapped more than one township. Conversely, there are also instances of several manors within a township, such as in

Kirkby, which after 1252 was divided into Kirkby Beetham and Kirkby Gerrard. Two manors also existed in Huyton.

Early modern Liverpool – the changing landscape

Maps should always be consulted when studying areas of research to get a clear idea of the extent of suburban development, as this may well determine where records are held. Extensions to the town boundaries of Liverpool were being made in the 1830s, while Birkenhead was yet to be planned as a formal grid layout, and in South Wirral the town of Ellesmere Port did not exist beyond a few cottages around a canal terminus known as 'Whitby Locks'.

Liverpool still had its medieval townfield as late as 1700. But by the late seventeenth and early eighteenth century, many of these old townfield systems were being swept away on a tide of enclosure – one of the new methods of farming that was part of the huge changes in husbandry that were collectively known as the Agricultural Revolution. Locally, for example, the Earl of Derby was an advocate of these new methods. He had surveys taken of his land and applied improvements wherever possible. His home estate was and still is in Knowsley, but his landed estate extended throughout south-west Lancashire. His tenants had no say in developments and Acts of Parliament to enclose land were pushed through without opposition.

Improvements in Agriculture: Enclosure

During the fifteenth and sixteenth centuries, as farming methods in England and Wales began to change and the desire for grassland gradually increased, a pattern of mixed agriculture and pastoral farming became the norm. In the local Liverpool townships all had a fully enclosed arable farming system by the early nineteenth century. In fact, no Enclosure Acts for arable farming survive for the district and measures were probably of a piecemeal nature. In Liverpool town, cultivation of the waste began as early as 1300, when Salthouse Moor was enclosed prior to 1309 during a period of economic prosperity under Thomas, Earl of Lancaster. This was, however, the only important encroachment upon the waste until the seventeenth century. The enclosed area was divided among ninety-eight tenants, occupying approximately forty-five acres. Of the total, thirty-two were new burgesses and had not held land on the Townfield before.

Enclosure of the Townfield rapidly increased during the early eighteenth century, although the map drawn of the Breckshot immediately prior to its enclosure shows 'William Cliff's Old Enclosure' – land most likely enclosed by the Moores in the sixteenth century. A deed of 1739 mentions four lands 'recently' enclosed and one of 1724 refers to ten enclosed lands on the west side of Pinfold Green. In fact, much of this type of enclosure was merely redistribution, as the later Eyes' 1785 map of Liverpool suggests. A comparison of the field patterns around the Townfield area, compared with those on the former Great Heath, shows firstly the clear antiquity of the Townfield area against the later haphazard, piecemeal division of the heath, and secondly the pattern of small narrow enclosed fields rather than a wholesale redivision into larger units seen elsewhere. The growing prosperity of the port prevented any such agricultural modernisation and within fifty years much of the former Townfield had been subject to urban sprawl, while lands sloping down to the foreshore had made way for the docks and associated development, which by now had encroached into Kirkdale Township. (Held in Liverpool Record Office is *A Plan of Liverpool Townfield called 'Breck Shute' as it lay before the division was made amongst the several Land Owners in Octr 1733 by J.Eyes*, a copy can be found in **Stewart-Brown, R.**, *The Townfield of Liverpool, 1207–1807*, 1916.)

In the outer regions, an Act to enclose the commons and waste of Childwall, Little Woolton and Much Woolton was passed in 1805. In fact, an agreement between landowners to enclose the commons of Much Woolton had occurred as early as 1613, when 150 acres were divided between Lord Derby, Sir William Norris of Speke, John Ireland of Hale and the remaining small landowners. Lord Derby had purchased the manorial

Old Hutt Gatehouse, 1820. The former Manor House of Hale.

rights only three years earlier, which shows how keen he was to see a swift return on his investment, prompted no doubt by the massive debt he had inherited from his father. The plan that was drawn for their preliminary discussions is the earliest known map of the village. The land covered by the 1805 Act included the common of Little Woolton, which lay on Woolton Hill, and the commons of Much Woolton, which were bounded approximately by a line running along the sandstone ridge from Camphill to Reynolds Park, running down to the township boundary with Allerton. Much of this land, of course, is still open parkland today. In Childwall the same Act covered the common pasture land on the high ridge to the west of the Hall, although today it is largely woodland (part of which is Childwall Woods).

What happened in Halewood gives an insight into agricultural management of the locality, both by the small yeoman farmer and his superior lord of the landed estate. In the western end of the township (known as Halewood) land was gradually cleared piecemeal over a long period, while in the eastern end of the township (known as Halebank), an open field system appears to have existed based around Lovel's Hall. A general enclosure Act of Parliament to modernise the open fields was therefore unnecessary. Nevertheless, there was still a fair amount of unused waste land in Halewood. The roads were also in bad condition and some were no longer used. The roads that were used were untidy and quite wide in some places – all this space could be added into the fields and be exploited. In 'North End' a hamlet surrounded a large common, while in Halebank there was a smaller village green near the Higher Lane crossroads. This was also felt by the major landowners to be surplus to requirements. In 1800, the two lords who owned most of the land in Halewood – Lord Derby, whose holdings were centred around the North End and Lovel's Hall areas, and Sir John Irelande-Blackburne of Hale, who owned most of the Halebank End – wanted to divide up all the common and wasteland of the township. They also wanted to exchange and consolidate a number of scattered holdings. A meeting was called in the village to discuss the plans and more than four-fifths of the landowners, the majority required, voted to enclose the wastes. The 'Enclosure Award' was granted by Act of Parliament on 6 January 1803. Although the enclosures of 1803 were not on a scale found elsewhere, especially in the Midlands, and only affected commons and wastes, the changes must have been felt by certain sections of the township, especially tenants and landless labourers. The biggest changes were witnessed around Halewood Green. Villagers had lost their right to graze their animals and their common was now divided up among several landowners – none of whom lived in Halewood. Some of their roads had been closed, other roads were made private and all were to be fenced or hedged, preventing roadside grazing. On maps made forty years later, many of the fenced roadside wastes had still not been included in the farmed fields alongside them – maybe the farmers realised this land was not very good after all.

The Halewood Green hamlet disintegrated, although in the late 19th century there was a minor resurgence when a small public house (the British Lion) was opened facing Church Road and a couple of cottages were built nearby. There was little change until the 1960s, when the remainder of the cottages around Halewood Green were demolished and the land became earmarked for housing, while North End hamlet grew marginally. On the former north-eastern border of the common the isolated Georgian farmhouse of Foxhill House can still be seen overlooking the Green. Near the centre of the Green was once a corn mill, which appeared to have been in use from the seventeenth to the end of the eighteenth century. After the enclosure award, the mill was dismantled and became a modest cottage. From the air, the site of the corn mill appears as a clear crop-mark, while at ground level a break in the hedgerow on Church Road indicates the original gateway, and a pronounced rise in the field betrays its position. Part of the common was finally destroyed in 1990 when the housing development hinted at thirty years earlier was finally completed.

Using local tithe maps, census and church records, quite an insight can be gained into the structure of the community. Family groups can be quite easily discovered – a great many of which have been present in the township over centuries. 'Incomers' clearly stand out, and are often arriving to carry out domestic work as house servants. The enclosure award of Halewood records the names of villagers (and their land) who are directly affected by the changes and takes research back another step into the late eighteenth century. Such an approach can be applied to any of the townships surrounding the port where similar records exist.

Forests and Parks

Medieval settlement documents reveal the extent of forest clearance around Liverpool. Halewood had become deforested by the early thirteenth century, while Croxteth township had been enclosed into small fields for agricultural use by 1769. The legal process to develop Toxteth Park was begun by Lord Derby in the late sixteenth century, and there were twenty farm holdings with tenants by 1596. By 1604, when the Molyneux family paid £1,100 for the estate, there were twenty-three tenants with holdings, but only thirteen farms had houses built on them. It is estimated that this number had more than trebled to forty-three by 1717, following a period of high turnover.

Toxteth Park was ripe for development now that the planning controls had been effectively lifted by the local courts. Furthermore, as it was an extra-parochial territory (not belonging to any particular parish) it was also a land of opportunity for dissidents. Field and farm boundaries on the 1769 estate map of Toxteth Park show clearly the regimented lines favoured by many enclosure commissioners of the day, the result of which was a pattern of dispersed farmsteads without apparent nucleus. Paradoxically, the community was tight-knit and comprised originally of a group of Puritans from Bolton seeking their promised land, naming one of their farms Jericho and renaming the Otters Brook the River Jordan. Although urbanisation soon swallowed up swathes of the former park, well over 400 acres of the park remain as relatively open landscape today, within the municipal parklands of Sefton, Princes and Greenbank.

Settlement and Buildings

At the beginning of this period, by far the most prominent building in the village was the church, usually the only one that was built of stone. The second substantial building was usually the manor house, sometimes built of stone although timber was more common. The majority of village buildings were also built of wood in this earlier period and those who could afford it would often erect cruck houses with a curved oak timber supporting the roof. The majority of cottages, however, were little more than hovels of wattle and daub construction. It is hardly surprising that such primitive dwellings had a short life. It was not unusual for them to be rebuilt every 25 or 30 years due to the flimsy materials used. Villages surrounding Liverpool, soon to be swamped by its suburbs, originated in three distinct forms: the street village, with the houses strung in a line along one street, such as at Hale; the 'green village', with a large open space or village green dominating the centre of the village, such as at North End in Halewood; and the agglomerated, or compact, village, having no distinct shape and made up of a formless tangle of houses and lanes. In some of the more prosperous villages, schools and almshouses had been founded by the seventeenth century, for example at Huyton (1555) and Much Woolton and Walton (early 1600s). Materials were usually brick and stone – in the case of Woolton the local sandstone quarry was heavily exploited. Inns and ale houses were also common. Although there was a general growth in population during the 1500s and villages began to expand, there is no evidence of new villages being founded, although several small settlements appear to have formed following the enclosure of areas such as Allerton and Little Woolton.

Out in the townships, even by the mid-nineteenth century the landscape was still agricultural and most villages consisted of small clusters of cottages and farm buildings. It would not be until the early twentieth century before accelerated change would be witnessed, and even then only in certain areas, mainly Much Woolton and West Derby. Most houses were the simple rectangular cottages typical of the seventeenth and eighteenth-century agricultural labourer, while at the other end of the scale the growing prosperity of the yeoman farmer was reflected in the more substantial sandstone farmhouses. During the eighteenth century this spread of wealth was evident in the increased numbers of scattered or isolated brick-built farmhouses and cottages.

Seddon's Cottage, Garston, in the late nineteenth century.

Seventeenth-century cruck-framed cottages have survived in Tarbock and Cronton, but the only surviving timber box-frame building is Georgeson's Farm, also in Tarbock. There are also buildings of early construction where the timber has been replaced by brick. The use of thatch for roofs was once quite widespread, with several examples surviving into the early nineteenth century. Apart from several in Hale, the only other surviving example is Rose Cottage in Tarbock.

In Allerton the greater part of the sixteenth-century manor consisted of furze, rough waste and common land, as indicated on the map of 1568. The low-lying ground between Allerton Road and Mossley Hill, and towards Garston, was probably under cultivation, but it would not be until the enclosures that the bulk of the manor would be developed. At the beginning of the seventeenth century there were still hundreds of acres of heathland upon which the tenants had grazing and other common rights, but by the end of the eighteenth, enclosure had resulted in an increase in dispersed farms. One concentrated settlement had sprung up by 1771 in the north-east of the township (Harthill area), which had been recorded as common pasture in 1568. A second settlement lay in what is now Greenhill Road (between Mather Avenue and Booker Avenue). One cottage still stands in Greenhill Road. Although it has a nineteenth-century brick façade it is likely to be of early eighteenth-century construction. The outbuildings survive, but partly as extensively modernised dwellings. A thatched, timber-framed, single-hearth building, probably of the early seventeenth century, also stood nearby on Greenhill Road. This building has long since disappeared, but a nineteenth-century photograph still exists. In close proximity, near Mather Avenue, the oldest surviving example is the listed Springhill/Brocklebank Cottage dating from the seventeenth century. The third settlement lay around the demesne land of Allerton Hall in the south. Allerton Hall cottage, a two-storey sandstone construction, has a 1639 date stone above the main door. Further south towards Hillfoot is Oak Farm, also sandstone, two-storeyed with mullioned windows and later additions. Shortbutts Farm, also part of this settlement and dating from the early eighteenth century, lay to the south-west of the Hall on land later acquired by Liverpool Corporation for the cemetery. The lord's mill stood on the hill to the north of the Hall on Mill Lane (now Woolton Road). The first reference to a mill in the township is when Edward de Lathom purchased '6 messuages a mill and land in Allerton' in 1441 and a sketch appears on the map of 1568. The mill or its site is mentioned on maps of the late eighteenth century and 'the road to the mill' is referred to on the Woolton and Childwall Enclosure Act of 1805. Later land purchases suggest the mill was demolished between 1825 and 1829. This mill may have been a later construction, as a field name on the 1771 estate map implies that an earlier mill existed in the field to the north-west of the eighteenth-century mill. This may have been Lathom's original mill.

By the nineteenth century Childwall was also still exclusively rural, with a small village centred around the parish church and several isolated farms around the margins of the township. This nucleated village of Childwall, although possibly shrunken, consisted of a manor house and outbuildings, a vicarage and two farms. The vicarage, which had been established as early as 1307 on land opposite the church known as 'Green land' and was documented as having 'five Bays of building' in 1728 no longer exists, the Parish Hall having been erected on the site in 1932. The two farms, eighteenth and nineteenth-century sandstone buildings and outbuildings still exist.

The mid-nineteenth century nucleated village of Fazakerley, shown on maps of the period, which lay in a straggling linear plan along Higher Lane, was probably on the site of the original medieval village. The most likely area of medieval open field arable close by supports this view. Only two settlements still remain; an eighteenth/nineteenth-century brick house and barn and, several hundred metres to the north, the unused barn of a demolished farmhouse.

Four settlements had developed in Little Woolton by the mid-nineteenth century. One lay along Belle Vale/Wambo Lane and was probably the main settlement at the time of Domesday, known as 'Ulventune'. A second area, also probably part of Ulventune, lay on the higher sandstone ridge to the west. Throughout the medieval and post-medieval period this land was the common pasture for Little Woolton and may have been the location of 'half a league of wood' recorded at the time of Domesday. This settlement resulted from the 1805 enclosure of the common. The settlement developed in the Rose Brow/Woolton Hill Road area, but an earlier concentrated village grew along the Portway (Halewood Road), part of which was in Much Woolton. The earliest reference to this is when Hugh Whitfield of Gateacre is mentioned in court rolls. Two early buildings survive here on the Grange Lane section, both of which are probably seventeenth-century. One is probably a former farm and consists of a two-storey sandstone house with mullioned windows, while the other is part of a row of sandstone cottages. On the south-east edge of the township lay the final nucleated settlement, the Domesday manor of 'Wibaldslei', or Lee Park as it became. The settlement, which probably originated in the seventeenth century, still partly survives as standing buildings on Gerrards Lane. Originally it consisted of five small farms and cottages.

Two medieval settlements are apparent in Much Woolton. The main site was a linear development along Woolton Street/Ashton Square, which is also marked on the enclosure map of 1613. There has been continuity on this site to the present, although most of the houses are nineteenth-century brick houses with late eighteenth-century buildings interspersed. A medieval site may have existed out at Carkington on the southern margins, but this appears to have disappeared by the post-medieval period. The second main settlement was on the northern slopes at Gateacre, bordering Little Woolton and standing on the Portway cross road. The earliest documentary record is not until 1559, but the site may even have pre-Conquest

Stanlawe Grange, Aigburth, photographed in the late nineteenth century. Thought to be the oldest residence in Liverpool still occupied, it dates from the thirteenth century.

Threshing at Stanlawe Grange in the late nineteenth century.

origins, as the Domesday entry suggests land holdings large enough to support the settlement. The modern village is part of the Gateacre Conservation Area, the buildings being mainly nineteenth-century, except for the late eighteenth-century Unitarian chapel.

In West Derby, the largest township in the Liverpool district, a document of 1298 describes lands belonging to Earl Edmund, brother of Edward I, as '30 burgages with cottages let'. This suggests an established settlement and more than likely corresponds with the modern village of West Derby. Here still survives a mid-seventeenth-century sandstone former farmhouse, the 'Yeoman's House'. Across the road is the contemporary Court House, a single-storey sandstone building dating from about 1663 and probably on the site of the earlier manor court mentioned in a thirteenth-century land grant. Between the two buildings, on what was probably the village green, lay the chapel dating from 1786 (demolished in the mid-nineteenth century). But again there is documentary reference to an earlier building in 1360. A row of eighteenth-century cottages remains in Meadow Lane. The stocks and the village pound both add credence to the view that this was the main village of the township. There was an extension to the village to the south known as Town Row. This was probably medieval in origin and several nineteenth-century houses survive. Among them is a remnant, possibly dating from the sixteenth century, where an oak cruck from a timber cottage which once stood on the site was incorporated into a late eighteenth-century brick cottage (a detailed account can be consulted in Cooper & Power's *History of West Derby*). Clearance of the woodland and waste of the township is documented from the thirteenth century onwards, which must have resulted in the expansion of settlement. Several concentrated settlements existed by the eighteenth century. Another outlying settlement was in the West Derby/Mill Bank area, in what was formerly the nucleated settlement of Tuebrook. The second-oldest tenanted house in Liverpool (after Stanlawe Grange) is Tew Brook House. This brick-built, two-storey cottage with mullioned windows, with a date stone of 1615, represents the farm of a prosperous seventeenth-century yeoman farmer. A smaller, one-and-a-half storey sandstone cottage of similar date lies opposite. It may once have been a farm, although it is likely to have been occupied by someone of lesser status.

Further research

So much for the local landscape, but what of the people who inhabited these local townships? Of course, the census will reveal much about the nature of nineteenth-century settlements, but when combined with other sources it can be quite rewarding to see continuity of occupation by extended families.

The Tithe Commutation Act of 1836 replaced the ancient system of payment of tithes in kind with monetary payments. The Act substituted a

Tew Brook House.

variable monetary payment (known as the 'corn rent') for any existing tithe in kind. This payment was originally calculated on the basis of a seven-year average price of wheat, barley, and oats, with each grain contributing an equal part to the total. In many areas tithes had already been commutated and were unaffected. The majority of the survey took place before 1841, and it was largely completed by 1851. Three copies of each map and apportionment were made. The original copy was kept by the National Archives; the other two copies were deposited with the local diocesan registrar and parish. (Many of the latter copies have been transferred to local archives.) These maps and apportionments are a valuable source for historical researchers. This was a kind of Domesday of its time; all land ownership and land use was shown, as were names of tenants. All fields and buildings were numbered and named in the accompanying apportionment. Several exist for most of the suburbs around Liverpool, including Everton, Wavertree, Garston and Halewood. The originals are in the county record office, but local record offices hold certain copies. These maps of land ownership were drawn up in this area in the 1840s. They determined the taxes due when the payment of tithes to local clergy was abolished. They consist of a map and a schedule, which shows who owned and who rented the land and what it was used for. For a useful study of how enclosure impacted upon a local community see **Royden, M.W.** *The Effects of Enclosure: Halewood Township by the Mid Nineteenth Century*, Liverpool University BA thesis, unpublished, 1989. (Copies in Knowsley

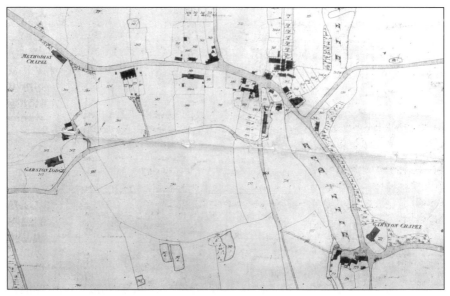

Detail from the Tithe Map of Garston, showing the Mill Dam Pool.

RO and Halewood Library, or online at www.roydenhistory.co.uk. Select Mike Royden's Local History Pages.)

Agricultural labourer, the 'ag lab' of the census, was the most common occupation throughout this area until the turn of the nineteenth century. The majority of the rural population were involved in agriculture despite the close proximity of the port. It would not be until the development of the local railway infrastructure that changes began to be seen in this occupational structure. For example, in Halewood, nine miles south of Liverpool centre, it was not until the construction of the Cheshire Lines railway and Halewood station in the 1870s that commuters began to move in to this quiet township. In fact the railway made a great impact during the period of construction, as it cut through most of the townships surrounding Liverpool. Sleepy backwaters were suddenly invaded by industrial workers, bringing change that often altered the social structure for good. There were new dangers on the railway: rural folk soon learned the difference between being hit by a train or by a horse. Nine people buried in St Nicholas's churchyard in Halewood between 1875 and 1888 had died on the railways. In the burial records there was a noticeable attitude, hostile or otherwise, of the incumbent to the railway. No causes of death are recorded in the burial registers of St Nicholas *except* those on the railways. In fact, any relationship to the new railway was recorded: ' . . . of new Railway Cottages . . . died at Railway Cottage . . . wife of station master . . . ' and so on. Does this reflect a general feeling in the community, of hostility or awe, or just that of the presiding vicar? We can only surmise. **Royden, M.W.** *The Impact of the Coming of the Railway on 19th Century Halewood* – copies deposited and online as noted above – contains a study of the local society, occupations and lifestyle and how these were affected by the railway. It can be seen as an example study of the experience of townships surrounding the town at this time. John Cooper and David Powers's books on West Derby are also excellent in this regard (*A History of West Derby* and *The People of West Derby*) and contain a wealth of photographs of local people and brief studies of many of the families featured.

There is no single set of records that can be used to track down agricultural labourers. In fact it was the census of 1841 that grouped various rural occupations together under this catch-all description. Before that they were husbandry servants, labourers, or farm servants. Local Record offices carry numerous photographs depicting their daily life, from posed scenes among the crop fields to the industrious scenes when the threshing machine came to visit. Quarter Sessions Papers found in the county record offices detail proceedings for petty offences such as licensing and poaching. Once dates are pinpointed a search of local newspapers can prove fruitful. They are often very detailed and could cover local misdemeanours, incidents of fire, accidents and deaths and other issues affecting rural life. Owners of large farms and estates kept records such as wages, cottage rents and land transfer, all of which detail names and where labourers may have lived. Overseer's records also need to be consulted as most families would have claimed relief of some kind. Other records relevant to this section held by the County Record Office are parish charities, diaries, estate records, local newspapers, census returns and parish registers.

Enclosure Maps and the accompanying apportionment book are held there also. Even if the map does not show names, tenants may appear in the apportionment. Liverpool Record Office holds the 1613 Enclosure Award for Much Woolton, otherwise local county record offices should be consulted.

Manorial records

The thought of consulting manorial records can be daunting for the inexperienced, but many are easily accessible and can provide unexpected glimpses of ancestors' lives in the community. Documents include court rolls, surveys, maps, terriers, documents and books of every description relating to the boundaries, wastes, customs or courts of a manor. In other words, any documents which were generated by the internal administration. The manor was basically an administrative unit of a landed estate. It could vary in size from a few acres within a parish, to many square miles within several parishes. In some cases, the bounds of a manor may have been the same as the boundaries of a village; sometimes a single village may have been part of several manors; in other cases a manor may have been a group of scattered lands and farmsteads interspersed with the lands of other manors. Tenants paid rent and service to the lord of the manor, they had to abide by the customs of the manor, and the succession of their land was governed by the manor court, which often also acted as the local court of law for routine offences. Manors were an important feature of local communities. There were two basic courts in this system; the court leet and the court baron. Court barons were held around every three weeks and all bound tenants were expected to attend. Small claims could be brought, such as disputes with neighbours, and property transactions were also recorded. Leets took place only twice a year. All tenants over the age of twelve had to swear fealty to their lord and attend the sessions. This was usually the first court for both civil and criminal cases brought by tenants. Local officials, such as constables and waywardens, were appointed by these courts. Any wrongdoings, disputes or breaking of byelaws were brought before this court. The lord of the manor or his steward presided over both courts, but members of the community took an active part in deciding the outcome and collecting fines. If tenants could not pay, animals were often impounded in the village pinfold. Where these documents exist quite a picture can be drawn up of the villagers within their small communities in the rural hinterland of the town. Many names crop up again and again and, when tied in with maps, enclosure, tithe and census, family groups can be pieced together and continuity of occupation traced back several generations. A useful example is summarised by Janet Hollinshead in *Halewood Township – A Community in the Early Eighteenth Century*, THSLC

Vol.130, 1981 (although this is only part of a much broader, unpublished doctoral thesis looking at South-West Lancashire, held at Liverpool University).

A most useful magazine article to introduce the researcher to manorial records, by Peter Foden, can be found in *Who Do You Think You Are?* No.16, BBC, December 2008. Likewise Denis Stuart's *Manorial Records: An introduction to their transcription and translation*, Phillimore, 1992, is recommended. Another very useful introduction in layman's terms is the 'Medieval Roots' section within *Explore Your Family's Past*, Readers Digest, 2000. With regard to manorial records, the TNA manorial document register is a useful online resource for finding out what is available and where to track it down. Some may be in private hands or with solicitors - see www.nationalarchives.gov.uk/mdr. The TNA also contains the Poor Law Commission records, estate records, assize and civil court records and records of emigration. The University of Nottingham has produced a useful online resource to help in learning to use manorial records. See www.nottingham.ac.uk/mss/learning/skills/manorial.

As the Earls of Derby held vast tracts of land throughout the West Derby Hundred and beyond it is inevitable that researchers will come across documents that will need to be consulted. They cover estate maps, land conveyances, court leets and court barons. A comprehensive catalogue is now online at the TNA Access to Archives (use the search path 'Lancashire Record Office/Stanley, Earl of Derby/ref DDK'). In a similar fashion, searches can also be made online for records of the other major local landowner, the Molyneuxs, Earls of Sefton (ref DDM). Much of the original material is held in Lancashire Record Office, although Liverpool Record Office does hold copies of much requested items such as tithe awards.

Wills

Wills and related documents, such as inventories, can be very useful sources of information. They are a great resource for local and family historians, as they can give details about personal possessions and even establish family relationships which might not otherwise be known.

Apprenticeship indenture records are useful for discovering an ancestor's trade or industry. This extract shows a James Gerrard apprenticed to Alexander Royden in 1707 to learn the trade of bricklaying. Their location can be found via the TNA online Access to Archives section.

Unfortunately, only a small proportion of the population made wills, as most of the labouring class were not in a position to do so. Tracking down a surviving will can also be difficult. Liverpool Record Office holds very few original or copy wills. Before 12 January 1858 the church courts dealt with the process of probate. If a person left a will it went to the appropriate court of probate to be proved. If they died without making a will ('intestate'), or did not appoint an executor, an administration bond was issued by the court to a named person or persons to administer the deceased's estate. After 1858 the process was passed to the civil courts.

Wills before 1858

Before 1541 Lancashire south of the River Ribble, including Liverpool, was in the Diocese of Lichfield. Surviving wills are at the Lichfield Record Office, Lichfield Library, The Friary, Lichfield, WS13 6QG.

From 1541 until 1880 Liverpool was in the Diocese of Chester. Wills for the Archdeaconry of Chester in Lancashire, which was the area south of the River Ribble including Liverpool, are held at the Lancashire Record Office. Indexes to these wills have been published by the Record Society of Lancashire and Cheshire. Copies of the indexes are held at Liverpool Record Office (see their online archive reference guide No.13).

For the years 1831–1858 there are typescript indexes available at both Lancashire Record Office and Cheshire and Chester Archives. Not all of the wills listed in the indexes still survive. Wills for Cheshire are at Cheshire and Chester Archives. There is an index for 1492–1940 at www.cheshire.gov.uk/recordoffice/wills/home.htm. The National Archives website also gives excellent guidance at www.nationalarchives.gov.uk/documentsonline/wills.

Wills after 1858

From 12 January 1858, a Principal Probate Registry was set up in London, along with forty District Probate Registries, including one at Liverpool. Indexes are available for England and Wales and record key details of all wills proved and letters of administration granted. Liverpool Record Office holds large volumes on open shelves covering 1858 to the 1950s. For later copies these are with the District Probate Registry at Queen Elizabeth II Law Court, Derby Square, Liverpool. Registered copies of wills for the Liverpool Registry are at Lancashire Record Office for 1858–1940, although some of the registers were damaged during the Second World War and are too fragile to consult. Copies of wills for England and Wales can be obtained for a fee by writing to the Postal Searches and Copies Department, York Probate Sub-Registry, 1st Floor, Castle Chambers, Clifford Street, York, YO1 9RG, with full details of the name and address of the deceased or by contacting your local Probate Registry. A search will be made for four years forward from the date of death.

Further Reading

The following contain useful studies on the local communities which now form part of Liverpool's suburbs:

Cooper, John and Power, David, *A History of West Derby*, 1982.

—— *The People of West Derby*, 1987.

King, A. *Huyton & Roby – A History of Two Townships*, Liverpool, 1984.

Lally, J.E. and Gnosspelius, J.B. *History of Much Woolton*, Liverpool, 1975.

Cox, E.W. 'Some Account of Garston, and of the Ancient Chapel of St Michael formerly existing there', THSLC Vol.40, New Series Vol.4, 1888.

Booth, P. 'From Medieval Park to Puritan Republic' in **Crosby, A. (Ed.)** *Lancashire Local Studies*, 1993.

Booth, P. 'The Background, People and Place' in *Sefton Park*, 1984.

Stewart-Brown, R. *A History of the Manor and Township of Allerton*, 1911.

Griffiths, R. *A History of the Royal and Ancient Park of Toxteth*, 1907.

Hatton, P.B. *The History of Hale*, 2nd ed., 1978.

Stewart-Brown, R. 'The Townfield of Liverpool' THSLC, Vol.68, 1916.

Cowell, R. *Knowsley Rural Fringes Survey*, National Museums on Merseyside.

Hollinshead, J. *The People of S.W. Lancashire During the Second Half of the Sixteenth Century*, 1986, unpublished PhD thesis, Sydney Jones Library, University of Liverpool.

—— *Halewood Township during the first quarter of the eighteenth century*, M.Phil thesis, Liverpool University, 1980.

The following papers are online at www.roydenhistory.co.uk:

Royden, M.W. *The Impact of the Coming of the Railway on Nineteenth century Halewood*, Liverpool University, unpublished, 1988.

—— *The Moated Sites of Halewood*

—— *The Effects of Enclosure: Halewood Township by the Mid Nineteenth Century*, Liverpool University BA thesis, unpublished, 1989.

Chapter Five

TRANSPORT

During the period of the early Industrial Revolution there were three crucial stages of development in local communications: the improvement of roads from Liverpool, the construction of canals with their terminal points in Liverpool and the opening of the Liverpool to Manchester Railway in 1830. As a direct consequence, within fifty years Liverpool's isolation and remoteness had ended.

Early roads and trackways

The state of the road network in the parishes of Childwall and Walton by the end of the eighteenth century can be best observed by using William Yates's Map of Lancashire, published in 1786. Certain roads can be easily dated, such as the then recently constructed turnpikes. However, the dating of the roads thought to be ancient trackways is very difficult. Two roads of significance had existed since ancient times. Evidence existed in the nineteenth century of a Roman road running through Grassendale and Otterspool (no doubt linking the Pool – later to be Liverpool – with the Within Way route to the river cossing at Hale). The other was the Portway, which ran from the Mersey near Oglet through Speke and Childwall, heading north.

Responsibility for the upkeep of the highways fell upon the holder of the land through which the route passed. This was usually the lord of the manor, who passed the obligation on to his manor constables, with the duty of supervision determined by the court leet (manorial court). The officers were also charged with ensuring that highways and footpaths to the church, mill or market were not stopped or hedged up. Bridges also had to be maintained.

In the Highways Act of 1555 responsibility for the upkeep of the king's highways was transferred to the parishes. Each parishioner owning a ploughland in tillage, or keeping a draught or plough, was liable to supply a cart for four days a year for use in road repair. Each able-bodied householder or tenant was required to give four days 'statute' labour a year (increased to six in 1691). It was possible to pay a fine to commute this or else to provide a substitute. One (or more) surveyors were appointed by each parish. Usually, the selection of such an officer was made by the churchwardens, the constable and some parishioners; from 1622 the selection was made by the majority of parishioners. The procedure was altered once more in 1691 when it became the custom for the parish officers to supply a suitable list of people who could act as surveyors. This was forwarded to the justices, who then made the appointment.

Although maps of the seventeenth century show a road from Liverpool to Warrington, this was little more than a farm trackway and was impassable by coaches. To send letters or goods further afield, therefore, it was necessary to send them via packhorse to Warrington, where a link could be made with the Preston to London highway, which traversed the town. This crossing of the Mersey was the key to the whole road system in south-west Lancashire and it was clear to Liverpool merchants that it was imperative to improve communications to this route if there was to be any chance of exploiting the port and ending the relative remoteness of the area. Such isolation certainly hindered development.

Turnpikes

Wheeled traffic prior to the seventeenth century was rare. The primitive system of road maintenance could cope with the wear and tear of horse traffic, but by the later half of the seventeenth century, when wheeled traffic was beginning to increase, parishes were unable to maintain standards, especially as most villagers were unwilling to meet their obligations. Pressure began to mount on Parliament to allow tolls to be collected from the users of main roads in order to cover the costs of maintenance. The first Turnpike Act was passed in 1663 in Cambridgeshire and covered a section of the London to York road. It was a slow beginning, however, with a lull of nearly thirty years before the next Act was passed. Almost 2,000 Acts followed in the eighteenth century and in 1773 a General Turnpike Act was passed to speed up the process.

Local Turnpikes

The first local Act, passed in 1725, was the first of a series dealing with the improvement of the Liverpool to Prescot Road, the last of which was passed in 1831. The route, which left Liverpool via London Road and passed through Old Swan, Broadgreen and Roby, had clearly been a great hindrance to trade and travel by the early eighteenth century. The original application from Liverpool Council began:

This Councill, takeing into Consideration that the Road between this town and Prescott hath been almost unpassable, and that the Inhabitants of this Town have suffer'd much for want of getting their Coales home Dureing the Sumer season, thro' the Great Rains . . . and that it would be highly necessary to Gett an Act of Parliam't for the Repairing that Road, so that it may be passable att all times of the year, and for Erecting A turnpike thereon, It is Now Order'd that a Petition to the Parliam't for that purpose be prepar'd. (Liverpool Town Books, November 1725)

While half of the cost was met by the Borough, the annual rate levied on the inhabitants was soon found to be inadequate to keep the road in good repair. Furthermore, inhabitants of the townships were still liable to complete three days statutory work to help upkeep the road, so in June 1728 it was resolved to prosecute 'those persons, Inhabitants of West Derby, that neglected to do their Statute Work last Year upon Summons'.

The impetus behind the Liverpool to Prescot turnpike was the desire to improve the coal supply from the mines in the vicinity of Prescot and St Helens, and it was Liverpool merchants who petitioned for the Act. The tolls were farmed out to the highest bidder, toll gates being erected at

South Liverpool section from William Yates's map of Lancashire, showing the local turnpikes.

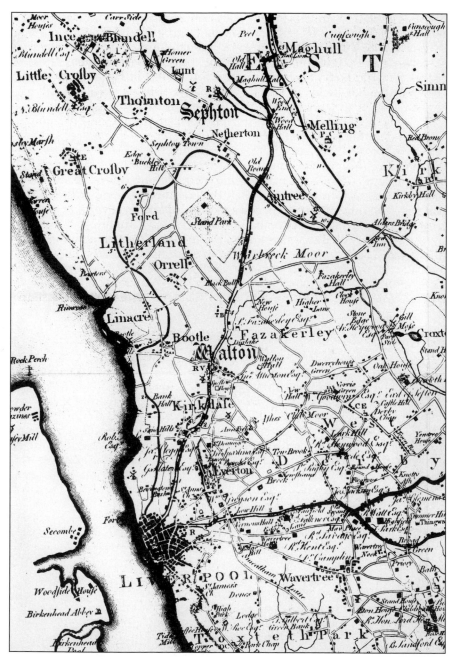

North Liverpool section from William Yates's map of Lancashire, showing the local turnpikes to Manchester and Warrington.

suitable points, controlled by the pikemen, who received low pay and a toll-house, rent free. In 1842 the wages ranged from 2s to 21s a week. Pikemen wore a distinctive dress: tall black glazed hats, stockings and knee breeches, and short aprons with large pockets for money.

The Liverpool to Prescot Turnpike was later extended to St Helens (1746), as the old packhorse track of cobbled stones was in bad repair as a result of the heavy coal traffic. Extensions to Warrington and Ashton followed in 1753. The period of transition was not altogether smooth as, shortly after this extension, cases occurred rather frequently of 'persons abusing the collector' and 'pulling down gates'. Entries in the Liverpool Town Books refer to the 'insults of the Prescot mob' and the 'danger of being plundered, by a mob of country people and colliers in and about Prescot'. Consequently, the Council ordered sixty good 'musketts and bayonetts' to defend the town, presumably against those who objected to the tolls. (Liverpool Town Books, 3 October 1759)

Within a year of the completion of the turnpike to Warrington, regular direct stage coach services from Liverpool to Manchester and London were opened in 1761. A coach also ran to Runcorn via Childwall, Woolton and Hale, returning daily (although it may have run only as far as the Mersey ferry at Hale).

Canals

The opening up of the salt fields of Cheshire and coalfields of south-west Lancashire following the construction of the Weaver Navigation and Sankey Canal was to be the catalyst for the development of Liverpool. The involvement of Liverpool merchants and surveyors from the outset was testament both to the desperate need for such projects, and to the growth of trade and economy in the area. The completion of the Bridgewater extension to Runcorn in 1773, and the Trent and Mersey in 1777, linking the Potteries with the Mersey, improved trade still further, but it was the opening of the Leeds and Liverpool Canal, with its terminal close to the central docks in the town, which gave the greatest boost to its trade and economy.

The idea for the canal was first mooted in Bradford in 1764, where local merchants were keen to meet the demand for limestone. From the early meetings between local men it was also apparent that if the canal was to be cut to Liverpool it would increase exports of local woollens to the expanding colonial markets abroad. However, in the preliminary meetings with Liverpool financiers it was clear that a compromise would have to be reached over the route, as funding would only be forthcoming from the Liverpool entrepreneurs if the town's now insatiable demand for coal was satisfied by the provision of a link with the coalfields of Wigan and Chorley.

After a protracted dispute it was agreed to commence the digging from each town simultaneously, thus enabling a swifter completion of the

Bradford link to Craven and its lime, and at the Liverpool end early access into the coalfields. Although this local section into Wigan via the Douglas Navigation was completed by 1774, the entire network would not be finished until well into the 1800s.

During the early 1800s the canal route, on its final approach to Liverpool, passed through an almost entirely rural landscape, from the point where it entered the township of Kirkdale, near Bank Hall, until it reached the industrial site of Moore and Gouthwaite's glass bottle works at Gerard Bridge. (Later the dock branch would be constructed nearby). Industry was still in its infancy in this area and the route continued through the open country as far as Chisenhale Bridge, where it passed the newly-erected lead works. A short distance beyond, the canal terminated at a basin near the end of Old Hall Street.

The town was now achieving increasing recognition as an international port and was able to retain enough raw materials passing through to become a sizable industrial area itself. The abundance of salt was soon capitalised upon and led to an expansion in the brewing trade. Thirty-nine breweries produced nearly 50,000 hogsheads of ale a year in the 1780s and another sixty-nine brewers produced table beer. There were eight sugar houses refining 6,000 hogsheads a year, while limekilns and brickfields produced more material than was needed to build the houses, docks and warehouses of the rapidly expanding city. Four iron foundries, three glass-works, seven tobacco-pipe manufacturers, several potteries and the thirty-nine copper works consuming 10-12,000 tons of coal per year all contributed to significant industrial growth.

A stocking factory was opened in the 1780s and in the following decade four cotton mills and a sulphuric acid plant were established, giving rise to Gores's observation, in his Liverpool Directory of 1794, that 'now in the town and its vicinity are numerous erections for most of the manufacturers hitherto carried on in the inland towns . . . to which give a new character and spirit to the place', which, he explained, had only happened 'of late'. This expansion of smelting, boiling, melting and steam-powered industry was due mainly to cheap high-quality coal supplies pouring into Liverpool after the completion of the Sankey Navigation in 1757 and the Leeds and Liverpool Canal in 1794.

This rate of industrial expansion was not to last, however. It was becoming apparent that Liverpool manufacturers could not compete with those of the specialized establishments situated at the source of one of the heavy materials they used, especially when sited along the banks of the inland waterways. Many of the new industries closed down. The salt-works moved upriver in 1798; the breweries proved inadequate and increasing quantities of ale had to be imported from the surrounding area; the copperworks ceased production in 1794 and the textile industries were short-lived. Thus a pattern was becoming established in the relationship between Liverpool and the rest of south-west Lancashire, which was to be followed even more strongly into the nineteenth century.

The waterways had created an integrated industrial system in north-west England and the continued developments through competition between manufacturers in different parts of the area consistently disadvantaged industry in Liverpool. Whereas the hinterlands were able to industrialize around the canal system, Liverpool's status as an industrial centre was to decline, and instead it would become an entrepôt for the masses of raw materials and manufactured goods fed into the port.

Railways

Into the new century the problems posed by the inadequacies of the turnpikes multiplied as traffic increased. Packhorses, farmers' carts, stage coaches and lumbering wagons would flow daily along the poorly main-

The entrance tunnels to the Liverpool to Manchester Railway, 1831. The right tunnel led to the Liverpool terminus at Crown Street, the centre tunnel ran down an incline to the dockside station at Wapping and the left tunnel led to a goods yard.

tained tracks, described as 'circuitous, crooked and rough, with an infamous surface', often hampered by impossible conditions caused by the weather or frequent accidents. The canals too were proving inadequate for the demands for an efficient supply and swift turnaround. Bales of cotton would often be left on the Liverpool dockside for so long that it led to the criticism that the cotton took less time to reach Liverpool from the Americas than it did to reach Manchester from Liverpool. Furthermore, the longer a consignment was en route to its destination, the less likely it was to arrive intact and in good condition. Despite the slow circuitous routes, frozen surfaces in winter, low water levels in summer and the frequent pilferage, the canal operators became rich and powerful. They often ran over-priced monopolies, leaving merchants little alternative but to pay up.

It was hardly surprising that a more efficient form of transport would be born from such disenchantment. While the Leeds and Liverpool Canal took a meandering fifty-eight miles to reach Manchester, the proposed new railway would complete the distance in thirty-one. After a protracted battle, the new Liverpool to Manchester Railway opened on 15 September 1830. It was the first railway to incorporate everything – it was public and carried both freight and passengers. It was worked by locomotives, was promoted by Act of Parliament and was run on business principles. The 'Railway Age' had begun.

In Liverpool the main terminus was sited at Edge Hill, where John Foster's Moorish Arch would represent the gateway to the town. A 1¼-mile tunnel down to Wapping, providing a link to the docks, was commenced in 1826 and was completed three years later after being whitewashed throughout and lit by gas. Here gravity took trains down, while they were recovered to Edge Hill by a cable. The Moorish Arch also housed the stationary engines required to haul the trains. This method, which hauled the trains up a gradient rise of 123 feet, continued until 1896. It was surely one of the most underrated engineering achievements of the industrial age, given the primitive conditions. This preceded the more lauded Mersey Tunnel by over a hundred years. Understandably, the construction workers were often terrified. According to Ferneyhough:

> '. . . On some occasions . . . the men refused to work . . . nor is this surprising, considering the nature of the operations: boring their way almost in the dark, with the water streaming around them, and uncertain whether the props or stays would bear the pressure from above till the arch-work should be completed . . . the light of a few candles . . . barely sufficient to show the dreariness of the place'. (*Liverpool and Manchester Railway 1830–1980*)

To promote public relations, and to dispel potential panic among future passengers riding in unlit carriages under the bowels of the town, 3,000 people were allowed to walk its length in the summer of 1829 at a shilling a time.

A second tunnel, shorter at 290 yards, was cut from Edge Hill to Crown Street, where the main railway premises, the principal station for railway carriages and a depot for coal would be situated. Its use as a passenger terminal would be short-lived, however, as a third tunnel, this time to the newly-erected Lime Street Station, was opened on 15 August 1836. Again, locomotives were not permitted along the steep gradient and trains were hauled back up to Crown Street by the use of a long rope attached to a counter-weight, which was allowed to sink into a sixty-foot well.

The approach to Liverpool was laid as level as possible, the result of which was yet another major feat of engineering, this time at Olive Mount, where it was necessary to excavate a cutting, originally only 20 feet wide at a depth of 70 feet. Later the cut was enlarged from a double to a quadruple track, but it remains an impressive sight. Cut by hand, almost 480,000 cubic yards of material were removed, much of which was reused in the construction of the embankment at Roby.

The effect of the railway on the rural townships was, in certain areas, overwhelming, and would often change a sleepy agricultural area into one of bustling activity, sometimes merely because it was where routes crossed, rather than through the exploitation of local trade or resources. Earlestown, near Newton-le-Willows, and Monks Coppenhall, which grew into Crewe, were clear examples. In Liverpool, the desire to service the docks later in the century resulted in the dissection of a number of townships, especially after the Cheshire Lines failed to gain access via the south end route. This led to an extension circumnavigating the outskirts of the town to enter the dock at the north end.

By the early twentieth century, several competing companies had a complex network of passenger and goods lines in Liverpool and its environs, including the London & North Western Railway, the Lancashire & Yorkshire, the Midland, and the Cheshire Lines Committee. Added to this was the famous 'Docker's Umbrella', the Liverpool Overhead Railway.

Liverpool Overhead Railway

The Liverpool Overhead Railway was commenced in 1889, completed in January 1893 and opened on 4 February 1893. The railway ran from Alexandra Dock in the north to Herculaneum Dock in the south, a distance of six miles. It used standard gauge track and there were eleven stations along the line. This was the first electrically powered overhead railway in the world. On 30 April 1894, the line was extended northwards to Seaforth Sands and southwards to the Dingle on 21 December 1896. Dingle was the line's only underground station and was located on Park Road. However, to reach the Dingle a 200-foot lattice girder bridge had to be built from Herculaneum to the raised tunnel entrance, which ran half a mile through the sandstone rock to the terminus. Finally, on 2 July 1905, a northward extension was connected to the Lancashire and Yorkshire Railway's North Mersey Branch.

A significant target during the Blitz, Liverpool docks suffered extensive damage during the raids and the Overhead Railway suffered badly due to its close proximity. After the war, as the railway was a local undertaking, it was not nationalised in 1948 with the rest of the British railway system. Some modernisation did take place, and although it was still heavily used by passengers, especially dock workers, structural surveys revealed that expensive repairs estimated at £2 million would be needed to ensure the line's long-term survival. The Liverpool Overhead Railway Company could not afford such costs and went into voluntary liquidation. Despite considerable protest, the line was closed on the evening of 30 December 1956. The final trains each left either end of the line, marking the closure with a loud bang as they passed each other. Both trains were full to capacity with well-wishers and employees of the company. By 1958 the entire structure had been removed, leaving very little trace of the railway, save for a small number of upright columns found in the walls at Wapping and the tunnel portal at Dingle. The station at Dingle still exists as an underground garage.

The former southern terminus of the Overhead Railway at Dingle, now an underground garage.

Aviation

Flat land on the banks of the Mersey estuary has offered useful facilities to aviators almost since the beginning of powered flight. In November 1917, the Cunard Steamship Company were given a contract to build 500 Bristol F.2B fighters at Aintree (later the site of Courtaulds) and tests were flown on the racecourse. The following year the factory was taken over by the Government and it became National Aircraft Factory No.3. Only 126 aircraft had been delivered before production ceased in March 1919. Five years later, Northern Airlines at Aintree began to operate a daily mail service to Belfast using de Havilland 50s and passengers were also carried. It was clear that a purpose-built aerodrome was necessary for a city the size of Liverpool and in 1927 the Liverpool Organisation (partly financed by Liverpool City Council) lobbied for a municipal aerodrome. In 1928 there was still no suitable site put forward and Hooton Airfield was used. This was a former racecourse that had been used as an army training ground and airstrip during the First World War. Meanwhile, later that year, Liverpool City Council purchased 2,200 acres, part of the Speke Estate, from the executors of its former owner Miss Adelaide Watt (of Speke Hall). As well as being earmarked for housing and industrial estates, provision was to be made for a municipal aerodrome. In February 1929 the Government sanctioned a loan of £162,150 to purchase 1,726 acres of land, and the balance of the area was bought in 1933. During September/October 1928, Liverpool Organisation operated an experimental mail/passenger service from Liverpool to Belfast using a Short Calcutta Flying Boat of Imperial Airways operating from the River Mersey. Liverpool Maritime Aerodrome was operated by the Mersey Docks and Harbour Board between Rock Ferry Pier and Garston Docks until the war, although no trace of further flights has been found.

In 1929 the Town Council proposed five sites for the new airport: two within the site of the now Old Airport, one site within the present airport site, one site straddling Woodend Avenue and even one within Walton Hall Park. The 'northern airfield' site was chosen and construction began in March 1930. Enough work had been completed by 16 June 1930, when a licence was granted for a private-use aerodrome. Later that day an Armstrong-Whitworth Argosy airliner of Imperial Airways arrived to begin a service from Croydon to Speke via Birmingham and Manchester, which ran successfully until September. On 1 July 1933 the airfield was

An Armstrong-Whitworth Argosy airliner at Croydon. The first aeroplane service to use Liverpool airport?

P-51 Mustangs pictured on Allerton Road on their way for completion at Lockheeds.

officially opened to the public, although the only aerodrome building was a wooden structure on the north-east side of the landing ground. The new airport terminal building was finally opened in 1938.

During the war, the airport was taken over by the Royal Air Force and was known as RAF Speke. Hundreds of local people joined the war effort when Rootes built many bombers in a shadow factory here, including Bristol Blenheims and 1,070 Handley Page Halifaxes. Lockheed Aircraft Corporation assembled numerous planes, including Hudsons and Mustangs, which had been shipped from the United States to Liverpool Docks. The airport was also home to the Merchant Ship Fighter Unit.

Civil airline operations resumed on a normal basis after VE Day, and although growth was witnessed initially, ownership by the Ministry of Aviation proved to be a hindrance and Manchester began to gain the lead. The City Council took over control of the airport on 1 January 1961 and, in 1966, a new 7,500-foot (2,286m) runway was opened on a new site to the south-east of the existing airfield. A new modern passenger terminal, adjacent to the runway on the southern airfield site, opened in 1986, and this was followed by the closure of the original 1930s building. However, the old airport building has recently been renovated and adapted as a hotel, preserving its Grade II-listed Art Deco style. The apron is also listed and several historical aircraft are preserved either side of the old terminal. The two Art Deco style hangars that flank the terminal and apron have also been converted to new uses.

Further research

Liverpool Record Office – see online local catalogues and information sheets

The City Council generated huge amounts of material on roads and various forms of road transport, including a succession of major plans for the city's transport networks, during the twentieth century. Its role in licensing taxis and managing the bus and tram systems has also produced many publications: search the catalogues for 'hackney carriages', 'buses', 'tramways' and 'road safety'. See also the reading guides on 'Horses'.

Port Cities

www.mersey-gateway.org – numerous pages under transport.

Further reading

Road transport

Tupling, G.H. 'The Turnpike Trusts of Lancashire' *Memoirs and Proceedings of the Manchester Literary and Philosophical Society*, Vol.94, 1952–3.

Horses and carters

Harry Wooding, *Liverpool's working horses*, Liverpool, 1991. A detailed personal account by a young Liverpool carter; has an appendix with lists of firms, horses and carters.
Edward N. Clark, *The carthorse and the quay: The story of the Liverpool cart horses*, Garstang, 1989. An excellent study with great detail and photographs, tracing the rise and fall of the industry.
Paul Smith, "'A proud Liverpool union': The Liverpool and District Carters' and Motormen's Union, 1889–1946", *Historical Studies in Industrial Relations*,16, 2003, pp.1–38. A recent study of the carters' efforts to unionise, and the transition to motor transport in the twentieth century.

Canals

Canal Museum help for researchers: www.canalmuseum.org.uk/collection /family-history.htm.

Census: The master of a canal boat filled in a special schedule for all on board his vessel on the day of the census. This would appear at the end of an enumeration district.

John Roberts's *Waterway Index* contains the names of more than 9,500 men connected to the waterways (such as boatman, waterman, flatman, boat-builder, lock-keeper, toll-collector, canal or river company clerk, canal agent, boat owner, navigator (navvies), wharfinger, etc). Contact John Roberts, 52 St Andrews Road, Sutton Coldfield, B75 6UH.

Barker, T.C. 'The Sankey Navigation – The First Lancashire Canal', *THSLC*, Vol.100, 1948.

Clarke, Mike, *The Leeds and Liverpool Canal: A History and Guide*, Carnegie, 1990.

McIntyre, W. 'The First Scheme for Docks at Birkenhead and the Proposed Canal Across Wirral' *THSLC*, Vol.124, 1972.

Willan, T.S 'The Navigation of the River Weaver in the Eighteenth Century', *Chetham Society Transactions*, Vol.3, 3rd series, 1951.

Railways

Bolger, P. *Illustrated History of The Cheshire Lines Committee*, 1984.
Prys Griffiths, R., *The Cheshire Lines Railway*, 1947.
Singleton, D., *Liverpool and Manchester Railway*, Dalesman, 1975.
Thomas, R.H.G., *The Liverpool and Manchester Railway*, Batsford, 1980.
Ferneyhough, F., *Liverpool and Manchester Railway 1830–1980*, 1980.

The effect of the railway on local communities:
Royden, M.W., *The Impact of the Coming of the Railway on 19th Century Halewood*, BA (Hons.) dissertation, Liverpool University, 1989. Copies lodged at Halewood, Huyton and Liverpool Central Libraries.

Smith, L.J. 'The Impact of the Liverpool and Manchester Railway on a South Lancashire Township: Newton-le-Willows 1821–1851', *THSLC*, Vol.129, 1979.

Tramways

The Liverpool Tramways Company was authorised by Act of Parliament in 1868. It opened in November 1869 and its successors ran trams until 14 September 1957. The system ran from the Pier Head throughout the city.

Horne, J.B. and Maund, T.B., *Liverpool transport* (four volumes, London, 1975–89). Very detailed illustrated histories of Liverpool's tram and bus systems, 1830–1957.

Merseyside Tramway Preservation Society www.mtps.co.uk.

Birkenhead Tramway and Wirral Transport Museum: 1 Taylor Street, Birkenhead, Wirral, Merseyside, CH41 1B6. Tel: 0151 647 2128.

Overhead Railway

Gahan, John W., *Seventeen Stations to Dingle: Liverpool Overhead Railway Remembered*, Countyvise, 1982.
Bolger, Paul, *Docker's Umbrella: History of Liverpool Overhead Railway*, The Bluecoat Press, 1992.

Local Airport/Airfields

Under the catalogue entry for 'Airport' in the LRO there is a great deal of material generated by Liverpool City Council's Airport Committee in the 1960s, including a 20-year plan published in 1964. It also has records relating to successive airport managers, from the first manager, Harold Andrews in the 1930s.

Butler, Phil, *Liverpool Airport: An illustrated history*, Stroud, 2004.
Bowdler, Roger et al, *Berlin-Tempelhof, Liverpool-Speke, Paris-Le Bourget*, Paris, 2000. Nicely illustrated accounts of three important airports of the 1930s, including the original terminal at Speke.
History of local air travel – Port Cities – www.mersey-gateway.org (search for Liverpool Airport)
History of Hooton Airfield www.hootonparktrust.co.uk/history.html.

Section Two

SOCIETY

Chapter Six

A BLACK SPOT ON THE MERSEY OR A HOUSE IN THE PARK

Urban and suburban development during the nineteenth century

Spend a short time on Merseyside and you will soon hear strong views about the town planners, from those who marvel at the new post-millennium impetus reflected in the ivory towers that now dominate the old shore line behind the Three Graces, to those, in marked contrast, who quickly refer you to those areas of deprivation that seemed to have been forgotten about in the sheen of the 2007 Borough anniversary and the 2008 Capital of Culture. According to Ramsay Muir, it was no different 200 years earlier:

> Neither in 1785, nor in 1825, nor at any later date, did the Town Council make any attempt to control the character or direction of the new streets which were being created with such rapidity during this age of growth, so as to make the town healthy or beautiful. A glorious opportunity was lost. For Liverpool, throned on her long range of hill and looking over a magnificent estuary to the distant hills of Wales, might easily have been one of the most beautiful cities of Europe, if due care had been taken to ensure that the streets running down the hill should command uninterrupted vistas. The fact that in modern Liverpool these fine possible prospects do not anywhere refresh the vision of the treader of pavements must be attributed above all to the lack of foresight of the governors of the town in the age when it was so rapidly extended. (*A History of Liverpool*, 1907)

Muir suggested the Town Council were not left without guidance:

In 1816 for example, a memorial was sent up by a number of leading townsmen suggesting that a 'spacious handsome public road with wide footpaths planted on each side with two rows of trees' should be laid out, to run the whole boundary of the old township. Such a scheme could have been carried out at very little expense at that time; and how vastly it would have improved the aspect of the modern city! But the Council only curtly replied that 'the memorial cannot be entertained.'

The same townsmen also suggested that 'open pieces of land in the outskirts of the town [later to be covered with crowded housing] should be appropriated to the amusements of the working classes'. This would appear to be the first attempt to create parks or playgrounds, but again the proposal fell on deaf ears, such luxuries not yet felt to be necessary in the atmosphere of growing industrialisation and commerce.

Indeed, one of the most striking features of the town at this time was the absence of any pleasant green areas for the use of the general public. What green spaces there had been were being utilised for the densely packed housing concentrated around the docks.

While the planners failed to foresee the effects of allowing uncontrolled growth, the port expanded rapidly and so did the housing, to cope with the influx of its essential workforce, much of which was coming from Wales and Ireland. Meanwhile, while the slum areas increased, in sharply contrasting situations the new merchant classes were wasting little time in taking advantage of the wealth and opportunity there was for those prepared or able to exploit it. Their home was, during demanding periods, the large town house on the perimeter of the borough, especially those surrounding the neatly laid out squares of Abercromby and Falkner. For many, the aim was a mansion in the country, with an estate to go with it. But soon, what was once an idyllic rural backwater would be swallowed up by the suburban sprawl of the late nineteenth and early twentieth century, which would see the departure of many of the merchant families from the plethora of substantial Georgian and Victorian houses dotted around practically every surrounding township.

Expansion of town boundaries

The 1830s saw the end of an era regarding the political status of the town. On the passing of the Reform Bill in 1832, the days of the old corrupt Parliamentary Borough of Liverpool were numbered. At that time only 3,000 freemen voters out of a population of 165,000 were eligible to vote and the forthcoming increase in the franchise was sorely awaited. The Municipal Reform Act followed in 1835, which finally swept away the old Borough of Liverpool, with its minority of privileged freemen and self-electing council, replacing it with a democratic Borough Council elected by ratepayers. Powers were also granted by the Act to enlarge the new

Borough and following this the townships of Kirkdale, Everton and much of Toxteth and West Derby were taken in.

In fact, to ensure accurate assessment of the new borough areas, several detailed plans were commissioned and published during the mid-1830s (now of great value to historians): Jonathan Bennison's 'Map of the Town and Port of Liverpool' (1835); Michael Gage's 'Trigonometrical Plan of the Town and Port of Liverpool' (1836); and Austin's 'Liverpool and its Environs', (1836). (Copies held at Liverpool Record Office.)

Housing – the Black Spot on the Mersey

The new council brought with it significant change as it reconstructed the whole system of borough government. The old and separate Watching, Lighting and Cleansing Boards were taken over and the council immediately proceeded to reorganise the police force. Several sub-committees were created to suggest schemes for administrative reform, one of which concerned itself with the appalling housing problem, which was now reaching overwhelming proportions. The number of unhealthy and unsafe houses had now become so high that a building surveyor was appointed to demolish dangerous houses at the owner's cost.

So great was the problem that even these measures were inadequate. Hundreds of houses, although not in imminent danger of collapse, were dangerous due to their unsanitary condition and the appalling state in which their inhabitants had to live. To remedy this, the council obtained powers to impose certain building regulations on all new buildings erected in the town, to close existing houses which were not merely dangerous but filthy or unwholesome, and to appoint a Health Committee to regulate the sanitary condition of the town. As a result of these proposals the Building Act was passed in 1842, which was the pioneer Act of its kind in England and the model for other towns.

Following the Act, the improvement of sanitation and housing was vigorously tackled. Further attention was focused on the problems of the town after Dr William Henry Duncan, a lecturer at the Royal Infirmary School of Medicine, published a pamphlet drawing attention to the squalid conditions of the housing. His report revealed that half of the working-class population of the town dwelt in narrow enclosed courts, devoid of all sanitary provisions, or in dank underground cellars. Only the streets of the 'well-to-do' were provided with sewers, while the lodging houses in which many of the poorer population lived were crowded together in reeking cellars covered with dirty straw. His calculations showed a staggering ratio of 100,000 people per square mile, which also included the spacious and airy abodes of the wealthy. No town in England was so unhealthy. There was unparalleled mortality; one in twenty-five people died from diseases such as cholera and typhoid every year. Overall he drew a picture of squalor, disease, misery and vice as in no other English city.

The council, meanwhile, secured a new Act in 1846, which added further powers to those granted by the 1842 Building Act. By this, proper sewers were regulated for all streets; powers were provided to carry out regular inspections of lodging houses; smoke pollution from factories could now be controlled; powers were given to the council to provide an adequate water supply; and for the first time an expert Medical Officer responsible for general health of the town was to be appointed. Duncan was the appropriate choice – the first such appointment in the country.

The great campaign against unsanitary dwellings began the following year, in 1847. A health committee under Duncan was formed, which inspected, measured and registered a total of 14,085 inhabited cellars. Of those, 5,841 had wells or muddy and stagnant water on or under the floors. During the year over 5,000 cellars were cleared of their inhabitants. This could only be a temporary solution, but the Sanitary Amendment Act of 1864 enabled the Medical Officer to recommend buildings for condemnation, and for the council itself to alter or demolish all dwellings they condemned, after purchasing them or paying compensation to the owners.

Two problem areas clearly stood out: the Toxteth quarter near to Parliament Street and the Docks, and Vauxhall to the north. This was highlighted on an intriguing map produced by Abraham Hume, vicar of Vauxhall, in 1858 entitled *Liverpool, Ecclesiastical and Social*. On the map were recorded pauper streets, semi-pauper streets and streets of crime, vice, immorality and disease. Hume also highlighted the ratio of churches to the local population figures, contrasting the affluent well-served merchant-class areas (27 churches serving 10,000 people) with the deprived slum areas (12 churches serving 35,000), arguing that it was the lack of support by the church which must shoulder part of the blame (copy held at Liverpool Record Office).

These squalid houses had begun to appear towards the end of the eighteenth century and into the early nineteenth, without restriction regarding size, provision for light and air or sanitary conditions. Quite often families would use cellars once part of dockland warehouses, or even cellars of merchant houses in the dock areas where formerly rich and poor lived together. As the multitudes swarmed into the docklands, crowded slums were inevitable. It was so different to the contrasting fortunes of the rising merchant and ship-owning class of the same period.

A house in the park

While the working class and paupers crowded into the central areas, merchants and the rich removed to the urban outskirts and rural hinterland. Large Georgian townhouses increasingly appeared on the periphery, such as those in Duke Street and Hanover Street. Rodney Street was one of the earliest and largest of the new residential areas springing up on the boundary at that time.

The programme began slowly, but by 1807 most of Rodney Street had been developed, and formed part of a larger line of similar housing stretching northwards along Clarence Street, Russell Street and Seymour Street towards St Anne Street. However, it was the laying out of the former Mosslake Fields which has left the greatest legacy from this early display of merchant affluence. In 1800 the Corporation Surveyor, John Foster Senior, prepared a grid iron plan for the development of this extensive former peat bog. Again building was initially slow, but within twenty years the northern area was developed around Abercromby Square, although it would not be until after 1835 that the Canning Street and Falkner Street plans would see fruition. Today what remains is one of the largest areas of Georgian townhousing outside London. So impressive is this heritage that it has now become a popular alternative to the capital as a period location for film-makers.

As the port and its merchants prospered, it became fashionable to secure a house with an estate in the country. Most townships already had large mansion houses, but these were usually the manor house, such as Speke Hall, Allerton Hall, Old Hutt, Bank Hall, Woolton Hall and Childwall Hall. During the nineteenth century, however, a plethora of mansions appeared, while large areas of former agricultural lands were turned into estates and landscaped. There were three phases in the erection and use of such housing. The first was of the result of early enterprise; the slavers and privateers, who erected homes such as Carnatic Hall in Mossley Hill, Allerton (not to be confused with Allerton Hall) and St Domingo in Everton. A second wave was built for the nineteenth-century industrialists and businessmen, who were responsible for expansive homes such as Allerton Tower, Larkhill, Roby Hall, Wavertree Hall, Hart Hill, Calderstone and Otterspool, and many more which came to litter the outlying townships.

Childwall Abbey.

Allerton, to take one township for example, was clearly an attractive proposition and was extensively divided by the new landowning class. In the north end, on the Wavertree border, Joseph Need Walker, a shot manufacturer of Chester and Liverpool, purchased the Old Hall of Calderstone in 1828 and erected a new mansion house in its place (the same building stands today in Calderstones Park, part of it being used as the tea room). Meanwhile, Walker began to systematically acquire adjoining land until he had amassed 93 acres, which he passed onto his son in 1865. The estate was later secured by the shipowner Charles MacIver in 1873, but following his death it was purchased by Liverpool Corporation in 1902 for £43,000 and formally opened as parkland on 20 February 1905.

Nearby was 'Hart Hill', an estate once owned by the Percevals, who had the house erected in 1825. The estate and house were purchased in 1848 by John Bibby, a Liverpool iron and copper merchant. The house was later demolished, apart from the lodges and stables. By 1964 Calderstones Park and the former Harthill Estate in particular had assumed the role of Liverpool's Botanic Garden, although the glasshouses were allowed to fall into such a dilapidated condition that they had to be demolished. The vestibule still remains, in which are housed the prehistoric Calderstones.

To the west of Calderstones, now either side of Mather Avenue, was the Wyncote Estate, with its early nineteenth-century house. Formerly the home of a merchant banker, it was later occupied by Henry MacIver, brother of the aforementioned Charles. In 1920 the estate was purchased by the University of Liverpool following a gift of £25,000 from Sir Thomas Harrison Hughes, the shipowner. The house was demolished in the mid-1960s, while the open land now forms an impressive University sports complex.

Towards the southern Woolton boundary of the township a number of substantial houses were erected in leafy surroundings, including 'Allerton' and 'Allerton Tower'. The former replaced an earlier house of the same name destroyed by fire, which had been constructed in the early 1800s. The second house, erected in 1815, was occupied by Joseph and Caleb Fletcher, sons of Captain Caleb Fletcher, a well-known Liverpool privateer. 'Allerton' was also purchased by Liverpool Corporation, which paid £40,000 for the house and estate in 1921. In 1923 it was opened as a municipal golf course with the house functioning as the club house. 'Allerton' was gutted by fire in 1944. Part of the building still remains, although the upper floor was removed due to its dangerous condition.

The latter house, 'Allerton Tower', stood between 'Allerton' and 'Allerton Hall' and was designed in 1847 by Harvey Londsdale Elmes, (architect of St George's Hall), as the residence of Sir Hardman Earle, one of the first directors of the Liverpool–Manchester Railway. It stood within 78 acres of land formerly part of the manor of Allerton, and was acquired by the Corporation in 1924 and developed as a park. Again there was no provision for the upkeep of the house and the dilapidated building had to be demolished in 1937. The orangery and outbuildings remain.

To the west of the township lies Springwood Hall, completed in 1839 by William Shand, a merchant in the West Indies trade, which was bought by the shipowner Thomas Brocklebank in 1844. Liverpool Corporation obtained the 123-acre estate in 1921 and it was later taken over by the Springwood Tenants' Association. After various uses it was opened in 1967 as a Leonard Cheshire Home. This home has now moved to a new site nearby, while the now privately owned 'Springwood Mansion Nursing Home' reopened in 1992 in the original hall. This brief study of Allerton also highlights the third phase affecting these estates; decline and reuse.

The later history of many of these mansions reflects the downturn in the fortunes of the port. Often merchants' business interests took them elsewhere, usually to the south, or profits became losses and houses had to be sold. As family inheritances were sometimes split between family members, owners were left with an impossible burden in the upkeep of such spacious homes. The swift appearance of these houses around the locality was matched by their rapid desertion in the twentieth century. A number were purchased by the Corporation, mainly where the estate could also be secured, usually with intention of providing parkland.

They have been reused in a variety of ways. Calderstone House and outbuildings now contain the offices of the city's recreation and open spaces department and a cafe. Nearby the Children's Playground was opened in June 2000 by Sir Paul McCartney and is dedicated to the late Linda McCartney. Sudley was bequeathed by the Holts and is now an art gallery. Other houses have been left to rack and ruin, leaving demolition as the only viable alternative.

Victorian Residential Parks

In the early to mid-nineteenth century, Grassendale and Cressington Parks were laid out as a private speculative venture. An administering body – the Trustees of the Parks – was set up to manage the restrictive covenants which govern the operation of the estate. Situated below St Mary's Road, both parks feature a carefully planned network of roads leading down the elegant riverside promenade.

Detached and semi-detached villas were sited in large plots of land, while a strong discipline in design was applied in the planning of boundary walls and use of external materials. Today the whole area is a conservation area and still has a timeless Victorian air, even down to the restored station which serves the park.

Fulwood Park, situated near the southern border of the ancient Toxteth Park, formed a long cul-de-sac running from Aigburth Road down towards the river. Again operated as a private estate, with entrance gates and a lodge, the area was laid out in the 1840s, with large, grand houses set in generous plots of land. Many of the Italianate houses had common features, such as square columned entrances, window mouldings and cornices, probably the work of the same architect.

Less substantial estates were laid out throughout the peripheral areas of the town, where Victorian villas lay in secluded leafy avenues, especially evident at Sandown Park, Victoria Park, Sandfield Park and Fairfield. As at Fulwood and Cressington, entrances were often provided with lodges and gates. At Sandfield privacy was encouraged by the sign at the entrance lodge, which read 'For daily use of Park Roads – all vehicles 1 penny per wheel'.

Garden Suburbs

Following the examples set by William Lever at Port Sunlight village and Hartley's Village at Aintree (and the much earlier experiment at Price's Patent Candle Company village at Bromborough Pool), with their low-density housing with gardens at reasonable rates and local amenities in peaceful, pleasant and healthy surroundings, elsewhere other industrialists followed suit, most notably at Cadbury's Bournville village, and Rowntree's New Earswick.

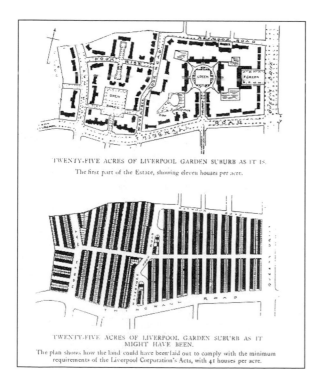

TWENTY-FIVE ACRES OF LIVERPOOL GARDEN SUBURB AS IT IS.
The first part of the Estate, showing eleven houses per acre.

TWENTY-FIVE ACRES OF LIVERPOOL GARDEN SUBURB AS IT MIGHT HAVE BEEN.
The plan shows how the land could have been laid out to comply with the minimum requirements of the Liverpool Corporation's Acts, with 41 houses per acre.

Wavertree Garden Suburb. The bottom plan shows what might have been, with rows of dense terraces, compared to the spacious garden design shown in the top plan.

Yet planners argued that such housing need not only be for the attached local factory worker. These 'communities', they claimed, were only extensions of the factories that they were built to serve. Following the views expressed by Ebenezer Howard in *Garden Cities of Tomorrow* (1902), the idea of utilising the best aspects of the factory village and removing it into a leafy 'garden suburb' were put into practice at Letchworth (commenced 1903), Hampstead Garden Suburb (1906) and Welwyn Garden City (1920).

While these designs were on a large scale, in Liverpool such ideas, although adopted, were not capitalised upon as much as they might have been, with only Wavertree Garden Suburb remaining as an example of what these pioneers were trying to achieve. In 1909 the Liverpool Garden Suburb Tenants Limited were set up as a workers' co-operative. Under the auspices of Co-partnership Tenants Limited, which had been formed two years earlier, the first 100 houses were completed at Wavertree and occupied by 1912, following the laying of the foundation stone of the first house on 20 July 1910.

The first part of the suburb to the west of Wavertree Nook Road was laid out in 1910 by Raymond Unwin, who, with his partner Barry Parker, had

New Corporation housing at Bevington Street, 1912.

already laid out Letchworth, Hampstead and New Earswick. All houses were provided with gardens, and the estate benefited from open spaces, tree-lined roads and amenities such as a bowling green, tennis courts, a children's playground and an Institute (formerly two farm cottages knocked together). The original plan was to extend the suburb as far as Childwall, near to the five-ways, but war curtailed the programme in 1915 and only 360 of the planned 1,800 houses were built. Originally the area was to have been a suburb of Liverpool, of which the present area is only part, and would, no doubt, have taken the name 'Liverpool Garden Suburb'. However, after the rationalisation of plans it became known under its present localised title.

Expansion of the Dock Estate

Changes to the shoreline showed no signs of slowing. The remarkable system of enclosed docks continued to expand north and south during the nineteenth century until they covered nine miles of the waterfront, stretching from Hornby at Kirkdale in the north, to the Herculaneum at Toxteth in the south. By the end of the eighteenth century eight docks had been completed: the Old Dock (built by Steers and opened in 1715), Canning (c.1737), Salthouse (1753), George's (1771), Duke's (1773), Manchester Basin (1785), King's (1788) and Queen's (1796). As trade with the Americas increased, so did the demand for dock facilities. New warehouses – the Goree Piazzas – were constructed on the lower half of Water Street in 1793. A tobacco warehouse was erected at King's Dock in 1795 and an even larger building was added in 1812.

The advent of steam power generated significant expansion in the growth of the port. The first steamship entered the Mersey in 1815 and, together with the coming of the railway in 1830, this brought a huge increase in tonnage cleared at Liverpool. Following the end of the East India Company's trade monopoly in 1813 imports were boosted on a vast scale. From that date until 1857, imports of cotton multiplied five times, sugar and West Indian rum doubled, with the greatest increase in wheat from the United States and Canada, which rose tenfold. Meanwhile, salt exports trebled.

Expansion of the dock estate continued so as to meet the enormous demands placed upon the facilities of the port. To the north of the old Pool five docks were opened in 1848 (Bramley Moore, Collingwood, Nelson, Salisbury and Stanley), and four more by 1855 (Wellington (1850), Sandon (1851), Huskisson (1852) and Wapping (1855)). The Albert Dock had opened a few years earlier in 1845.

Following a further extension on the Cheshire side of the river at Birkenhead during the 1840s, it was decided on the recommendation of a Royal Commission in 1853 that a new body was needed to operate the Mersey docks as a whole. Consequently an Act was passed in 1857 which removed control from the Liverpool Borough and handed it to the newly created, and independent, Mersey Docks and Harbour Board. Interests of the shipping companies were to be equally served by the formation of the Liverpool Steam Ship Owners' Association the following year. Liverpool was set to move into a golden era as one of the leading ports in the world.

The first important dock built by the new Board was Jesse Hartley's last and largest – Canada – opened in 1859. The smaller Herculaneum, named after the pottery which once stood on the foreshore nearby, was completed by 1866 and marked the southernmost extension of the Liverpool system. There was, however, a small independent complex further south at Garston. There construction of the Old Dock had begun as early as 1846, which effectively swept away the picturesque Mill Dale, while a second dock – the North Dock – was opened in 1874. A third – Stalbridge – followed in 1909. Expansion of the main dock estate continued unabated into the 1880s. Four docks were added towards the North End: Brunswick (1878), Alexandra (1881), Langton (1881) and Hornby (1884); and two to the south: Harrington (1882) and Toxteth (1888 – replaced a small basin originally opened in 1841). By 1882, Liverpool had at last achieved city status.

As in other cities, Liverpool exported much of its inner-city population in the twentieth century, creating satellite towns in the hinterland like Halewood, Speke, Skelmersdale and Kirkby. It may have been a sincere attempt to save people from the slums and squalid conditions. But life was often disrupted, communities became isolated and women and children were particularly affected. Planners were obsessed with tower blocks and concrete and many have been demolished already, a short life-span that is truly a mark of a failed experiment. In the early twenty-first century, housing remains controversial, with yet another demolition programme underway in the inner suburbs, a huge expansion in city-centre apartment-building, and a continuing gulf between Liverpool's best and worst housing districts.

Further research and reading

Any research of the expanding nineteenth-century town will be dominated by the use of the census, street directories, maps and church records. Liverpool and Wirral have been well mapped in a variety of scales and most are held in the local record offices. Copies of certain eighteenth and nineteenth-century maps are available for sale at Liverpool Record Office. Critical to genealogists are the local parish maps, to determine which church an ancestor may have attended. Especially useful in this regard, and also available for purchase from Liverpool Record Office, is the *Map of Church of England Parishes in Liverpool and District*. The parish information dates from around 1900 and has been clearly superimposed on Philip's *Map of Greater Liverpool* dated 1921, which is at a scale of nearly 5in to 1 mile. Street directories are essential to determine where ancestors may have lived, while census records give more detailed information about family groups. (See Appendix 1).

Housing

Belchem, John (Ed.), 'Living in Liverpool' and 'City of change and challenge' in *Liverpool 800,* Liverpool, 2006. These chapters in this definitive work are the best starting point for the history of Liverpool's housing in the modern era. The footnotes refer to a large amount of original evidence and sources.

Burnett, John *A social history of housing, 1815–1985,* London, 1986. A major survey with many references to Liverpool.

Tarn, John *Five percent philanthropy: An account of housing in urban areas between 1840 and 1914,* Cambridge, 1973. A general study containing some material on Merseyside housing.

Barker, E. *In and Around Broadgreen,* pp.143–151, 1991. A useful summary of the foundation and operation of Wavertree Garden Suburb.

Sharples, J. *Liverpool,* Pevsner Architectural Guides, New Haven, 2004. Has sections on residential (and former residential) areas of the city centre and inner suburbs. As well as being a major work in its own right, this has a useful guide to further reading, discussing significant recent publications.

Taylor, I., 'The court and cellar dwelling: The eighteenth-century origin of the Liverpool slum', *THSLC,* Vol.122, 1970, pp.67–90. A pioneering study of Liverpool's poorest housing.

Sharples, Joseph, *Merchant Palaces: Liverpool and Wirral Mansions* (photographed by Bedford Lemere), Bluecoat Press, 2007. Rich businessmen increasingly chose to live away from the noisy crowded centre and chose private estates such as Fulwood, Cressington and Sandfield Parks, as well as prime spots around the newly created Sefton Park. The leading architectural photographer in the country, Henry Bedford Lemere, photographed the homes of the wealthy and his many commissions in Liverpool give a fascinating insight into the private world of the city's elite.

Architecture and buildings

Liverpool Heritage Bureau, *Buildings of Liverpool,* 1978.

'Liverpool: Work in progress', a special issue of the *Architectural Review,* Vol.1331, January 2008. A well-illustrated survey of Liverpool's historic built environment, with discussion of future directions and projects.

De Figueiredo, Peter, 'Symbols of empire: The buildings of the Liverpool waterfront', *Architectural History,* Vol.46, 2003, pp.229–54. A recent assessment of the Three Graces.

Stenhouse, D. K. 'Liverpool's office district, 1875–1905', *THSLC,* Vol.133, 1984, pp.71–87. An important analysis of the late nineteenth-century office-building boom and its consequences for the city centre.

Hughes, Quentin *Seaport: Architecture and townscape in Liverpool,* London,

1964; new edition, Liverpool, 1993. The classic work that brought Liverpool's monumental built environment to the attention of the wider world.

Cottrell, David, *The Little Book of Liver Birds*, Breedon Books, Derby, 2006. A thoroughly-researched and beautifully illustrated book revealing the huge number of Liver bird paintings and statues to be found in and on the city's buildings: an excellent demonstration of how this key Liverpool icon has permeated the city.

Hemm, Gordon, *St George's Hall, Liverpool*, Liverpool, 1949. A history and description of the hall.

Parrott, Kay *Portrait of Liverpool*, Bluecoat Press. Former archivist of Liverpool Record Office Kay Parrott has produced a study of the artist Allan Peel Tankard, who produced a series of views of the city of Liverpool in the decade after the Second World War. They show the devastating effects of German bombing raids, particularly on the city centre, but also some of the gems of Liverpool's architecture, which survived the war only to succumb to the redevelopment plans of later years. This book is also illustrated with pictures from the collection in Liverpool Record Office, in the Central Library, William Brown Street.

English Heritage series

The fruit of a major research effort to document the city's historic built environment, this series is producing well-illustrated, informative commentaries on often neglected questions. These books are part of the Historic Environment of Liverpool Project (HELP). The project was created by English Heritage to ensure that the historic characteristics of today's city – the buildings, streets, open spaces and archaeology – play a key role in its future. The six books exploring Liverpool's historic environment are:

Giles, Colum and Hawkins, Bob, *Storehouses of Empire: Liverpool's historic warehouses*, 2004. During the nineteenth century Liverpool's warehouses handled the cargoes of Britain's maritime empire and the book provides a fascinating insight into the development of the nation's foremost provincial seaport.

Giles, Colum and Goodall, Ian, *Building a Better Society: Liverpool's historic institutional buildings*, 2008. How the city responded to the needs of its poor and vulnerable during the eighteenth and nineteenth centuries is told via the buildings erected to help sailors and their families, to provide better health for the poor, and to ensure better education and higher morals.

Layton-Jones, Katy and Lee, Robert, *Places of Health and Amusement: Liverpool's historic parks and gardens*, 2008. Liverpool's rich legacy of parks is explored, from the early private eighteenth-century walks of the growing town, through the period of municipal expansion and two world wars, to the post-war period of decline and today's revival.

Sharples, Joseph and Stonard, John, *Built on Commerce: Liverpool's central business district*, 2008. As Liverpool developed into one of the country's great nineteenth-century ports, towering offices, banks and warehouses packed the streets of the city's commercial district, all built to help oil the wheels of trade.

Brown, Sarah, *Religion and Place: Liverpool's historic places of worship*, 2008. Religious faith dominates the skyline of Liverpool and the cathedrals, chapels and churches, mosques, synagogues and temples are constant reminders of the part played by religion in the city's history.

Menuge, Adam, *Ordinary Landscapes, Special Places: Anfield, Breckfield and the growth of Liverpool's suburbs*, 2008. As Liverpool's suburbs enter a new period of change, their historic value becomes more and more important. Anfield and Breckfield are two such suburbs, whose history can be deciphered in the stones of their streets, houses and stadium.

Parks

Twist, Colin, *A History of the Liverpool Parks*, Southport, 2000. Short histories and descriptions of more than 20 parks and open spaces.

McInniss, Jean *Birkenhead Park*, Birkenhead, 1984. An illustrated pamphlet outlining the history of the park. Appendices include lists of sports teams, bands, buildings and surrounding householders in the nineteenth century.

Channon, Howard *A pride of parks*, Liverpool, 1974. A local council booklet with short descriptions, illustrations, maps and histories.

Crompton, John 'The role of the proximate principle in the emergence of urban parks in the United Kingdom and in the United States', *Leisure Studies*,Vol.26, 2007, pp.213–34. A recent analysis featuring Birkenhead Park and Prince's Park, not forgetting that the scale and design of Birkenhead Park inspired the creators of Central Park in New York.

Katy Layton-Jones and Robert Lee *Places of Health and Amusement: Liverpool's Historic Parks and Gardens*, Informed Conservation, English Heritage.

George, Susan, *Liverpool Park Estates: Their Legal Basis, Creation and Early Management*, Liverpool Historical Studies, Vol.16, 1999.

Photographic Record

As well as the archive collections in the Local Record Offices, the following are also of use:

City Engineer's Collection

In 1896 it was decided by the Liverpool Corporation to keep a photographic record of the work done by the City Engineer's department. The images were initially used to support the work of the City Engineer, the Surveyor, the Housing Department and the Medical Officer of Health, showing everyday work such as road improvements, refuse collection and the laying of sewers and major projects, events and general developments in the city. This immense collection is available to researchers at Liverpool Record Office and some are available online. Colin Wilkinson has made excellent use of the collection and his selections are reflected in the variety of the books he has published within his Bluecoat Press.

Wilkinson, Colin *Liverpool from the Air*, Bluecoat Press. The book compares two time periods – the 1930s and 1990s – to show through aerial photography some of the effects of urban change.

—— *The Streets of Liverpool A Photographic Record*, 1993, Bluecoat Press.

Fagan, Ged, *In a City Living – The Story of the Tenements Vols.1–3, 2007.* (Website: www.inacityliving.piczo.com – over 5,000 photographs and details about his publications.)

Cooke, Terry, *Scotland Road 'The Old Neighbourhood'*.

O'Connor, Freddy, *It all Came Tumbling Down*. This book catalogues the streets and houses of Liverpool, so many of which are now only memories. The bulldozers may have destroyed our city, but the famous Liverpool 'spirit' will always remain.

—— *Liverpool – Our City Our Heritage*.

—— *A Pub on Every Corner*.

Hughes, Quentin, *Liverpool – City of Architecture*, Bluecoat Press. This volume is beautifully illustrated showing, through the careful selection of key buildings, why Liverpool has become the finest city of architecture in this country outside London.

Fallon, Bernard, *Bernard Fallon's Liverpool*, Bluecoat Press. A photographic landscape of once-familiar faces and streets, many around the Scotland Road area in the late 1960s.

Edward Chambré Hardman Archive

From 1923 to 1965, Edward Chambré Hardman ran a photographic studio in Liverpool, first in Bold Street and later in Rodney Street. During this time he photographed thousands of Liverpool people, along with those who travelled to be photographed by him. Formal portraits, wedding photographs and more relaxed family photographs form a large part of the collection, now held in Liverpool Record Office. Alongside images of the countryside, Hardman took many photographs in Liverpool itself, which document the changing face of the city over more than sixty years. See the advice sheets on the Liverpool Record Office website or the dedicated pages within the Mersey-Gateway Portal site www.mersey-gateway.org/chambrehardman.

Liverpool in Print Reading Guides

See the Liverpool Record Office website to consult the reading guides, which are very useful when beginning research. Select 'Urban History, Building and Planning' on their webpage to access advice relevant to this chapter. Guides are available on: Architecture and buildings, Eighteenth-century Liverpool, Fires and fire-fighting, General histories of Liverpool, Liverpool guidebooks, Medieval Liverpool, Nineteenth-century Liverpool, Parks, Religious buildings, Sixteenth and seventeenth-century Liverpool, Town planning, Twentieth-century Liverpool and Water, baths and wash-houses.

Chapter Seven

POVERTY AND THE LABOURING POOR

During the early nineteenth century, the Poor Law was often heavily criticised for its leniency and was said to discourage the unemployed from seeking work, while at the same time placing an enormous burden upon the ratepayer. The period of transition between the Old and New Poor Law, which took place in the 1830–40s, was a difficult one, made all the harder by the contrasting demands placed upon it by the urban expansion of the port and the surrounding rural hinterlands.

The seeds of the Poor Law are in the Elizabethan desire to remove vagrants and beggars from the streets and to introduce a legislative framework to deal with the growing problem of the poor. In 1601, during the reign of Elizabeth I, an Act of Relief of the Poor was passed which was to be the basis of Poor Law administration for the next two centuries. It divided the poor receiving relief into three categories: the able-bodied who were to have work provided for them; the rogues, vagabonds, and beggars, who were to be whipped or otherwise punished for their unwillingness to work and the 'impotent' poor (the old, the sick and the handicapped), who were to be relieved in almshouses.

By the provisions of the Act, each parish was made responsible for its poor. It would appoint its own Overseers of the Poor (usually the churchwardens and a couple of large landowners), who would collect the poor rate. The money would then be spent in four main ways:

(i) for setting to work the children of all such whose parents shall not be thought able to maintain them.

(ii) for setting to work all such persons married or unmarried, having no means to maintain them, and who use no ordinary or daily trade of life to get their living by. (That is, the able-bodied pauper).

(iii) for providing a convenient stock of flax, hemp, wood, thread, iron, and other ware, and stuff to set the poor on work.

(iv) for the necessary relief of the lame, impotent, old, blind and such other among them being poor and not able to work.

The Act also made it legal 'to erect, build and set up convenient houses or dwellings for the said impotent poor and also place inmates or more families than one in one cottage or house' – the initial authority for the erection of workhouses. A number of parishes took up this option, realising there was a considerable saving to be made compared with supporting paupers within their own homes or as vagrants.

Further Acts were passed over the next two centuries to extend the administration or to prevent abuse of the system. However, there was a disparity between the size of parishes in the north of the country compared with those in the south, which was ignored in the initial implementation of the 1601 Act. Childwall, for example, comprised nine townships, each of which was of similar size to parishes in the south. This anomaly was largely addressed by the settlement Act of 1662, which made each township responsible for its own poor, especially if they had resettled elsewhere. Parishes were permitted to send paupers back to their own parish to receive relief if they became a burden. (This stayed in place until 1945). In Liverpool, following the devastation of the Civil War (1648), displaced 'yong Children and Beggars wch… are found Wandring and begging contrarie to Lawe…' shall be 'shipt for the Barbadoes or otherwise to be put apprentices if ye belong to this Towne'. The New World was now receiving the poor of Liverpool – this was the earliest known reference to emigrants from the town. Numbers steadily increased as paupers were transported over the next century, many of whom were apprenticed for four to eleven years on plantations.

Liverpool was already acting independently of the parish of Walton-on-the-Hill (of which it was a part) in administering its own poor relief. In 1656 it was 'ordered that hereafter this towne shall keep and maintaine their own poore, and that the poor of all other places shalbe kept out from begging here'. To further reduce expenditure, a Beadle was appointed to keep out the beggars, with a bonus of 6d for every rogue whipped.

A second key development in Poor Law legislation was Knatchbull's General Workhouse Act of 1723, which enabled single parishes to erect a workhouse if they wished, so that they could enforce labour on the able-bodied poor in return for relief. This 'workhouse test' would enable parishes to refuse relief to those paupers who would not enter them. Nationally, the building of workhouses increased considerably under this Act, and by the end of the century their number had increased to almost 2,000, most holding between 20 and 50 inmates. In Liverpool, a small workhouse was used in Pool Lane, South Castle Street, from 1723 but, as the system became more complicated and expensive, a building was erected on a plot of land behind the Bluecoat Hospital on the corner of College Lane and Hanover Street in 1732. The poor rate was reduced by a third, especially now that the poor were suffering the workhouse test and there was strict application of the law; for example, there would be no relief for the outdoor poor, unless a written order was given by the mayor or a Justice of the Peace.

In the surrounding parishes and townships, if a workhouse existed it was usually a small cottage rented for the purpose. Records in many cases appear to no longer exist and although certain references have been found, the existence of the building itself is often still dubious. In West Derby, however, we can be more certain; the parish workhouse, known as the Old Poor House, is known to have stood since 1731 on the northern side of Low Hill, near to the present site of the Coach and Horses, and was in use until the late 1830s. Other rural workhouses were known at Halewood (1723–1837), Huyton (1732), Prescot (1732–50), Speke (1742–76), and Woolton (1834–37). Others may have existed, probably for a short period, at Allerton (1776), Childwall (1776), Ditton (1776), Hale (1776), Cronton (1770–89), and Wavertree (1776), where a local parishioner was paid to marry a woman and take her off the poor relief!

Halewood is a typical example of a township that largely dealt with its own poor. Records show that overseers spent money on outdoor relief, mainly to the sick and unemployed on a short-term basis, and more permanently on orphans and the elderly. Paupers were boarded out for a year at a time in the community, while others received money for board, clothes, shoes, coal and the services of a doctor. A copy of the new Act was purchased for 7d in 1722, following which a cottage was rented from the Earl of Derby at 6d per year. Most of the overseers' time and expense was spent dealing with the problem of policing the settlement issue. Inevitably, much of what is written about this period reveals the grim face of the Poor Law administration. Attitudes in the local townships were probably more informal and sympathetic than those of the hard-pressed overseers of the Liverpool Vestry, constantly battling against the huge demand placed upon them. As Janet Hollinshead observed in her study of eighteenth-century Halewood:

> When the Overseers of the Poor could provide Hannah Hitchmough, an elderly lady, with not only her board and clothes, but also with tobacco to smoke, and when they also gathered flowers for a pauper, Samuel Stevenson's funeral, it does suggest that they knew the people concerned and that they cared.

In Liverpool it was inevitable that, given the expanding size of the town and poor, the impracticalities of the 1723 law would be revealed. Consequently, following an unacceptably high level in the poor rate, outdoor relief was reintroduced as the workhouse could not cope with the numbers. In 1771 a new purpose-built workhouse was opened on the outskirts of the town, high up on Brownlow Hill. Despite several alterations and additions to the building, it soon became inadequate at coping with the rapidly expanding pauper population and the poor health suffered by so many of the inmates. In 1801 it became necessary to erect a Fever Hospital to the south of the main building (it was bigger than all the other Liverpool hospitals put together) and a smallpox ward was added in 1823.

In Liverpool, where the committee of overseers had evolved into the 'Liverpool Select Vestry' in 1821, a more rigorous implementation of the Poor Law followed to combat the heavy operating cost. Abuses in relief were investigated; the labour test became more stringent; able-bodied men were put to work building roads, cultivating land, and breaking stones; while pauper inmates whitewashed cellar dwellings in the town. Meanwhile, the facilities at 'Hotel du Brownlow' were made even grimmer. Not surprisingly there was a steep drop in expenditure.

Generally, management of the Poor Law across the country was inefficient and the high costs of indoor relief had led to Gilbert's Act in 1782, which provided rigid guidelines on how parishes could combine into 'unions'. The Act gave instructions on how to manage a workhouse and, together with a recommended set of rules, the aim was to produce standardisation as far as possible. Now the unemployed able-bodied poor would be provided first with outdoor relief and then with employment, while indoor relief in poorhouses was confined to the care of the old, sick, infirm and their dependant children.

The later years of the century saw an economic depression, where during times of extreme hardship emergency measures were taken by parishes rather than the raising of wages by employers. The Speenhamland system introduced after 1795 was largely applied in the southern agrarian areas, where wages were brought up to subsistence level by the issue of a weekly dole. Farmers took advantage of this and lowered wages paid to their labourers, knowing that parishes would take the burden of the difference. The economic problems this caused over the following decades, attitudes to the pauper and the demands for a right to a standardised

The Old Poor House (right) and cottages, Low Hill, West Derby, 1821.

system of relief, pressured the Government into setting up a Royal Commission in 1832 to investigate the Poor Law.

When the Commissioners concentrated their inquiry on the extra costs paid out by overseers, the replies from the parish officials in the West Derby Hundred were either unhelpful or curt. Walton, Much Woolton and West Derby, for example, paid no extra money to able-bodied men in their parishes, Toxteth Park and Everton gave little detail in their replies, while Liverpool, Ormskirk and Prescot were more forthcoming, suggesting that demands increased during the winter and relief was largely unnecessary in the vicinity of an expanding prosperous port like Liverpool. The overall conclusion of the Commission was that most of the poor were aged, infirm or widows. In the rural villages further away from the town, handloom weavers were the only major group who required relief while still in full employment, but they were quite literally a dying breed as the shift towards factory production was expanding.

The New Poor Law

Following the conclusions of the Commission, the Government introduced a Bill which contained most of its recommendations and, while there was great opposition to the proposals from many quarters, there was too much disunity for it to be effective. Royal Assent was granted on 14 August 1834 and the Poor Law Amendment Act was placed on the Statute Book.

The new Act minimised the provision of outdoor relief and made confinement in a workhouse the central element of the new system. To qualify for relief, it was not sufficient for the able-bodied to be poor, they had to be destitute. The measure of this was their willingness to enter the workhouse, and it was originally planned that this was to be the only provision for relief. Only the truly deserving – in the opinion of the government – would be those 'desiring' to reside in such a repellent institution. To help them in their decision, the surroundings were made as unpleasant as possible as an obvious deterrent to those seeking relief.

Married couples were separated and children taken from their parents. Overall, inmates were segregated into seven groups according to age and sex; aged or infirm men or women; able-bodied men or women over 16; boys or girls aged 7–15; and children under seven. Each group was assigned its own day rooms, sleeping rooms and exercise yards. They could see each other, but not speak, during communal meals or at chapel, and could only meet at infrequent intervals at the discretion of the guardians.

By the terms of the Act, a central administrative body was created, the Poor Law Commission, which in turn ordered that parishes were to be grouped together into Poor Law unions to provide the finance to build the workhouses. Each union was to be run by professional officers under the jurisdiction of an elected Board of Guardians.

In Liverpool, opposition to the changes was vehement, the Vestry believing they were already operating in the spirit of the Law. Indeed, when Gilbert Henderson was sent to investigate Liverpool on behalf of the Commissioners, he was most impressed with what he saw. For example, he witnessed the thorough investigation each poor relief applicant was subjected to by members of the Vestry. In one morning he saw 250 cases dealt with, most of whom were refused relief. His report to the Commissioners was a favourable one – his only complaint was that the Thursday 'liberty hours' were being scandalously abused by the paupers. The poor rate was especially looked upon in a favourable light by the investigator – the national average in 1832/3 was 9s 9d, while in Liverpool it was only 4s per head.

Despite opposition to the New Poor Law in Liverpool, the changes finally took place in March 1841 when the Liverpool Poor Law Union was established. The Select Vestry was duly replaced by a Board of Guardians, who planned in early 1842 to reconstruct the Brownlow Hill workhouse at a cost of £52,000 to house 1,800 inmates – a figure that would soon prove to be totally inadequate. However, opposition was so vigorous that an Act was passed in June the following year to exempt Liverpool from the New Poor Law Act and the Select Vestry was given legal authority to assume the role of the Board of Guardians.

In the surrounding rural areas, twenty-three parishes, stretching from Ince Blundell in the north to Garston in the south, combined to form the West Derby Union, one of the largest in the country. Formed in 1837, it was to be run by a Board of Guardians, the members of which were elected representatives from each parish. That same year the Poor Law Commissioners despatched their first order to the West Derby Union, instructing them that under the terms of the new Act the united parishes should: 'contribute and be assessed to a common fund for purchasing, building, hiring or providing, altering or enlarging any workhouse or other place for the reception and relief of the poor of such Parishes.'

The Guardians immediately declared that the old parish poor houses, now under their jurisdiction, were totally inadequate to cater for the demands of the new legislation. A search was begun to find a site suitable for the erection of a new workhouse, large enough to provide accommodation for the poor of the entire West Derby Union.

Before the end of the decade, the Board had succeeded in purchasing land from Thomas Shaw, either side of Mill Lane (Kensington), among the local sandstone quarries and brick-fields.

By 1841 the workhouse was complete and the transfer of inmates from the Old Poor House on Low Hill took place during the summer of that year. This was the first occupation of the Mill Road Institution, although it soon suffered a setback when the building caught fire in March 1843, damaging a considerable quantity of clothing and bedding.

No sooner had the occupants moved out of the Old Poor House, than the Liverpool Select Vestry applied in March 1842 to rent the building to alleviate the overcrowding at Brownlow Hill. The rent was payable quarterly at a rate of £80 per year, which seems to have been misappropriated by Mr Dolling, the Overseer of West Derby. It was a considerable sum given that he probably earned around the same figure each year.

The new Mill Road Workhouse of the West Derby Union was barely complete before it was realised that it was already too small. The Guardians soon pressed the new Poor Law Board for permission to extend the site. Their calls, however, went unheeded until the Poor Law Board permitted a makeshift measure which entailed the erection of a new chapel and school (on the site later occupied by the Nurses' Home), thereby providing room for additional dormitories in the main block, which formerly housed such facilities. Further alterations were carried out after additional space was created following the Guardians' resolution to send all sick patients to the fever hospital in Netherfield Road.

It was intended that the 'fever sheds' and 'any other spare rooms' were to be used as workshops, 'in which competent persons would be employed in the instruction of the boys in some useful trade or occupation'. The men were not to be left idle either, the Guardians added, 'further, that a quantity of land be taken in the neighbourhood for spade husbandry to employ adult and able-bodied paupers'.

Problems caused by the lack of suitable accommodation for the sick came to a head in 1852, when it was decided to build a new hospital fronting West Derby Road (on a site now lying between Home Street and Hygeia Street). It would be known as the West Derby Union Workhouse Hospital. No illustrations or views of Mill Road Workhouse (or the hospital) appear to exist, and nothing survives of personal accounts. However, in the early 1860s the Reverend John Jones, a congregational minister from Kirkdale, who was convinced that 99 per cent of pauperism was due to the temptation of alcohol, set out on a mission to prove his case. In search of evidence, he inevitably toured the three workhouses of the locality; Liverpool (Brownlow Hill), Toxteth (now Sefton General) and West Derby (Mill Road). At last we have a first-hand account of what lay within:

> We come first of all to the West Derby Union Workhouse. As we pass in through the gate, a building of moderate proportions stands before us. We have seen structures having a far more imposing aspect; but still how unlike it is to the 'Parish Poor House' which the poet has revealed to us.

After comparing what he saw with the image conjured up by the poet Crabbe's description of the pitiful rural poor house, he moved inside and again noted the contrast:

> How different the scene around it is! Here we have commodious and amply lit apartments, made cheerful by blazing fires, while the floor, and tile walls, and the furniture, in point of cleanliness, must please

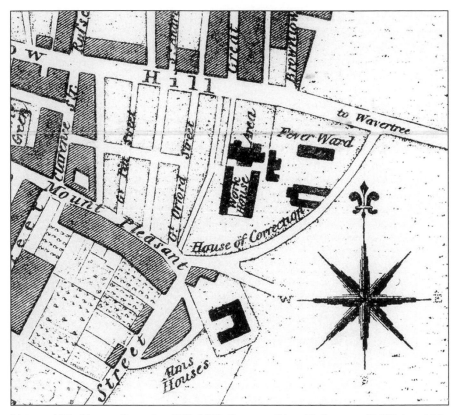

Liverpool Workhouse, Brownlow Hill, 1810. Compare this with the map of 1905, by which time there had been extensive expansion.

the most fastidious, and be found to meet the requirements of the most stringent of sanitary officers.

And here, too, are the men and women with their uniform attire, some of them more or less decrepit, forming themselves into a circle around the fire; others more active, standing or moving about; and others darning stockings or sewing a garment.

But here is another class – these are bedridden, most of them will probably rise up no more. How feeble does this one look, how wan the other; how distressing the cough of a third; they feel they have come to the workhouse to die, but they seem resigned to their fate and thankful for the care and attention bestowed upon them. But for such a provision they know it would fare badly with them, huddled up as they would be in some corner of a dark cellar on a heap of straw; but here they repose on a comfortable couch, attended to by the nurse, cared for by the doctor, ministered by the chaplain, and often cheered by the kind look and word of the governor: Yes, they may well indeed feel thankful that their last days shall pass away under such circumstances, although a pauper's burial and a pauper's grave await them . . .

This is a not too distressing account, compared to contemporary descriptions of the horrors witnessed at the notorious Brownlow Hill workhouse, and far removed from Dickensian imagery.

In Brownlow Hill, scores of sick persons in every stage of nearly every known illness (a large proportion of them incurable or very old and entirely helpless) were nursed, if it could be called nursing, by able-bodied pauper women selected from the adult wards of the workhouse. Seldom of reliable or compassionate character, it is unlikely that any of the 'nurses' had received formal training. In 1865, Agnes Jones, a Nightingale nurse who tried to improve the nursing at Liverpool Workhouse, wrote: 'I am

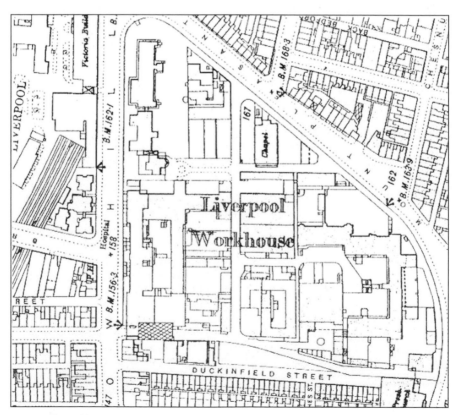

Liverpool Workhouse, Brownlow Hill, 1905.

almost distracted between sickness and anxiety and drunkenness. I have one head nurse in great danger. These ex-pauper women whom we are training were paid their wages on Friday, and the next day five came in tipsy . . . How little I can do!'

At Mill Road similar problems were encountered. Several times nurses were dismissed for drunkenness or fighting on the ward. In September 1863, for example, Elizabeth Hamilton, a nurse on the fever ward, was finding the horrors of her job too much. The ward was already over full and patients were being turned away and sent to the Netherfield Road fever hospital. Temptation proved her undoing and she sought solace in the entire supply of wines and spirits that had been ordered for the patients under her care. Not surprisingly she was found in an extreme state of drunkenness while on duty, whereupon she was given a month's notice to leave her £18-a-year job.

Within three years of her arrival in Liverpool, Agnes Jones had worked herself to death, dying from typhoid contracted from her patients. Nevertheless, her work was carried on, and Liverpool Select Vestry resolved to adopt her reforms in the Brownlow Hill workhouse. Florence Nightingale said of her:

In less than three years she reduced one of the most disorderly populations in the world to something like Christian discipline. She

Liverpool Workhouse, Brownlow Hill.

converted the Liverpool Select Vestry to the conviction, as well as the humanity; of nursing the pauper sick by trained nurses, the first instance of its kind in England.

Three Unions

It was clear that the West Derby Union was far too large to manage efficiently, thus the Toxteth Park Union was formed on 13 May 1857 to lift the increasing burden being placed upon the Mill Road Workhouse. A new workhouse for Toxteth was erected in Smithdown Road, which could take 600 paupers, plus a further 100 in its new Infirmary (later Sefton General Hospital). To further alleviate the cramped conditions at Mill Road, the Guardians placed an advertisement in the local press in May 1862, indicating their desire to secure land of not less than 20 acres, on which they intended to erect a new workhouse. It had been reported that:

> . . . the present workhouse has long been inadequate to the requirements of a rapidly increasing Union . . . the Guardians have for years been patching and adding to a building which was originally never contemplated to afford accommodation for a Union containing 156,000 inhabitants and provide accommodation for a rapidly increasing number of casual wayfarers which exceeded 4,000 during the last six months.

Within a couple of months, 37 acres belonging to the Earl of Sefton, situated at Walton-on-the-Hill, had been purchased at a cost of just over £11,000. The Guardians had already sold the West Derby Union Hospital on West Derby Road for the same figure and intended to raise a similar sum to cover the costs of the new building by the sale of Mill Road.

The first stone of Walton Workhouse was laid on 29 March 1864 by Thomas Haigh, Chairman of the West Derby Union Board of Guardians. The work on the new building (later to become known as Walton Hospital) was expected to take four years.

During October and November of 1867, Mr Crane, an Officer from the Poor Law Board, visited the local workhouses of Liverpool, Toxteth and West Derby in order to report on their condition. His report on Mill Road Workhouse described the workings shortly before their transfer to Walton:

> . . . the workhouse is wholly, insufficient for the wants of the Union. By the removal of the schools and by other means, it has been of the most part converted into a hospital and infirmary. Nevertheless, it is not large enough even for the sick and infirm poor. No detached infirmary seems to have been erected, nor is there any detached fever hospital. Contagious and infectious cases are placed in separate

wards in the main building. At present there are 427 cases on the medical list. There is no resident medical officer, but 2 medical officers constantly attend. There are 15 resident nurses with salaries varying from £15-30 per year with rations etc. for each. Four of these act as cost night nurses. The Guardians provide all drugs at about £400 a year. They have also appointed a dispenser who is in attendance during the whole of each day. The fever wards especially are too full. Great attention is evidently bestowed on ventilation, which is effectively kept up as far as possible: and the utmost cleanliness prevails throughout the establishment. It is only by such precautions that so large a number of cases have hitherto been congregated with safety in so limited a space.

And, regarding Walton:

I visited the new workhouse which is in an advanced state. It is highly desirable that the new hospitals there should be completed with as little delay as possible, so that the sick may be removed from the old workhouse and placed under the care of a medical officer who should reside in the new workhouse and devote his whole time to the duties of his office.

Walton Workhouse was formally opened on 15 April 1868, at a final cost, including the land purchase, of £65,000. It had accommodation for 1,000 'inmates' and was almost full by the opening day. The former Mill Road inmates enjoyed a 'good dinner and a half pint of ale each (oranges for the youngsters), and tobacco and snuff for the aged'. During the afternoon, guests toured the building to the accompaniment of various airs played by the juvenile band of the workhouse. Later that night, dignitaries dined at the Adelphi Hotel, where the Chairman of the Guardians praised the Union with an oratory of self-glorification, concluding: 'No doubt in many of the metropolitan workhouses the poor were harshly and unfairly treated, but in the provinces workhouses were as a rule, fairly and charitably conducted.'

As we have seen in both Brownlow Hill and Mill Road, even before Walton opened it was realised that space would soon be short. Consequently, Mill Road Workhouse, originally due to be sold to help fund the new Walton institution, was reprieved. While the new workhouse was under construction, a programme of alteration was put into operation to turn Mill Road into a workhouse hospital for the sick poor, to help prevent the anticipated strain on the hospital wards at Walton. After the transfer of inmates in 1868, the conversion plan was stepped up on the now vacated building.

The period of transition was difficult. Wards had to be opened at Mill Road earlier than expected when smallpox became rife at Walton in 1870. The Board of Guardians issued a directive in January 1871 ordering the

Medical Officer to vaccinate all children in the Mill Road workhouse ' . . . as soon as practicable after admission or birth, and do give to the Master certificates stating the cause why any particular child cannot be vaccinated.'

The following week the Guardians took a step further in an attempt to control the spread of infection, when a special sub-committee entitled the 'Smallpox and Infectious Diseases Committee' was formed, which was given full powers to 'act as they may deem most advisable in the present emergency.' (The emergency being described as an 'epidemic of smallpox and relapsing fever'.) Meanwhile, the Board found time to send a petition to Parliament objecting to the Bill presently in the Commons which called for the prevention of the removal of poor persons to Ireland. The ramifications for workhouses would be considerable should such legislation be placed on the Statute Book. The Liverpool workhouses, which had witnessed a massive influx of Irish since the 1840s, the majority of whom were now consigned to poverty, would be greatly affected.

Boards of Guardians had the power to send paupers back to the parish from which they came, unless that parish paid for their upkeep in the workhouse of their new abode. Not a penny would be spent on those who did not qualify for relief within that Union. Nor were the Guardians averse to sending paupers abroad to the colonies. Canada was their usual choice. In April 1884, the Board decided that 'the several poor persons . . . being desirous of emigrating to Canada, the necessary steps to be immediately taken to effect the emigration and that a sum not exceeding £14.3.0d be expended for each person upon the common fund of the Union . . . ' The oldest of these poor persons was sixteen, and the youngest a girl aged four and a boy just two. It begs the question how children aged two and four, without parents, could 'desire' to sail on a crowded boat halfway across the world into the unknown. This was not an isolated incident; several transportations were underwritten by the West Derby Board before the end of the century, in an effort to alleviate the 'burden' they placed on the Union.

One man in particular, however, was concerned about transportation. Harris P. Cleaver, Clerk to the West Derby Guardians and a man noted for his devotion to his work (his father had been the Clerk before him, from 1847 until his death in 1880), had deep reservations regarding the transportation of such young children. Fearing for their treatment, he travelled to Canada at his own expense to investigate their situation.

So distressed was he at what he observed, that upon his return he persuaded the Guardians to discontinue this policy and find an alternative to keeping the children in the workhouse. A short while later, funding was made available and in the late 1880s the Cottage Homes were opened in Fazakerley to house school children. Liverpool Select Vestry followed suit and shortly afterwards a similar scheme was carried out to erect Olive Mount Children's Homes. The West Derby Union widened their facilities for children when a Children's Convalescent Home was opened in Heswall, later to be renamed the Cleaver Sanatorium.

The spectre of incurable disease lay over the workhouse for the greater part of half a century following the opening of Mill Road. Due to widespread squalor, poverty, and poor sanitary conditions, smallpox, cholera and typhoid claimed thousands of victims. Even for those illnesses that could be treated, medicines were in short supply and cases would be referred to professional vaccinators, who had to provide their own drugs. Even the post of Medical Officer was hardly a position of autonomy. The final word on many decisions frequently lay with the Guardians, while action would rarely be determined until the following Board meeting. Consider the ludicrous situation caused by this procedure when such lay people (none of whom had a medical qualification) were required to give authorisation to the Medical Officer to amputate the foot of a woman named Smith, an inmate of Mill Road Workhouse.

Nevertheless, the latter years of the nineteenth century were a period of great medical progress and, together with new attitudes within the nursing profession, foundations were being laid to take care for the sick and poor into the twentieth century. Many new institutions, taking advantage of modern developments and techniques, were being opened in Liverpool, such as the Royal Southern (rebuilt in 1872), the Hospital for Women in Shaw Street (1883), the Homeopathic (1884) and the new Royal Infirmary (1890). Workhouse Infirmaries, however, were clearly not at the forefront of such developments, yet change was undoubtedly necessary.

Despite the fact that Mill Road had been reprieved and altered to take on a new role in the early 1870s, it was becoming increasingly obvious that the building was inadequate, outdated and, above all, unhealthy. There was no alternative. It would have to be condemned. The old building had in the past been adapted where possible, but it was generally agreed that a completely new purpose-built establishment was necessary to provide modern hospital facilities.

The old building was pulled down in its entirety, leaving only the detached Lower Hospital for 'imbeciles' (built in the 1850s) at the rear of the main block close to Atwell Street. The sick patients, meanwhile, were transferred to the Test House in Belmont Road, the vagrant workhouse of the West Derby Union (later known as Newsham General Hospital). The foundation stone for the new building was formally laid on 18 March 1891.

As work continued into the mid-1890s, Mr Jenner-Fust, the Local Government Board Inspector, told the West Derby Guardians at their weekly meeting in March 1893 that 'the Mill Road Infirmary when quite completed would be one of the best specimens of a workhouse infirmary in the country'. 'Workhouse' was the crucial word. The new venture, although a modern building, was still not up to the standard of the voluntary hospitals, and it would be another 50 years before it came anywhere near losing the 'poor relation' tag among its regional counterparts.

Poverty in England throughout the Victorian period was largely equated with immorality, irreligion and intemperance. Furthermore, there was little chance of overturning a Poor Law that was outdated and based on a profound misconception about the causes of poverty. It was ironic that when another local civil servant, Mr Holding, commented, '... party politics are coming more and more to the one thing – to the idea of social reform – we are getting nearer and nearer every year to the idea that the young and the old who cannot work and cannot keep themselves have a right to be kept by the community. . .', he was merely outlining the provision of the Old Poor Law, which had been so ruthlessly cast aside over fifty years earlier.

The initial care of the destitute fell largely on the shoulders of the parish doctors, who worked for a meagre salary in impossible conditions. They could admit serious cases to the Poor Law hospitals, but it was less easy to admit patients to the better-equipped voluntary hospitals. Even as late as 1909, the stigma and fear attached to the workhouse infirmary showed no sign of abatement:

> . . . the parish doctor is always available. But the poor do not like the parish doctor and they will adopt any device rather than summon him. They dread what they know to be too often the burden of his message: 'You must go into the Workhouse Hospital'. Of course, we know it is very silly of them to dread the workhouse hospital but that does not alter the fact that they do dread it and that they dread the parish doctor.

The respectable poor preferred to endure almost any degree of neglect or misery at home rather than be sent to the workhouse.

Dissatisfaction with the Poor Law and disagreement over its objectives again led to the setting up of a Royal Commission in 1905. It concentrated on the relevance of the old Act within a modern urban industrial society, how far charity was funding areas originally covered by the Act, and to what extent new welfare agencies were undermining the provisions of the Poor Law.

The Commission found it impossible to find common ground as a united body, issuing conflicting Majority and Minority Reports in 1909. Both were ignored by the Liberal government, but the Local Government Board responded to them by tightening up its administration, especially regarding indoor relief, while Asquith prophesied: 'You will find that Boards of Guardians will die hard'.

Meanwhile, 'Lloyd George's Ambulance Wagon,' that vast programme of social reform which might eventually make the Poor Law unnecessary, gained momentum, and an opportunity to finally bury the 1834 Act was squandered.

Over the next three decades the Poor Law was gradually dismantled. Already in 1908 the Children's Act had given local authorities new powers to keep underprivileged children out of the workhouse. On New Year's Day 1909 old-age pensions were introduced; in the same year labour exchanges were set up to help anyone without work find a job, and in 1911 the National Health Insurance Act was passed, which provided state benefit for sickness and maternity. The term 'workhouse' was dropped in 1913 in favour of 'Poor Law Institution' and indoor relief was increasingly confined to the 'helpless poor': children, old people and the sick.

In an attempt to improve the administration and financing of what was now three unions operating in the same city, the West Derby Union was enlarged by its amalgamation with the Select Vestry of Liverpool and the Township of Toxteth Park. This merger formally commenced on 1 April 1922 by the terms of the Liverpool Corporation Act passed the previous year. The new authority would operate under the retained name of the West Derby Union. Chamberlain's Local Government Act of 1929 was the death knell for the Poor Law. Unions and their Boards of Guardians were finally swept aside and responsibility for the destitute passed to the new Public Assistance Committees within County and Borough Councils. So began a difficult period of transition in the face of Local Government cuts and stringent economies in Liverpool, where demonstrations and riots against the tough measures occurred as early as 1931.

Poor Law Records and further research

www.workhouses.org

This is an excellent, unsurpassed web site by Peter Higginbothom on all aspects of the history of the workhouse and the Poor Law. For example, view a useful introduction to the study of Brownlow Hill at www.work-houses.org.uk/index.html?Liverpool/Liverpool.shtml.

Archives

Taylor, I., *Liverpool Workhouse Records Collection*, Liverpool FHS, spring 1978.
An example of some of the archives held at LRO:
Guardians' minutes (1852–1922)
Brownlow Workhouse – Admissions (1869–1925); Births (1841–1914); Baptisms (1831–58, 1874–1928); Deaths (1914–24); Creed register (1841–1928)
Kirkdale Industrial School – Admissions and discharges (1862–1965); Classification registers (1845–97); Creed register (1869–1904)
Kirkdale Homes – Creed registers (1913–1969); Registers of deaths (1924–1971)
Township of Toxteth Park Board of Guardians Archives
West Derby Union Minute Books
See the Liverpool Record Office online information leaflet No.17 for the Poor Law and for more about hospital records please consult leaflet No.18 – Hospital Records.

For listings of the Board of Guardians Select Vestry Archives deposited at Liverpool Record Office see the TNA Access to Archives: www.nationalarchives.gov.uk (type the LRO reference number '353 SEL' into the site search engine).

Further reading

Bickerton, T.H., *A Medical History of Liverpool*, Liverpool, 1936.

Oxley, G.W., 'The Permanent Poor in South West Lancashire under the Old Poor Law' *Liverpool and Merseyside* Ed. Harris, J.R., pp.16–49, Frank Cass, London, 1969.

Oxley, G.W., *The Administration of the Poor Law in the West Derby Hundred of Lancashire 1601–1837*, MA thesis, University of Liverpool, 1966.

Royden, M.W. *The People's Hospital – A History of Mill Road*, Liverpool, 1993.

Midwinter, E.C. 'Liverpool and the New Poor Law' in *Old Liverpool*, David & Charles, Devon, 1971.

Chapter Eight

HEALTH AND CHARITY

The laissez-faire politics of the late eighteenth and early nineteenth century were embraced by the political and intellectual elite who were determined to provide for those less fortunate. Public and private subscription transformed civic pride with the construction of facilities such as the Seaman's Hospital, the Royal School for the Blind and the Lying-in Hospital for Women. Liverpool Corporation appointed Dr William Duncan as the country's first Medical Officer of Health as the town became overwhelmed by overcrowding and poor conditions, resulting in several epidemics of typhoid and cholera. The demon drink claimed many more as the average life expectancy plummeted to below twenty in the 1840s. Consequently, Liverpool has a prominent place in the history of public health, partly for its disastrous record in the mid-nineteenth century, and partly for its pioneering efforts to solve the problems.

In 1795 it was calculated that every seventh house was open for the sale of liquor, supplied by the large breweries of the locality, while rum was imported in large quantities from the West Indies. The streets were frequently scenes of drunkenness, fighting, riots and press-gangs. Local politics were constantly anarchical and corrupt. William Moss, in his *A Familiar Medical Survey of Liverpool*, published in 1784, gave a doctor's perspective:

> The situation of the town as it affects the health of the inhabitants has many natural advantages . . . the west side of the town becomes freely exposed to the fresh and unpolluted air of the sea . . . The town is kept regularly purified, ventilated and freed from the lodgement and accumulation of vapours, and effluvia of various kinds which by retention, become highly deleterious and unfavourable to mankind. The strong gusts of wind which come from the western quarter so frequently throughout the year are most singularly effacious in these respects . . .

In Liverpool, as in many other provincial towns, hospitals, dispensaries, medical schools and societies came into being from the enthusiasm and spirit of liberal, intelligent and often radical individuals born of this period of Enlightenment, in an attempt to improve the conditions of all members of society. Within a period of phenomenal growth in the arts and scientific knowledge, it was an era when doctors began to rise from 'quack' or apothecary status – and barber-surgeons too – to a respected, university-educated level.

The rapid growth and expansion of towns of the Industrial Revolution would present doctors with challenges to their skills and knowledge, and in a thriving seaport such as Liverpool, with its background of social extremes, average life expectancy remained worryingly low. The change in quality of Liverpool doctors during the mid-eighteenth century was certainly affected by the establishment of the Infirmary, which provided a focus where physicians and surgeons could work together, exchanging ideas instead of remaining in competition as individuals. The health of the people of Liverpool was dependent on the provision of such hospitals and other welfare institutions. This was determined by personal income and the medical knowledge at the time. Access to care was not a problem for the rich, although treatment was usually no better than that offered to the poor, but they could usually afford to pay for a doctor to visit their home. Most families were dependent on healthcare set up by charitable or voluntary organisations.

In 1749 the Infirmary was ready to accommodate 100 patients, although there was still much to be desired regarding its universal treatment of the sick. Barred were those who could pay for their own medicines, as were those who could not provide a reference from a Trustee (except in cases of casualty). So too were the 'incurable, children under seven, lunatics, sufferers of small-pox or women big with child'.

The Infirmary had been sponsored by a group of 'Clergy, Physicians, Surgeons, Merchants and Tradesmen, with some neighbouring gentlemen' and was erected entirely on charitable subscription. The principles on which it was founded would set the pattern for numerous institutions which were to follow. Alongside the Infirmary in 1752 was erected the Seamen's Hospital for seamen and their families. Every mariner of the port had paid a compulsory contribution of 6d a month towards its support. (Both buildings stood on the site now occupied by St George's Hall).

In 1778, the Liverpool Dispensary was established in North John Street, which provided medical advice and medicine for the poor and was supported by voluntary subscriptions from the majority of the established surgeons or physicians in the town.

Yet, despite such positive steps made in a port increasingly influenced by its diverse cultural influx, it was, by the end of the eighteenth century, a town of much pauperism, appalling housing conditions and frequent violence. During the nineteenth century there was greater expansion – the Infirmary moved to Brownlow Hill in 1824 (rebuilt in 1890) and the Northern Hospital opened in 1834, followed by the Southern in 1842. By the turn of the century there were three general hospitals, four dispensaries and another twenty specialist hospitals. Subscription schemes helped some skilled workers (but not family), while others relied on Friendly Societies, savings, charity or support from family or neighbours. Not all could benefit, however, and many simply went without care. For the pauper there was always the option of entering the workhouse, coming under the care of its attached infirmary.

Care of Women and Babies

Today the city benefits from the recently opened Liverpool Maternity Hospital, but with a history reaching back two centuries, it can claim to be one of the oldest local hospitals in the country. Such roots lie in the foundation of the 'Ladies' Charity' in 1796, whose objects were to afford medical and other assistance in childbirth 'to reputable married women or widows resident in this town,' in their own homes.

Until the mid-sixteenth century it was universal practice throughout Europe that women were attended in confinement only by those of the same sex. Attitudes began to change due mainly to the work of Ambroise Paré (1510–90), with the result that the medical profession began to give the practice of midwifery a much higher profile. But it was not until the eighteenth century that greater advances began to be made, notably in 1726 when a professorship in obstetrics was founded in Edinburgh. Despite the acceptance by wealthier classes of the principle that the medical profession could give assistance to those in childbirth, public opinion was still, at first, largely prejudiced against the building of 'lying-in' hospitals for the poorer classes. Consequently, it was not until 1796 that a charitable obstetric organisation was founded in Liverpool. The first building to be utilised by the Ladies' Charity was at 13 School Lane, from where patients would be cared for by gifts of clothing, food, soap or money, loans of temporary requisites, such as changes of bed linen, and by the provision of the attendance of a midwife, and, if necessary, a doctor. Three medical officers were appointed, and the subscriptions given by the ladies of Liverpool rose from £256 in 1797 to £385 in 1800. The town was also divided into four administrative districts, each with its resident midwife working for the charity.

In its early years the Ladies' Charity had a remarkably fine record. About one third of the total average births in Liverpool came under its supervision and the death rate was remarkably low – somewhere in the region of 0.1 per cent. Most of these were due to disease or circumstances which would have proved fatal despite medical care. Thomas H. Bickerton, Opthalmic Surgeon and local medical historian, suggested that it was the general good health of country-bred wives of the new labourers coming to the port from Ireland and Scotland that largely explained the low maternal mortality.

Despite such statistics, obstetrics was still in a rather backward state during this period. English medical schools remained slow to include midwifery, despite advances being made on the Continent and in Edinburgh, where James Simpson had been appointed Professor of Midwifery in 1840. Small improvements had been made in the intervening years, although methods were still primitive. Caesarean section, for example – which was usually performed as a last resort after gross mismanagement of labour – was still an imperfect and highly dangerous technique. Local surgeon Richard Kay reported in the *Liverpool Medical Gazette* in 1833 that he had delivered a child by Caesarean section, but twice bled his patient (a practice still in use) until she lost consciousness. After the loss of twenty ounces of blood, his patient, not surprisingly, died.

Two documents held in the Library of the Liverpool Medical Institution are of particular use to researchers. The first was compiled by Henry Park (1745–1831), who, although primarily a surgeon, also practised medicine and obstetrics. His *Book of Genesis* lists all the births he attended, wherein he also recorded the names and addresses of all the mothers he delivered, the sex of each child and a brief clinical note. Although he did not record mortality of the mother or infant, it is occasionally inferred by mention of 'crotchet case' (extraction of a dead foetus by a crude instrument) and other complications which must have resulted in infant or maternal death. Such figures can be rather misleading, as he tended to practice in more affluent areas, although there is no record of his fees. (On 29 December 1809 Park recorded his delivery of William Gladstone, the future Prime Minister.) The second volume was kept by Dr John McCulloch, who attended on average 210 deliveries each year between 1797 and 1820. In his *Register of Births and Innoculations* he recorded the name and address of the mother, the sex of the child and his fee. Much of his work was carried out, in stark contrast to Henry Park, among the poor in the worst of the slums. Occasionally he entered a comment, mentioning deliveries taking place 'in a yard', 'in an opening', or 'in a court', frequently without charge. A better class of patient would pay one or two guineas.

The surgeons of the Ladies' Charity in its earliest years resided in the centre of the small town which was in close proximity to the districts they were attached to. Nevertheless, problems were encountered once the bounds of the town were extended, and in 1842, for instance, the suggested hire of a cab for the surgeon had to be refused on economical grounds, with the result that cases in Kirkdale township could not be attended. It was not until 1874 that cab hire was allowed to the surgeons of the charity. By the time the Ladies' Charity amalgamated with the Lying-in Hospital in 1869, the seventy-three years of its separate existence had undoubtedly resulted in an improvement in the management of childbirth in the homes of the deserving poor.

The first obstetrical and gynaecological hospital, the Lying-in Hospital and Dispensary for the Diseases of Women and Children, was established at 31 Horatio Street, Scotland Road, in November 1841. However, it was soon apparent that larger premises were necessary and the hospital was transferred to 21 Pembroke Place in October 1845. During the first four years of the hospital's existence, figures show only one death in labour. On the staff at that time was the surgeon Benjamin Blower, the inventor of the slipper bedpan. The organisation of the hospital was operated under clear rules and unmarried women were not admitted.

In December 1846, news reached Liverpool about the successful administration of ether during an operation in Boston, USA. Within days local surgeons were using the new technique, but it was not until 25 November 1847 that J. Parke gave the first paper on anaesthesia at the Liverpool Medical Institution: 'On the Moral propriety of administering ether in other than extraordinary cases'. This reflected the current arguments concerning the use of anaesthesia, particularly in obstetrics. He discussed the moral aspects and made much of the opinion that insanity might be induced by ether or chloroform (by this date chloroform was also in use). Others feared infantile convulsions if chloroform was given in labour. John Birkbeck Nevins, the recently appointed Medical Officer at Mill Road Workhouse Infirmary, reported that he had not witnessed a death in the general use of anaesthesia in eighty cases of labour.

Improvements in the training of nurses in Liverpool were undoubtedly influenced by the work of Florence Nightingale, although there had been some attempt to train nurses at the Lying-in Hospital as early as 1841. A Nurses' Institution opened in Soho Street in around 1855, but greater strides were made in 1862 when, through the efforts of William Rathbone, the 'Liverpool Training School and Home for Nurses' was founded, while in the same year the Royal Infirmary decided to build a Nurses' Home.

The dispensary at the Lying-in Hospital opened three days per week, each patient being required to pay one penny when medicine was provided. The number of patients, however, was not increasing in comparison with the population of the town, and in the autumn of 1853 the Board of Governors agreed that smaller premises would be preferable. Finally, it was decided to build a completely new hospital in Myrtle Street. This was erected at a cost of £3,000, contained thirty beds for in-patients and was officially opened by the Lord Bishop of Chester in July 1862. The site in Myrtle Street had been chosen in preference to one near the old hospital, although this meant the loss of an offer of £1,000; a £50 gift was also withdrawn because unmarried women were refused admission. It was becoming clear that there was an increasing overlap in the facilities provided by the Ladies' Charity and the new Myrtle Street Lying-in Hospital, so by 1869 the two charities combined on the Myrtle Street site. However, frequent outbreaks of fever raised the issue of treating maternity and gynaecological cases together in the same hospital. It was decided to separate maternity from obstetric cases and a new maternity hospital was built on the corner of Brownlow Hill and Brownlow Street, on the new isolation principle. The old site was sold to the Committee of the Hospital for Cancer and Diseases of the Skin in 1882. (The hospital still stands there today, adjacent to the Philharmonic Hall).

The Brownlow Hill Hospital was modernised in 1907 and became

The Brownlow Hill Lying-in Hospital, 1884.

known as Liverpool Maternity and Ladies' Charity, but by the early 1920s the site was deemed inadequate and a new site was found. In 1926 the new hospital in Oxford Street was opened and stood as the largest voluntary maternity hospital in Britain.

Meanwhile, the hospital for the general care of women moved from Myrtle Street to Shaw Street in 1883 and later amalgamated with the Samaritan Hospital for Women, which had opened in 36 Upper Parliament Street in 1900 (after short stays in 37 Upper Warwick Street (1895) and St James' Place (1897)). This amalgamation took place in 1932 in the newly opened Women's Hospital in Catherine Street. This stayed in operation until the move to the Liverpool Women's Hospital in the 1990s.

In March 1995, Liverpool Women's Hospital, the new £30 million hospital for women and babies, became fully operational. Officially opened by HRH The Princess of Wales, this was a coming together under one roof of the Maternity Hospital, the Women's Hospital and Mill Road Hospital, the latter a former workhouse infirmary.

In 1985 these three hospitals had been united under the control of the Liverpool Obstetric and Gynaecology Unit. This then became an NHS Trust in 1992 and changed its title to the Liverpool Women's Hospital NHS Trust in 1994. The move to the new Liverpool Women's Hospital maintained the links to the past with the transferral of the foundation stones and commemorative plaques from the three old hospitals. Hospital treatment of women in Liverpool has come a long way since the inception of the 'Ladies' Charity' in 1796, and over the last two centuries the women's hospitals have been understandably proud of their achievements.

Disease and epidemics

For the nineteenth-century poor, housing conditions in the dockland courts were horrific and living in the slums meant a constant struggle to survive overcrowded, damp, poorly ventilated buildings with no private toilet or washing facilities. Sewage ran through the streets and polluted the wells from which people collected their drinking water. Disease was widespread, but epidemics of cholera, typhus and typhoid decimated the population during the early to mid-nineteenth century. The first outbreak of Asiatic cholera in Britain was at Sunderland on the Durham coast during the autumn of 1831. From there the disease made its way northward into Scotland and southward toward London. Before it had run its course it claimed 52,000 lives, the main epidemic occurring during 1832. The disease caused severe diarrhoea, dehydration, collapse and often death. There was widespread public fear, and the political and medical response to this new disease was variable and inadequate. In the summer of 1832, a series of 'cholera riots' occurred in various towns and cities throughout Britain, frequently directed against the authorities, doctors, or both.

Liverpool experienced more riots than elsewhere. Between 29 May and 10 June 1832, eight major street riots occurred, with several other minor disturbances. The object of the crowd's anger was the local medical fraternity. The public perception was that cholera victims were being

The squalor of the court housing.

removed to the hospital to be killed by doctors who wanted to use them for anatomical dissection. 'Bring out the Burkers' was one cry of the Liverpool mobs, referring to the Burke and Hare scandal of four years earlier, when two men had murdered people in Edinburgh in order to sell their bodies for dissection to the local anatomy school. This issue was of special concern to the Liverpool citizens because in 1826 thirty-three bodies had been discovered on the Liverpool docks, about to be shipped to Scotland for dissection. Two years later a local surgeon, William Gill, was tried and found guilty of running an extensive local grave-robbing system to supply corpses for his dissection rooms. The widespread cholera rioting in Liverpool was thus as much related to local anatomical issues as it was to the national epidemic. The riots ended relatively abruptly, largely in response to an appeal by the Roman Catholic clergy read from church pulpits and also published in the local press. In addition, a respected local doctor, James Collins, published a passionate appeal for calm. The Liverpool Cholera Riots of 1832 demonstrate the complex social responses to epidemic disease, as well as the fragile interface between the public and the medical profession. (Recent research on this can be found in Sean Burrell and Geoffrey V. Gill, *The Liverpool Cholera Epidemic of 1832 and Anatomical Dissection – Medical Mistrust and Civil Unrest*, Journal of the History of Medicine and Allied Sciences, 2005, pp478–498.)

In 1846, as the potato famine struck Ireland, a virulent form of typhus appeared, cutting down large numbers of even well-to-do families. As Irish workers moved to cities like Liverpool, the 'Irish fever' moved with them. By 1847 the contagion, not all of it connected with immigration, had spread throughout England and Wales, accounting for over 30,000 deaths. As had happened a decade earlier, typhus occurred simultaneously with a severe influenza epidemic, which carried off almost thirteen thousand.

It is not hard to see why the idea of disease had such an impact in the last century. In his *Report on the Sanitary Condition of the Labouring*

Liverpool Infirmary, Brownlow Street.

Population of Gt. Britain, Edwin Chadwick included figures to show that in 1839, for every person who died of old age or violence, eight died of specific diseases. This helps explain why, during the second and third decades of the nineteenth century, nearly one infant in three in England failed to reach the age of five.

Generally, throughout the 1830s and the 1840s trade was experiencing a lull and food prices were high. The poorer classes, being underfed, were less resistant to contagion. Furthermore, during the more catastrophic years the weather was extremely variable, with heavy rains following prolonged droughts. Population, especially in the Midlands and in some seaport cities and towns, was growing rapidly, without a concurrent expansion in housing. Crowding contributed to the relatively fast spread of disease in these places. The Registrar General reported in 1841 that while average life expectancy in Surrey was forty-five years, it was only thirty-seven in London and twenty-six in Liverpool. The average age of 'labourers, mechanics, and servants', at time of death was only fifteen. Mortality figures for crowded districts surrounding the docks were worse still.

In 1853, the Health Committee of Liverpool contacted the West Derby Board of Guardians, requesting co-operation in taking precautionary measures to prevent the spread of Asiatic cholera. Local medical officers were to notify the Liverpool Authorities of all cases of diarrhoea and cholera in the area, and the relieving officers were to report similar instances and filthy housing conditions known to them. Two months later, the Guardians also appointed a Public Vaccinator, who would receive ls 6d for every successful case of vaccination. At this time, the disease seemed to be largely confined to Liverpool, but due to the close proximity of Mill Road all necessary steps were being taken to prevent it spreading. (By 1854,

Liverpool Hahnemann Homoeopathic Hospital, Hope Street.

representatives of the Board were being asked to visit a house in Walton-on-the-Hill to investigate a reported case of cholera).

From at least 1842, the Liverpool Homoeopathic Dispensary had been a free medical charity consisting of several dispensaries. The South End Homoeopathic Dispensary was established by Dr Drysdale in 1841 at 41 Frederick Street, later moving to a house in Benson Street, then to 2 Harford Street. Later the Dispensary moved to a building in Hardman Street, erected by public subscription in 1860, and transferred to Hope Street when the Hahnemann Hospital was built in 1887. Meanwhile, the North End Homoeopathic Dispensary opened in Wilbraham Street in 1866, moving to 10 Roscommon Street in 1872. The old Dispensary was pulled down and a new building erected by public subscription, which was formally opened in December 1905. The Roscommon Street Dispensary was closed in July 1940. Situated at 42 Hope Street and equipped by its benefactor Sir Henry Tate, the Liverpool sugar magnate, as a free gift to the citizens of Liverpool, the Hahnemann Hospital opened in September 1887. The hospital was incorporated with the Homoeopathic Dispensary, and took the name the 'Liverpool Hahnemann Hospital and Dispensary' for the treatment of the poor, as both in and out patients. The War Office requisitioned the hospital during the First World War and operated it as an Auxiliary Military Hospital. It became part of the Emergency Medical Service in the Second World War. After the formation of the NHS, the hospital came under the state, forming part of the South Liverpool Group of hospitals. It was then renamed the Liverpool Homoeopathic Hospital, and in 1969 changed again to the Hahnemann Hospital. After further reorganisation in the 1970s the Hahnemann became part of the United Liverpool Hospitals in 1972, but this was short-lived and the hospital finally closed in April 1976. In 2008, following campaigns by local people and the Victorian Society to prevent its demolition, English Heritage recognized the Hahnemann as a building of national significance, noting its Queen Anne Revival design, its early hydraulic lift and innovative heating and ventilation system. In an area that has witnessed intense redevelopment, its new Grade II listing may safeguard its future and ensure that any future design would incorporate its key features. (I have my own family connections with the hospital as my mother worked as a nurse there for twenty-five years.)

The year 1875 saw the passing of the Public Health Act and, despite the continuing problems of poor housing, conditions did improve from the 1870s, with the construction of new, healthier housing. The Act required local authorities to implement building regulations, or bye-laws, which insisted that each house should be self-contained, with its own sanitation and water. This change in the design of housing complemented the public investment in sewers and water supply. In the last quarter of the nineteenth century, huge numbers of new houses were constructed, with long rows of terraced housing, in grids of streets, easily cleaned and inspected. In 1890 a new Liverpool Infirmary building by Alfred Waterhouse was constructed on the Brownlow Street site, an impressive example of red-brick Victorian design. (In 1978 the building closed and was replaced by the nearby Royal Liverpool University Hospital. In 1994 the Infirmary was purchased by Liverpool University and was restored after being left empty since its closure).

By the inter-war years access to health and welfare services was improving, but provision was still dependant on a system of insurance or direct payment. The 'Penny-in-the-Pound' system was popular with those on low wages and this generated a steady flow of income into the voluntary hospitals on Merseyside. The health schemes provided free care as an in-patient and out-patient and some convalescence. Treatment by GPs was not included, nor that for infectious diseases such as TB, which was still prevalent during this period. This was treated through municipal care, especially within the increasing number of sanitoria being constructed for the purpose. By the early 1930s the scheme had over a quarter of a million contributors on Merseyside and ensured a wider access and better quality care than in many other localities. After 1929 municipal hospitals, which had previously been run by Poor Law Unions, combined with voluntary hospitals to provide hospital care towards the formation of the NHS.

In 1948 both voluntary and public hospitals came into the ownership of the National Health Service to be managed by local hospital management committees under the Liverpool Regional Health Board. A reorganisation of the National Health Service in 1974 saw Liverpool hospitals come under district health authorities as part of the Liverpool Area Health Authority, in turn part of the Mersey Regional Health Authority. Between 1991 and 1995 Liverpool hospitals became independent NHS trusts.

Further research and reading

The bulk of the surviving records date from the nineteenth century onwards, although some institutions have archives going back to the mid-eighteenth century. The major reorganisations of both local government and the NHS in 1974 led to the virtual disbandment of local authority public health departments and in many cases the loss of records. What remains up to 1974, therefore, is incomplete. What does survive are mainly minute books of the hospitals and local authority health committees, and annual reports of the Medical Officers of Health dating from 1840–1974. Much has been done since the 1990s to ensure the safe preservation of records and to collate catalogues and keep the issue of the importance of such records in the public eye. The Merseyside Archives Liaison Group and the Merseyside Records Users Group did much in this regard, as well as local archivists such as Margaret Proctor and Adrian Allan.

An excellent starting point, therefore, is **Margaret Procter, (Ed.),** *Public Health on Merseyside – A Guide to Sources*, Merseyside Archives Liaison Group, 1991. This is a comprehensive listing of archives and printed material covering local hospitals, public health committees, Poor Law infirmaries and a variety of other institutions across Merseyside. Listings are too detailed to include here, but copies are available for consultation in Liverpool Record Office. Online, a search for 'Liverpool Hospitals' under reference 614 on the Access to Archives website www.nationalarchives .gov.uk/a2a will also be productive, as will searching the online Liverpool Record Office catalogue in a similar fashion (see Information Leaflet No.18).

A discussion about the archives and their care can be found in **Allan, Adrian**, 'Caring for Records? Records of Healthcare on Merseyside as untapped resources for the Historian' in *Medical Historian: Bulletin of the Liverpool Medical History Society*, No.4, July 1991. Researchers should also be aware of the restrictions covering access to hospital records: medical or patient records less than 100 years old, and administrative records less than 30 years old, are not usually open for public access. However, bona fide researchers can often get permission for access – in each case contact the relevant local archivist. An indication is given in the *Guide to Sources* above.

A good starting point for a general study of the topic is **Colin Pooley**, 'Living in Liverpool', in **John Belchem, (Ed.)**, *Liverpool 800*, Liverpool, 2006. This chapter also includes many references to sources and further reading.

An earlier history is **Bickerton, T.H.**, *A Medical History of Liverpool*, Liverpool, 1936. Copies of this reference volume are held in certain local libraries, such as the Liverpool Medical Institution, while Liverpool Record Office also holds Bickerton's research notes and illustrations.

Shepherd, J.A., *A History of the Liverpool Medical Institution*, Liverpool, 1979, also provides a useful insight into the medical history of the city.

Studies of local hospitals and institutions

Royden, Michael W. *A History of Liverpool Maternity Hospital and the Women's Hospital*, Liverpool, 1995.

——*A History of Mill Road Hospital*, Liverpool, 1993.

—— *Pioneers and Perseverance: A History of the Royal School for the Blind, Liverpool, 1791–1991*, Countyvise, Birkenhead, 1991.

Ross, J.A., *History of the Liverpool teaching hospitals until 1907*, Liverpool, 1972.

McGloughlin, G. *A Short History of the First Liverpool Infirmary 1749–1824*, 1978.

A useful study on local nursing following an extensive collection of oral material can be found in **Starkey, P. (Ed.)**, *Nursing Memories* NMGM, 1994.

A recent sudy of the cholera epidemic of 1832 can found in **Burrell, Sean and Gill, Geoffrey V.**, *The Liverpool Cholera Epidemic of 1832 and Anatomical Dissection – Medical Mistrust and Civil Unrest*, Journal of the History of Medicine and Allied Sciences, Vol.60, Number 4, pp.478–498, Oxford University Press, 2005. Useful studies of public health include **John Ashton and Howard Seymour**, *The new public health: The Liverpool* *experience*, Milton Keynes, 1988; and **Loraine Knowles**, *Public health: The Liverpool School of Hygiene Museum collection*, Liverpool, 2003, a well-illustrated exhibition catalogue with detailed accompanying text. **John Ashton**, *The changing health of Mersey, 1948–1994*, Liverpool, 1994, is a mainly contemporary analysis with historical introduction. An important historical text on local public health written by the former Medical Officer of Health for the city and port of Liverpool is **Hope, E.W.**, *Health at the gateway: Problems and international obligations of a seaport city*, Cambridge, 1931. A more recent collection of essays which includes chapters on Liverpool is **Sally Sheard and Helen Power**, *Body and city: Histories of urban public health*, Aldershot, 2000. Local academic lecturer Maggi Morris and her husband John Ashton, Regional Medical Officer for the North West of England during the 1990s, have produced *The Pool of Life: A Public Health Walk in Liverpool*, 1997. This is the history of public health told through key buildings and people, arranged in a number of guided walks. This now has a net presence – see below. An insight into the operation of the medical services during the war and information regarding casualties is **C.L. Dunn (Ed.)**, *The Emergency Medical Services Vol II* from the series 'A History of the Second World War – United Kingdom Medical Series', 1953. Margaret Simey has written extensively on the history of local charity and a useful introduction is **Simey, Margaret** 'Charity Rediscovered: A Study of Charitable Effort in Nineteenth Century Liverpool', Liverpool University Press (reprint 1992).

Kelly, Mike, *The Life and Times of Kitty Wilkinson*, is the story of a remarkable woman who fought poverty and adversity to become a legend in her time. Living in a poor part of Liverpool, plagued by disease, particularly cholera, she disregarded her own safety to care for the sick and dying, to take in homeless children and to teach that cleanliness was the main weapon against disease, turning her own home into a washhouse for her neighbours' benefit. Kitty was honoured by the city of Liverpool and by Queen Victoria, and in Liverpool Cathedral there is a dedicated window.

Workhouse records

It must be remembered that some of Liverpool's hospitals began originally as workhouses and the changeover from workhouse infirmary to 'modern' hospital was a gradual one. Therefore, depending on the period, some of the patients may have been workhouse inmates. This is certainly applicable when researching Sefton General (formerly Toxteth Park Workhouse) in Liverpool Record Office under catalogue ref. 614 SEF, Mill Road (ref. 614 MIL) and Newsham General (formerly Belmont, ref. 614 NGN) where workhouse admission/discharge records can be consulted. (Refer to Liverpool Record Office leaflet No.17, available online).

On the net

The Pool of Life – A Public Health Walk in Liverpool at: www.nwph.net /liverpoolpublichealthwalk has evolved over more than 20 years. Maggi Morris's original book was first published by Bluecoat Press in 1997. It was updated in 2007 with her husband, John Ashton, in anticipation of Liverpool's year as European Capital of Culture. They are your guides for this audio version, which features the key elements of the walk but is necessarily abridged. The walk is divided into four quarters – the maritime, the merchant, the institutional and the academic – which reflect Liverpool's history from its origins as a fishing port, through to the slave trade, its role as second city of Empire and, finally, to the present day. The walk takes two to three hours in total and is accompanied by a self-guiding map. Maggi Morris is Director of Public Health for Central Lancashire. She lectured at the Liverpool School of Architecture and the Department of Public Health, University of Liverpool. John Ashton, formerly Regional Director of Public Health and Regional Medical Officer for the North West of England, is Director of Public Health for Cumbria. He is a visiting Professor of Public Health Policy and Strategy.

Further information about local architecture and the fight for the Hahnemann building, for example, can be found on the Victorian Society site at www.victorian-society.org.uk (see link for Liverpool region).

An online history of St Paul's Eye Hospital is at www.eyecharity .com/history.

Mike Royden's Local History Pages at www.roydenhistory.co.uk have two useful papers:

Royden, Michael W. *The Roots of the New Liverpool Women's Hospital: 'The early medical care of women and babies in the late 18th/early 19th century'*, 1999.
——*The 19th Century Poor Law in Liverpool and its Hinterland: Towards the Origins of the Workhouse Infirmary*, 2000.

Chapter Nine

THE WORLD IN ONE CITY: RELIGION AND MIGRATION

Religion

Despite the multi-racial cosmopolitan nature of the city today, Liverpool is presently 80 per cent Christian, 1.4 per cent Muslim and other religious groups account for less than 1 per cent. Almost 18 per cent have no religious leaning at all (2001 Census). All the main denominations are present, with a much larger Roman Catholic population than in many other parts of the country, largely down to the impact of the Irish migration. A census of 1851 that counted church attendance revealed that of the 45 per cent of the population who attended that day, 40 per cent were Church of England, 32 per cent Catholic and the remainder Non-conformist. Welsh migration was evidenced in the 3.2 per cent who attended the Welsh Calvinist chapels on the counting day.

The established church took some time to gain a foothold in the area and even by the end of the seventeenth century the traveller Celia Fiennes was still moved to comment, 'there are a great many dissenters in the town'. Half a century later, alongside the five Anglican churches in the town were two Baptist meeting houses, one synagogue, one Methodist meeting house, a Quaker meeting house, a Catholic church and Dissenter meeting houses. Even by 1800 there were still thirteen Dissenter Houses against fourteen Anglican churches. Despite the dominance of the Protestants and Catholics, many of Liverpool's wealthy merchant elite of the nineteenth century were Unitarians. A variety of religious tracts and sermons were also published with regularity during the late eighteenth and early nineteenth centuries, many of which survive in Liverpool Record Office. They also hold details about local religious groups and their leading figures. The *Diocese of Liverpool Yearbook* and the *Archdiocese of Liverpool Directory* lists clergy and other information about the two main denominations, covering much of the twentieth century.

Liverpool has some of the largest and most radically designed religious buildings in Britain, reflecting the importance of its various communities during the nineteenth and twentieth centuries. The massive Anglican cathedral dominates the skyline from its dramatic position on the sandstone ridge, while the Roman Catholic cathedral was the first in Britain to be built in a circular form. On Princes Road, the Greek Orthodox church was designed as an enlarged version of one that stood in Constantinople, while the adjacent synagogue has an extremely ornate interior. Britain's first mosque was built in Liverpool in the 1880s.

Liverpool Record Office holds a plethora of information about local churches, from lists and directories of churches and clergy from the nineteenth century, to the more specialised material about fabric such as church bells.

Further research

The most comprehensive and up-to-date study yet of Liverpool's diverse ethnic make up is **John Belchem and Donald MacRaild**, 'Cosmopolitan Liverpool', in **John Belchem, (Ed.)**, *Liverpool 800*, Liverpool, 2006, and should be consulted at an early opportunity as a solid introduction to the subject.

Shearer, M., *Quakers in Liverpool*, 1982. There have been several meeting houses of the Society of Friends, first in Hackin's Hey (next to Quaker's Alley), then Hunter Street and currently in School Lane.

Read, Gordon and Jebson, David, *A voice in the city: 150 years of the Liverpool City Mission*, Liverpool, 1979. A long-lived organisation managing missions to the poor and to particular occupations and workplaces.

Lewis, David, *The Churches of Liverpool*, Liverpool, 2001. Brief illustrated histories of several hundred individual buildings, many no longer standing.

Sharples, Joseph, *Liverpool*, New Haven, 2004.

Pollard, Richard, *Lancashire: Liverpool and the South-West*, New Haven, 2006. These volumes have many descriptions of current Liverpool religious buildings. For many demolished from the 1960s refer to the Liverpool volume of the original Pevsner series, *The Buildings of England*.

The cathedrals

Kennerley, Peter, *The building of Liverpool Cathedral*, Preston, 2001. Thorough account of the development of the Anglican cathedral.

Kennerley, Peter, and Wilkinson, Colin, *The Cathedral Church of Christ in Liverpool: Pictures from the first hundred years*, Liverpool, 2003. Includes new photography by Barry Hale.

Gibberd, Frederick, *Metropolitan Cathedral of Christ the King*, Liverpool, 1968. An account of the Catholic cathedral, by its architect.
Liverpool Anglican Cathedral website: www.liverpoolcathedral.org.uk.
Liverpool's Metropolitan Cathedral website: www.liverpoolmetrocathedral.org.uk.
There are numerous local websites that hold photographs of churches and chapels, for example:
www.toxteth.net (currently offline – use the wayback machine
www.archive.org/web/web.php);
www.old-liverpool.co.uk; http://pennylaneliverpool.merseyside.org.

Migration: The World in One City

Once the second city of the Empire, Liverpool was a global port city with an ethnically diverse 'cosmopolitan' population, although despite this head start, Colin Pooley's study *Liverpool 800* has shown that Liverpool has become one of the least ethnically varied cities in the country today, with only a small number of 'new commonwealth' migrants arriving after 1945. Studies of the Edwardian census have revealed that Manchester was more European in its mix than Liverpool, but Liverpool had a more global element, and had twice as many people of the Empire as Manchester.

On disembarking many migrants found themselves stranded in squalid housing conditions close to the docks, unable to fund further travel to their desired destinations. This was a vast floating, migrant and casual population. Most of the groups and individuals making up Liverpool's ethnic mix were directly or indirectly connected to the development and activity of the port, which created a constant interchange of people.

There is no suggestion that this ethnic mix was always cordial, with each group neatly dovetailing into a peaceful coexistence. Diverse it may have been, but prejudice and discrimination have been commonplace alongside the 'inclusive' rhetoric. Racial problems were common, with sectarian violence and murder being frequently reported. In fact, the earliest sectarian violence has been dated to 1819, when an Irish Catholic mob attacked a procession of Orangemen in Dale Street.

Liverpool's ethnic mix has made a difficult challenge for historians. On its own, the census does not fully reflect the diversity of daily life in the dockland areas of the city. In recent years, there has been an increasing volume of work on particular ethnic groups, often using oral history techniques or the study of archives of churches and community organisations to reach a greater level of understanding of Liverpool's multicultural history.

The Celtic Influx

Liverpool-Irish

This most common of ethnic groups has long suffered from caricature and stigma, frequently perpetuated in humour, writings and even the inverted snobbery of those who speak with pride of the evolution of the true Irish scouser. Even as early as 1836, the local Head Constable was critical of sectarianism, which had not been left at home. Indeed, the presence of a larger contingent of Ulstermen than in other cities seemed to awaken latent British anti-Catholicism. Orangeism soon became part of Liverpool civic culture, unmatched even in Glasgow. This emotive and populist presence in politics persisted right down to the interwar period. Consequently, the stigmatised stereotype of the Irish Catholic migrant as being low in morals and hygiene, and beyond British politics, was a difficult image to shake off. Migrants of the famine merely entrenched these local views. A local magistrate declared that within twelve hours of disembarkation the Famine Irish were to be 'found in one of three classes – paupers, vagrants, or thieves'. In 1847 alone 300,000 arrived, mostly in dreadful circumstances: 116,000 were said to be 'half naked and starving'. The local Poor Law was in crisis, while appeals to central government for assistance fell on deaf ears. Despite tougher rules to prevent settlement, many claimed irremovable status under the Five Year Residency Act of 1846.

It must be remembered, however, that 17 per cent of the Liverpool population before the famine was Irish. According to the 1841 census, the town was already home to 50,000 Catholic and Protestant Irish. Those that could not move on to America or elsewhere in 1847 were able to adapt into a Liverpool-Irish lifestyle and culture that was already present. However, the Irish migrant was the largest group of unskilled labourers and of the lowest socio-economic status, while the Irish middle class tended to use the town as a stepping stone rather than a destination. But others did remain and went on to occupy positions in local politics, law, journalism and the medical professions. Irish merchants frequently dominated the mercantile circles. William Brown became a role model for many (the Museum and Central Library building, which houses the Liverpool Record Office, was funded by him), while Richard Sheil (after whom Sheil Park was named) became the most prominent and influential merchant – and for a time the only Catholic member of the local council. A network of Irish Confederate pubs soon took hold, providing a link between the nationalist elite and the wider community. This was easily exploited by the Liverpool Fenians from the later nineteenth century onwards. Throughout the risings of 1916–23, Liverpool played a crucial role as the transatlantic centre in supplying arms and volunteers. Sanctuary and escape routes would also be provided for those on the run from the authorities. Nevertheless, many of the Catholic Irish shopkeepers and trading class engaged in electoral politics and began to challenge the previous Liberal alignment of the Catholic merchant elite. As the campaign for Home Rule gathered momentum in the 1870s, Irish Nationalists began to gain an increasing foothold in local politics. In fact, forty-eight Nationalists sat on Liverpool Council between 1875 and 1922

During the famine years, approximately 1.3 million Irish passed through the port. The living conditions of many of them were fairly poor. Low hygienic standards, high child mortality and epidemics like cholera and typhus were down to primitive sanitary facilities and little space. By 1851 the streets in the North End between Vauxhall Road and Scotland Road contained the greatest concentration of Irish immigrants in England, while in the South End, in the streets between the docks and a line running from Park Lane to Park Road, a smaller but still large Irish community was to be found. So by 1851 the Irish in Liverpool had risen to over 22 per cent (83,813) of the city's population, although the number of Irish in the city declined to 15.6 per cent (76,761) by 1871. By 1911 the Irish population was equal to the Scottish/Welsh/Manx influx combined.

Father James Nugent, 'the father of the poor', was born in Hunter Street, Liverpool on 3 March 1822. He trained for the priesthood and was ordained as a priest at St Nicholas's, Liverpool, in 1846, where he returned as curate three years later. Moved by the deprivation suffered by those in his community he encouraged those with power, money and influence to help. In 1849 he opened a Ragged School at Copperas Hill, to take homeless children off the streets by offering them shelter, food and clothing. He also brought the teaching order of Notre Dame to the city to staff the Catholic Poor Law Schools. He followed this by establishing a night shelter and refuge for homeless boys, but it was obvious that with over 48,000 boys receiving supper and 3,000 a night's lodging, something more substantial was required. The Boys' Refuge (a certified Industrial School) was opened in 1869 teaching shoe-making, tailoring, joinery and printing, which lasted until 1923. He continued to provide educational opportunities and was also a chaplain to Walton Prison, where he could see first-hand the plight of women after their discharge and helped provide a refuge. The result was the House of Providence, a home for mothers and their babies established in the Dingle. Father Nugent also pioneered child emigration to Canada from 1870, an activity that continued until 1930, although the benefit of this has undergone recent revision (see child emigration). The Nugent Care charity continues today.

Irish migration did not end in the famine years. By the late 1930s it was still a cause of dissent among some sections of the local community and politicians. A further wave of Irish settlement occurred at the end of the 1940s as Irish workers helped assist with the city's post-war regeneration. Irish cultural centres and associations were established in the community and music and dance featured prominently. Venues such as the Shamrock Club on Lime Street, which opened in the late 1940s, were very popular with their weekend céilídhs and dances. In 1957 a Liverpool branch of Comhaltas Céoltoirí Eireann (Association of Irish Musicians) was established and in 1964 the dedicated Irish Centre opened on Mount Pleasant, which became a focus for the community for many years.

Further research

Belchem, John *Irish, Catholic and Scouse: The history of the Liverpool Irish, 1800–1939*, Liverpool, 2007. A major new study.
Runaghan, Patricia, *Father Nugent's Liverpool 1849–1905*, Countyvise, 2003.
Grenham, John, *Tracing Your Irish Ancestors*.
Maxwell, Ian, *Tracing Your Irish Ancestors*, Pen & Sword, 2009.
O'Mara, Pat, *The Autobiography of a Liverpool Irish Slummy*, Bluecoat Press, new edition 2007, originally published 1933. This is a tale of working-class life in Liverpool at the turn of the twentieth century. A chronicle of a tough childhood and everyday life around Great George's Square.
Neal, Frank, *Sectarian Violence – The Liverpool Experience 1819–1914*, *Manchester University Press, 1982*. A a wide study that includes Irish society, migration, famine and the Liverpool reaction.
Kelly, Michael, *Liverpool's Irish Connection*, A.J.H. Publications, Liverpool, 2006. This tells the story of many notable Liverpool-Irish people during the development of Liverpool in the early part of the Industrial Revolution. Chapters include figures such as Nurse Agnes Jones, Michael James Whitty, James Muspratt, Percy French, Patrick (Dandy Pat) Byrne and James William Carling. Some of the people featured in this book are also briefly mentioned in the *Liverpool Notables* on the Liverpool Heritage Forum's website.
Gallman, J. Matthew *Receiving Erin's children: Philadelphia, Liverpool, and the Irish famine migration, 1845–1855*, Chapel Hill, 2000. The most recent major work on the famine migration.
Papworth, John, *The Liverpool Irish 1851–1871*,unpublished PhD thesis, University of Liverpool, 1982.

On the net

Hibernia: http://freepages.genealogy.rootsweb.ancestry.com/~hibernia
A useful Liverpool Irish Family History records portal by Patrick Neill.

Irish Holocaust: www.irishholocaust.org/liverpoolandthegreat
A view of the Irish experience as a Holocaust, which the author insists should be taught as such in schools. Section on disembarkation and local reaction in Liverpool.

University of Liverpool Institute of Irish Studies: www.liv.ac.uk/irish
Information about degree courses plus external lectures, conferences and publications.

Liverpool Irish Festival: www.liverpoolirishfestival.com
An annual event that celebrates Liverpool's Irish heritage. Performance, participation, entertainment and education in Irish traditions, music, literature, theatre and art, and reflecting their significance in defining Liverpool's culture as a great European city.

Irish Ancestors: www.ireland.com/ancestor/browse/links/index.htm#emigrant
Portal pages sponsored by the *Irish Times*. Useful passenger list database.

Olive Tree Genealogy: http://olivetreegenealogy.com/ships/

Your Irish Roots: www.youririshroots.com
This site provides a wealth of information on all aspects of tracing your Irish genealogy, history, Irish surnames, Irish coats of arms and the sort of life your Irish ancestors might have led in Ireland.

National Archives of Ireland: www.nationalarchives.ie/genealogy/index.html
Also has a searchable database of Ireland-Australia transportation records from 1791–1853). Ancestry.com has passenger lists for those coming into various North American ports.

National Library of Canada: http://collectionscanada.ca/genealogy/index-e.html

Liverpool Welsh

The Liverpool Welsh have been an integral part of the town since the last decade of the eighteenth century. They came in their thousands between 1780 and 1820 and in that period a large number of Welsh chapels and churches were built. In 1851 the Welsh-born population was 20,262 – 5.4 per cent of the population, and many could speak only their native tongue. By the end of the century that figure had doubled to 10 per cent of the population. The pattern of Welsh settlement tended to favour the newly-created residential developments, leading to Welsh clusters in Everton, Anfield and Bootle, and also in the southern areas of Toxteth Park. As the areas became Welsh in speech and in culture, the streets were often given Welsh names. In fact, the initials of the names of streets built by the father and son firm of Owen and William Owen Elias, spelt the name of their firm in alphabetical order. Another well-known builder was John Jones, nick-named Drinkwater because of his refusal to pay workmen the customary price of a pint of beer when the first house in a terrace was completed. Many of the labouring Welshmen who arrived in Liverpool moved into the building trade and worked on the construction of these new residential areas in the suburban expansion of the town. The network inevitably extended into land agency, surveying and finance.

The first Welsh chapel was built in 1787 in Pall Mall – an area later to be known as 'Little Wales'. Later, the 'Welsh Cathedral', the Gothic Welsh Presbyterian church with its impressive spire, was erected on the Princes Road Parliament Fields development in 1868 – an area which excluded public houses. Integral to Welsh society were the chapels – Calvinist Methodist, Wesleyan Methodist, Independent and Baptist. Attendance figures were greater than those at Catholic churches and help and support was available for those coming to settle to learn English, further their education, or aid those falling on hard times. In the case of the latter, only two per cent in public institutions claiming relief were Welsh.

The Royal National Eisteddfod was held several times in either Birkenhead or Liverpool, and this helped promote the image of Liverpool as the 'capital of Wales'. The Welsh Choral Union has been in existence since the National Eisteddfod came to Liverpool in 1900. Societies were formed to help give support and promote a non-militant Welsh Nationalism, such as the middle-class Liverpool Welsh National Society and the Liverpool Young Wales Society. Politically and ideologically Liberal, they were bound to civic duty and moral servitude. The community continued to embrace the chapel, Eisteddfod, and the Welsh language, as well as Welsh books and newspapers, many of which were edited and published in Liverpool. But this was no isolationist community. When the Liberal Review praised the Welsh as 'among the most peaceable, law-abiding, cleanly and provident of the Liverpool citizens… they retain their national customs and habits, and, in the midst of this great Saxon population, have a little Wales of their own', they were reflecting a view held by many that the community as a whole was benefiting from their presence.

Further research

Rees, Rev. D. Ben, and Jones, R. M., *The Liverpool Welsh and their religion: Two centuries of Welsh Calvinistic Methodism*, Liverpool, 1984. Has a chapter giving an overview of Welsh settlement in Liverpool.
Rees, Rev. D. Ben, *The Welsh of Merseyside — Volume 1*, Modern Welsh Publications.
—— *The Welsh of Merseyside in the Twentieth Century – Volume 2*, Modern Welsh Publications.
Jones, J.R., *The Welsh Builder on Merseyside: (the Annals and Lives), Interesting accounts of 19th Century entrepreneurs-craftsmen, their families, culture, religion, and statistical data*, 1948.
Doughty, Martin (Ed.), *Building the Industrial City*, 1986. Includes chapter on 'The Welsh Influence on the Building Industry in Victorian Liverpool.'

On the net

The Welsh in Liverpool: www.liverpool-welsh.com

The Scottie Press: www.scottiepress.org/projects/welsh.htm
A section on this informative local site is dedicated to a study of the Welsh in the Vauxhall/Walton area of the town and includes photographs of streets and chapels.

Liverpool Scottish

This is a group that has been little studied, which is surprising given that 4 per cent of the local population was Scots-born in 1871, and in size was second only to the Scottish community in Newcastle throughout the nineteenth century. Many early migrants were involved in merchant shipping, sugar refining and brewing. The new chair of 'Philosophy, Logic and Political Economy' at University College in 1882 was funded by a £10,000 subscription from over forty Scottish merchants. John Rankin, the Scottish chairman of the Royal Insurance Company, Pacific Steam Navigation and the Bank of Liverpool, was the university's greatest benefactor when it gained its royal charter. The Scottish presence was keenly felt in medicine when the town benefited from the arrival of many men trained in Edinburgh. James Currie, Thomas Traill and William Duncan (the first Medical Officer of Health) were all notables in their field. Skilled Scottish workers migrated towards the more salubrious outskirts of the North End, no doubt maintaining an intentional distance from the lower Irish class of manual labourers in the South End.

The Scottish church of St Andrew in Rodney Street, built in 1824.

One of the most impressive church buildings in the town was the Scottish church of St Andrew in Rodney Street, built in 1824 with its Greek revival façade. Further community support was found in the Liverpool Caledonian Association and Liverpool Scottish Regiment. The Liverpool Scottish was formed as an infantry battalion in 1900 in response to the crisis of the Boer War. It was raised from among the body of highly educated and professional young Scotsmen in the city as the 8th (Scottish) Volunteer Battalion, The King's (Liverpool Regiment). There was an annual subscription of 10 shillings and an entrance fee of £2, such costs certainly dissuading the low-paid unskilled labourer. The first Commanding Officer was Colonel C. Forbes Bell VD and his tartan was adopted by the regiment as full Highland dress. Before the First World War the battalion numbered over 700, many of whom were keen for adventure on the regular camps and to meet up with like-minded friends in the evenings. In 1908 the Battalion was established as a Territorial Force as the 10th (Scottish) Battalion, The King's (Liverpool Regiment).

Further research

Munro, Alasdair and Sim, Duncan, *The Merseyside Scots: A study of an expatriate community*, Birkenhead, 2001. Has detailed chapters on doctors, businessmen, the church and the army, as well as useful general material.
McGilchrist, A.M., *The Liverpool Scottish 1900–1919*, 1930, reprinted and available through the regimental website.
Reeves, Dennis, *Brief History of the Liverpool Scottish 1859 to 2006.*
—— *Special Service of A Hazardous Nature: The Story of the Liverpool Scottish Involvement in Special Forces Operations in World War Two 1939–1945.*

On the net

The Liverpool Scottish Regiment www.liverpoolscottish.org.uk
An excellent website containing regimental history, bookshop and research advice.

Scotland's Family www.scotlandsfamily.com
The Scottish genealogy portal designed to help you explore your Scottish family tree. The aim is to direct you to free on-line data and information in diverse Scotland family history records, wherever you live in the world.

Manx

There have long been close ties with the Isle of Man, with Liverpool being the main port for ferries and the Island becoming a resort for holiday-makers. These visitors were escaping the dwindling appeal of the local

Edwardian attractions closer to home, before the arrival of the foreign package holiday eventually sounded the Island's death knell as a tourist haven.

Many Manx workers coming to Liverpool in the nineteenth century were seasonal, deriving their income from the summer tourist trade, before travelling to Liverpool hoping for a position to tide them though to the following year. The Liverpool Manx Society was set up in 1895 to keep the Manx spirit alive and to help support these workers, and others who made their stay permanent. Vaughan Robinson (*The Isle of Man: Celebrating A Sense of Place*) shows the main distribution of Manx settlers to be in Liverpool, the Wirral and parts of the North Wales coast.

One such family were the Quilliams. William Quilliam was born in Liverpool to a wealthy Manx family in 1856, and was educated at the Liverpool Institute and King William's College on the Isle of Man. He began work as a solicitor in 1878, but he is remembered today as a nine-teenth-century convert from Christianity to Islam, who founded England's first mosque and Islamic centre. After a trip to Morocco in 1887 he converted, changed his name to Abdullah Quilliam and established the Liverpool Mosque and Islamic Institute at 8 Brougham Terrace in West Derby Street in 1889. The mosque, which could accommodate around a hundred Muslims, was soon followed by a Muslim college and a weekly Debating and Literary Society. Quilliam's book, *The Faith of Islam*, was translated into thirteen languages, gaining him fame across the Islamic world, and he produced a weekly paper, *The Crescent*, from 1893 until 1908. He died in 1932 and Western Muslims, particularly converts to Islam, see him as a pioneer. Today his legacy is maintained by the Abdullah Quilliam Society (formed in 1996), which has purchased 8–10 Brougham Terrace in order to restore the historic mosque and establish an educational centre. His name is also remembered in the Quilliam Foundation, a moderate Muslim think-tank aimed at challenging extremist Islamist ideologies, launched in 2008.

In 1992 the University of Liverpool founded the Centre for Manx Studies (part of the School of Archaeology, Classics and Egyptology), managed by a committee with representatives from the three partner organisations: Manx National Heritage, the University of Liverpool and the Isle of Man Department of Education. Its primary functions are to teach students, to carry out research in Manx archaeological, cultural, environmental and historical studies and to further the international recognition of the Isle of Man in these areas. A central aim is a project to bring A.W. Moore's *History of the Isle of Man*, still the standard textbook for the period 798–1830, up to date, as it was published over a century ago. The five-volume *New History of the Isle of Man* will present the most recent research and ideas from Manx scholars, in a readable, authoritative account from geological times to the present day. Almost 150 writers and researchers have been involved in the project. The first of the five volumes deals with the landscape and environ-ment, setting the scene for the arrival of early man and describing some of the effects which have resulted from his appearance. The second volume explores the prehistory of the Island and volumes three and four take a fresh look at the documentary evidence of the period from 1000–1830. Volume five examines the political, economic, legal and social developments of the past 170 years.

For more details, availability, details of conferences and further education see www.liv.ac.uk/manxstudies/index.htm.

Further research

Moore, A.W., *History of the Isle of Man*, 2 vols, 1900, reprinted by the Manx Museum and available in paperback.
Kinvig, R.H., *The Isle of Man*, Liverpool University Press, 1975. The third, and greatly expanded, edition of a slim volume that first appeared in 1944.
Robinson,V. and McCarroll, D., *The Isle of Man: Celebrating a Sense of Place*, Liverpool University Press, 1990. Covers much from geology through to post-Second World War changes in industry.

On the net

Isle of Man Family History Society: www.iomfhs.im
Formed in January 1979 to encourage the study of genealogy and family history, for those on the Island or those living abroad.

A Manx Note Book: www.isle-of-man.com/manxnotebook/
Useful history portal for all matters concerning the Manx and their history.

Greek

Among foreign merchants, the Greeks occupied a prominent and important place as gentlemen of position, wealth and intelligence. Five shipping lines exported to Greece: Leyland, Moss, Cunard, Papayanti Johnstone and Prince's Line. Of the first four companies, one boat of each line was sent every week. The goods which passed through Liverpool destined for Greece even included Yarmouth Herrings. Soda ash, caustic soda, steel, iron and many more Black Country commodities were shipped, together with manufactured articles from Manchester, Leeds, Sheffield, Nottingham and other parts of the kingdom. Return cargoes mostly comprised various kinds of fruit, oil, vegetables and wine. Until the 1870s the Greek community had no public place of worship, and assembled for service in a house in Sandon Terrace in Duke Street. The increasing prosperity of the Greek ship-owning and mercantile community was reflected in the commissioning of plans from local architect Henry Summers, and the Greek Orthodox Church of St

Nicholas was erected at the junction of Berkley Street and Princes Road in the Parliament Field development in Toxteth. Designed as an enlarged version of St Theodore's church in Constantinople, it was built in 1870 in the Neo-Byzantine architectural style. It is now a Grade II listed building. This was a period when many substantial mansions were being erected in the neighbourhood with churches to match, designed to advertise the wealth and status of a group of leaders of industry. Immediately adjacent are the equally impressive Princes Road Synagogue and the early French Gothic Welsh Presbyterian Church.

Further research

Crowther, Anne L., *The Greek Gentlemen,* a short article about the death of a local Greek gentleman and the Liverpool Greek Community (hosted on Mike Royden's Local History Pages. Links for various aspects of Greek family history research.)

Italian

Liverpool's 'Little Italy', concentrated around Gerard Street, was small and only numbered around 500 in 1915. Two recent works have been published on this little studied subject. Firstly, *Little Italy: A History of Liverpool's Italian Community* by Terry Cooke, in which he shows that Little Italy generally comprised the area around Circus Street, Gerard Street, Hunter Street, Lionel Street, Whale Street and part of Christian Street, Clare Street and Springfield Street. Italians worshipped mainly at St Joseph's Church, Grosvenor Street, and Holy Cross Church, Great Crosshall Street. Official records referring to the surnames of Italian immigrants show various spellings, many of which are only approximate, and during the 1940s there was a tendency for the spelling and pronunciation of some Italian surnames to become anglicised. The area they came to was far removed from the seaside beauty they had left behind, and the Italians introduced their own culture, colourful religious processions and unique community spirit to their new home. In the second publication, Debra D'Annunzio looks at Liverpool's Little Italy in the nineteenth century. Debra's family were part of the mass migration from Italy and settled in Liverpool as a part of this vibrant community. Copies can be obtained through the Anglo-Italian Family History website: www.anglo-italianfhs.org.uk.

Further research

Cooke, Terry, *Little Italy: A history of Liverpool's Italian Community,* Liverpool, 2002.

D'Annunzio, Debra, *Liverpool's Little Italy in the Nineteenth Century*, Liverpool, 2008.

On the net

Scottie Press Little Italy Project: www.scottiepress.org/projects/litaly.htm
Several pages full of photographs, maps, documents, and memories about Little Italy and the Liverpool Italian Community in this ongoing project. A recommended starting point.

Scandinavian

The scale of the Scandinavian emigration, particularly from the 1850s to the outbreak of the First World War, was unprecedented, reaching around 50,000. But in 1870 the Swedish-Norwegian Church Council in London had already recommended that there should be a mission present in the port to give support to the transient community. Consequently the first priest, Per August Tegner, arrived in Liverpool on 22 August 1870 and the first service was held six days later at South Bethel, while his brief entailed that he made innumerable visits to ships and local boarding houses. The Gustaf Adolfs Kyrka Seamen's Church was initially built in 1883/4 in order to respond to the needs of both seafarers and emigrants. The young architect, William Douglas Caroe, created a unique building, which contained many Scandinavian features, including stepped gables and a concave-sided lead-covered spire over the entrance. Construction costs amounted to 50,000 Swedish crowns, a mere £15,000 today. The church stands today as one of only four octagonal church buildings in the country. It was also the first Swedish church built overseas.

However, in early 2008, the future of the Scandinavian seamen's church was thrown into doubt when the Swedish leaders decided to leave the city. The Church of Sweden had decided to switch the focus of its international work to South-East Asia and the Americas. Speaking a year later in early 2009, Mette Royden, housemother at the church, disclosed that a decision as to the future of the Grade II listed building had yet to be decided. There were no definite plans about where the community would worship if the building was sold off. Her husband, Stan Royden, voluntary chairman of the church committee, said 'We don't know where services will be held once the church is closed, but one thing is certain and that's that the Scandinavian community will fall apart once the church disappears.' That would mean the end of 125 years of worship on the site for Liverpool's Scandinavian and Nordic communities, unless they are able to buy the building.

Further research

On the net

Genfind: – Scandinavian transmigration www.genfind.org/transmigration.htm
Useful advice and links for those tracing Norwegian/Scandinavian heritage.

Nordic Ancestry: www.nordicancestry.com
Professional researchers based near Salt Lake City, Utah.

Scandinavian Seamen's Church in Liverpool: www.svenskakyrkan.se/skut/liverpool

Jewish

The Liverpool Jewish community was the first organised Jewish community in the north of England, and until the mid-nineteenth century it was the largest in the provinces. Settlers arrived in the mid-eighteenth century and there is a record of an early synagogue in Stanley Street in 1753. Jews soon established a niche supplying chandlery and general provisions to the local seafaring quarter, while sending out hawkers into the local communities with cheaper goods. A second wave of settlers arrived from the late nineteenth century to 1914, when destitute Russian and Polish Jews arrived following the pogroms. Many passed through Liverpool and emigrated to America, but at least 5,000 stayed in Liverpool, settling in the Brownlow Hill/Copperas Hill/Pembroke Place/Crown

Princes Road Synagogue.

Street area. The Princes Road Synagogue, with its beautiful interior, was consecrated in 1874. The first provincial company of the Jewish Lads' Brigade was established in February 1897, and the Liverpool Hebrew Day School, in 1904. The Lads' Brigade moved to Harold House in Upper Parliament Street in 1926, which in turn relocated to Chatham Street three years later. The Greenbank Drive and Childwall synagogues were built in the 1930s, followed by the founding of the Merseyside Jewish Representative Council, created to protect Jewish communal life. The community today is centred around Dunbabin Road in Woolton. The primary and secondary school of King David are situated there, as is the social and cultural centre, Harold House, in its new home.

Further research

It is recommended that the information leaflet 'Merseyside Jewish Community Archives at Liverpool Record Office' is consulted before beginning research. What follows is a brief summary of this extensive collection. Liverpool Record Office holds the archives of the Merseyside Jewish Community from the eighteenth century to the present day and they cover five main themes: welfare, Zionism, education, synagogues and personal papers. The archive shows the Jewish population becoming part of the wider Merseyside community and their contributions to the city. Liverpool Record Office currently holds over 250 collections relating to the Jewish community. Catalogues are currently available electronically at Liverpool Record Office and all Liverpool libraries. Printed catalogues are also held at Liverpool Record Office.

NB. Certain sensitive records are still closed under the Data Protection Act 1998 – these restrictions are noted in the catalogues.

Synagogues

One of the most extensive collections in the Merseyside Jewish Community Archives is the records of the Old Hebrew Congregation (296 OHC). The earliest archive is the 'Register Book of the Jews in Liverpool', which records births, deaths and marriages from 1804 to 1816 (296 OHC/29/1). The register also includes information on members of the community from as early as 1722. The records give an insight into the life of many of the eighteenth-century members of the Liverpool Jewish Community. In the mid-nineteenth century there was a split which led to the formation of the New Hebrew Congregation. Other records include Greenbank Drive Synagogue (consecrated 1937), Fountains Road Synagogue (1888), the Progressive Synagogue Wavertree (1928), Allerton, Central Synagogue, Islington, Childwall, Crosby and Waterloo Hebrew Congregation, Fairfield, Great Synagogue, Grove Street, Nusach Ari Synagogue, Pride of Israel Congregation – Ullet Road Synagogue, and Wallasey Synagogue.

Education

The King David Primary School had its origins in 1841 when the Liverpool Hebrews' Educational Institution and Endowed Schools was established. In February 1844 a Girls' Department was added and in 1857 an Infants' Department was founded. As the community moved towards the more affluent suburbs of Childwall and Woolton, the King David High School was opened in Childwall in 1957. In 1964 the Primary School moved to the Childwall site. The admission and discharge registers of the school are of particular interest (1866–1960) for genealogical research. Records are also available for associated organisations such as the Association of Old Boys, the Association of Old Girls, and the Junior Association of Old Boys. Liverpool Talmudical College (Yeshiva Torat Chaim) was established in 1910 to provide advanced Jewish learning. In 1938 it accepted refugees from Nazi Germany and residential accommodation for the refugees was organised. Liverpool was a restricted area, excluding 'enemy aliens', and the college temporarily moved to St Asaph in North Wales. The minutes in the collection cover this period, 1935–1964.

Welfare

The principal synagogues originally carried out relief of the poor. The Liverpool Hebrew Philanthropic Society, established in 1811, provided charity outside of the synagogues. The Jewish Ladies' Benevolent Fund was founded in 1849, 'for the relief of poor married women during sickness and confinement'. Records also include those of the Board of Guardians for the Relief of the Jewish Poor, the Jewish Loan Society, the Liverpool branch of the Mansion House Fund, the Liverpool Hebrew Provident Society and the Society for Temporarily Sheltering and Assisting Poor Strangers of the Jewish Faith.

Personal papers

The personal papers in the Merseyside Jewish Community Archives provide insight into the process of emigration, as well as individuals' relationships with the wider community. The largest collection of personal papers is that of Bertram B.B. Benas. Benas was one of the most highly esteemed members of the Liverpool Jewish Community, which he continued to serve for over seventy years. The Benas Collection is a most valuable research tool because of the number of roles he played in the Jewish and wider community. The collection also documents Jewish life in Liverpool in the twentieth century. The organisations which are recorded in this collection include the Literary and Philosophical Society, the Athenaeum and the Historic Society of Lancashire and Cheshire, musical societies in Merseyside, papers relating to the integration of Jews in Britain, the Board of Deputies of British Jews and organisations dealing with

German Jewry, Zionist organisations and the development of Zionism. Other papers document the life stories of individuals fleeing Nazi persecution as well as the life of emigrants and travellers in the nineteenth and twentieth centuries. Correspondence exists from parents separated from their children sent to Britain from Bad Neustadt, Germany, between March and July 1942. There are also papers relating to George Behrend (born in 1826), a Liverpool merchant and shipowner. (See also **Behrend, Arthur**, *Portrait of a family firm: Bahr, Behrend & Co., 1793–1945*, 1970.)

Zionism

One of the earliest Zionist societies in Liverpool was the Chovevi Zion (Lovers of Zion), established in July 1891. Liverpool Record Office holds the first minute book of the society covering 1891–1898. Following the first Zionist Congress in 1897 there was intense Zionist activity in Liverpool and the Liverpool Young Men's Zionist Association was formed the following year. Records are held for the Liverpool Zionist Society formed in 1935, the Liverpool Ladies Zionist & Welfare Association and the Liverpool Zionist Central Council (originally the Liverpool Zionist Association). A selection of other Zionist records held are Jewish National Fund, Liverpool Daughters of Zion, Liverpool Habonim Youth Movement, Poale Zion – Jewish Labour Party, United Jewish Israel Appeal, Young Israel Society.

Further reading

Kolosalakis, N., *Ethnic identity and religion: Tradition and change in Liverpool Jewry*, Washington, 1982.
MacGregor, Jan, *In search of ethnicity: Jewish and Celtic identities in Liverpool and Glasgow 1850–1900*, University of Liverpool M.Phil. thesis, 2003.
Goodman, Mervyn, *From Toxteth to Tel Aviv: The contribution of Merseyside to the establishment of the state of Israel 1880–1948*, University of Liverpool M.Phil. thesis, 2000. Both theses can be consulted in the University Library.
Abrahams, K.L., *Merseyside Jewish Welfare Council, Centenary history*, Liverpool, 1975.

On the net

Moving Here: www.movinghere.org.uk/galleries/roots/jewish/jewish.htm
An excellent site for those researching Jewish ancestry and capitalises on the changes made following the opening up of Russian archives. An excellent starting point.

Liverpool Old Hebrew Congregation, Princes Road Synagogue:
www.princesroad.org
Includes photographs of the interior and history pages.

Chicken Soup & Scouse: www.chickensoupandscouse.com
This site provides information about the DVD of this name that was
produced in 2007 as a result of researches and interviews by Michael
Swerdlow and Arnold Lewis with senior citizens of the Jewish community.
The programme traces the history and personalities of the Liverpool Jewish
Community from the 1700s to the present day, with interviews, graphics,
photographs and archive film, and explores the contribution that members
of the Liverpool Jewish community have made to the culture and pros-
perity of the city of Liverpool. Available from the bookshop at Harold
House as well as the website.

JewishGen: The Home of Jewish Genealogy: www.jewishgen.org

The Changing Years: http://jeffmax.pwp.blueyonder.co.uk
A series of articles published in the Liverpool Jewish Gazette between 1968
and 1970.

Deane Road Cemetery: www.deaneroadcemetery.com
Cemetery of the nineteenth-century Liverpool Old Hebrew Congregation
and community.

Merseyside Jewish Community: www.merseyside-jewish-community.org.uk

Manchester University Centre for Jewish Studies: www.mucjs.org

British Jewry Website: www.british-jewry.org.uk
Databases, links and other information.

West Indian (see the section on the Slave Trade in Chapter One)

Lascar (Asian Indian sub-continent)

The Asian presence in Britain goes back to the early days of Empire and
forms a prelude to the larger-scale post-independence migration of Asians
to Britain. The imperial colonial link resulted in many South Asians visiting
Britain for a variety of reasons, but in Liverpool it was mainly as a result of
companies like the East India Company and British Merchant Marine
employing lascars (Indian seamen) on their ships. A significant number

settled in Britain permanently. By the 1890s ship owners were finding it increasingly difficult to staff their ships with good-quality British ratings because of the low wages and poor conditions afloat. They therefore began to employ growing numbers of foreign seafarers on their ocean-going ships. From 1890, the Brocklebank shipping company hired lascars from Singapore and Malaya as deck, engine room and saloon crew. Chinese crews were a feature of the Blue Funnel Line. The number of lascars engaged for service to the United Kingdom grew in the 1870s. Nevertheless, lascars encountered harsh conditions, substandard dietary provision and unequal treatment, including wages far lower than those of white seamen. Lascar desertion was a problem, and as a consequence lascar transfer officers were appointed by the Board of Trade at all major ports in 1871. These officers had the power to force Indian crews arriving in Britain to return on ships bound for India. Officers who engaged in crackdowns on lascars in Britain claimed to be motivated by humanitarian aims: they hoped to prevent potential deserters from wandering into a life of destitution on the streets of Britain. The Merchant Shipping Act of 1894 made legislation clear that lascar contracts bound sailors to return to their homeland, and it made provision for ship owners to place lascars on crews heading back to India. Nevertheless, desertion was still common and gradually a small community of Asian sailors grew up in Liverpool. Only a few shipping companies made warrants against the lascar deserters. Some ex-seamen felt free to apply to the High Commissioner for India to obtain Certificates of Nationality and the British Indian Seamen's Certificates of Identity, which are to all intents and purposes passports, and were regarded as such by their holders.

In 1937 there were only two shipping companies, the P&O and the Ellerman Lines, which took out warrants for the arrest of Indian seamen deserting their ships under the Merchant Shipping Act. The offenders were often arrested or became the subject of police inquiry (see the National Archives). The National Archives also holds Asiatic Seamen's Agreement and Crew Lists, and the Board of Trade: Registrar General of Shipping and Seamen, and its predecessor: Agreements and Crew Lists, Series II, 1861–1994, in the National Archives record series (PRO)BT 99. The Indian, Pakistan and Bangladesh Seamen's Services Records ('Pouches') for the period 1913–72 are in the National Archives record series (PRO)BT 372. When seamen were discharged, some or all of their documents (including the index cards) were placed in the pouches.

Further reading

Ashok Burman and Jennifer McCarthy (Ed.), *Indian presence in Liverpool*, Liverpool, 2002. A rare account of members of Liverpool's Indian community, published by the Museum of Liverpool Life.

Indian Presence website: www.liverpoolmuseums.org.uk/hamlyn/ip/index.html

Moving Here: www.movinghere.org.uk
Tracing Asian roots – some contributions have come from Liverpool.

Chinese and Eurasian

The first presence of Chinese people in Liverpool dates back to the early nineteenth century, with the main influx arriving at the end of the century. Liverpool was unique in that it had the highest concentration of Chinese residents in England. Immigrants from China came as sailors or stokers on the new steamships, often via the Blue Funnel line operated by Alfred Holt and Co. From the 1890s, those who settled lived near the docks, sometimes working in small businesses catering to the Chinese sailors working on Holt's lines or in the numerous laundries. During the First World War there were there were over 6,000 Chinese mariners in the city, but numbers escalated during the Second World War, when the population was estimated at 20,000. Some of these sailors married local women, resulting in a number of British-born Eurasian Chinese being born before the end of the war.

From February 1942 there was a four-month strike when Chinese mariners demanded equal pay and rights on a par with their white contemporaries. They were being paid about a third of the British seamen's rate, and they received no War Risk Bonus. In April the strike was settled when the Chinese were given a small increase in pay and the same War Risk Bonus as the British. However, many were now labelled as troublemakers by the ship owners and the British Government. Consequently, at the end of the war they were forbidden shore jobs, their pay was cut by two-thirds and they were offered only one-way voyages back to China. Hundreds of men were forced to leave their families. Some took their wives home to China, but most hoped one day to return to Liverpool. Most did not, and few saw their families again. They were to be denied again when ship owners blacklisted them and prevented their return to Britain. Over 300 women and approximately 1,000 Eurasian children were left destitute. Many of these Eurasian children continue to live in and around Liverpool's Chinatown to this day. A few Hong Kong seamen did settle in the city in the 1940s and 1950s, giving a small boost to the Eurasian population. But from the late 1950s onwards, complete families began to arrive from Hong Kong's rural New Territories. The Chinese population of Liverpool started to change dramatically and to form a truly separate entity.

Further research

Maria Lin Wong, *Chinese Liverpudlians: A history of the Chinese community in Liverpool*, Birkenhead, 1989.

Lee, Gregory B., *Chinas unlimited: Making the imaginaries of China and Chineseness*, London, 2003. An academic study of culture and representation, including testimony from the author's experience growing up in Liverpool.

On the net

Liverpool and its Chinese Seamen: www.halfandhalf.org.uk
The story of the Shanghai seamen by their children on a website created and authored by themselves.

Yvonne Foley's story: www.dimsum.co.uk/community/eurasians-the-first-british-born-chinese.html
The Eurasian daughter of an English mother and a Shanghai father.

Moving Here: www.movinghere.org.uk
Stories from Liverpool's Eurasians.

The Shanghai Sailors: www.bbc.co.uk/radio4/archivehour/pip/tqr27
Programme about the plight of the sailors that were forcibly repatriated, broadcast on Radio 4 on 13 September 2008.

Emigration and Passenger Lists

In the hundred years between 1830 and 1930 Liverpool's passenger liner companies carried up to nine million migrants, mostly to the United States, but also large numbers to Canada, Australia, New Zealand and South Africa. During this period of mass migration, the geographical location of Liverpool and its existing trade links put it at the centre of routes for migration and exodus of the Irish. Many ships sailed between Liverpool and Ireland, with some calling en route to and from the USA. The movement of people into and out of Liverpool is an important area of study for local and family history and integral to the study of the history of the city, but although there have been particular studies on specific areas of migration and the role shipping companies played, there is no general work on Liverpool migration as a whole.

Tracing migration is fraught with difficulties. The movements of ships and goods may have been recorded, but there was no requirement to record the details of people leaving the country – no *official* records were ever kept of passengers travelling by sea within the British Isles, including Ireland. Nor are there any lists of passengers departing the UK before 1890. The National Archives (TNA) holds Board of Trade passenger lists of vessels travelling to and from British ports, including Liverpool, from the 1890s to 1960. The only way to find out about emigrants before 1890 is to locate official lists of passengers arriving in the USA, where records were created due to immigration procedures.

Further research

The National Archives (TNA)

The TNA holds a lot of useful material on emigration in a number of different classes. These are outlined in a number of information leaflets available in Liverpool Record Office's miscellaneous information folders and on the TNA website. It is advisable that you read the information leaflets before visiting the National Archives or the Liverpool Record Office, although more and more is being made available online. The main classes of interest in the study of emigration and immigration are as follows:

- BT 26 Passenger Lists, Inwards, 1877–1888 and 1890–1960
- BT 27 Passenger Lists, Outward, 1890–1960

These classes contain the names of persons on ships leaving from or arriving at UK ports where the ship came from or was going to a final destination outside Europe and the Mediterranean. They include all passengers, not just those emigrating. There is no name index. To use them you need to know an approximate date of departure or arrival, the UK port and, if at all possible, the name of the ship. BT 32 Registers of Passenger Lists Received, 1906–60 acts as a finding aid for BT 26 and BT 27, if the name of the ship is known, but does not include passengers' names.

Transportation

Assize Records 1559–1972 (ASSI 1–80) can provide details on those transported. See TNA leaflets 'Transportation to America and the West Indies, 1615–1776' and 'Australian Convicts'.

Ancestors on Board: www.ancestorsonboard.com

This website, which is operated by Findmypast.com in conjunction with TNA, holds an extensive database of passenger lists with over 24 million records from ships that sailed to destinations all over the world. Much of the data is compiled from the TNA BT27 Outward Passenger Lists for long-distance voyages leaving the British Isles from 1960 right back to 1890. Searches can be made for records of individuals or groups of people leaving for destinations including Australia, Canada, India, New Zealand, South Africa and the USA, featuring ports such as Boston, Philadelphia and

New York. Passengers include not only immigrants and emigrants, but also businessmen, diplomats and tourists. Images of the passenger lists are available to download, view, save and print.

Liverpool Record Office

Liverpool Record Office does not hold any original passenger lists, although it does hold a great deal of contemporary and secondary material. This contains information about the reasons for migration, the ways and conditions in which it was undertaken, and the views of society on the subject. There are three transcripts of lists of emigrants, but these lists cover only limited dates and destinations:

French, Elizabeth, *List of Emigrants to America from Liverpool 1697–1707*, (Hq325.2 FRE). Taken from the Liverpool Town Books.

France, R. Sharpe, *List of Early Emigrants to America from Liverpool 1686*, (H325.2 QUA). Taken from the quarter sessions at Lancashire Record Office.

Hughes, Ian, *Passengers to Port Philip [Victoria, Australia] from Liverpool 1839–1851*, (Hq325.2 HUG). Taken from newspaper shipping columns.

(A copy of the passenger list for the *Titanic*'s final voyage is also available for consultation, although an extensive list including crew and biographies can be found here: www.encyclopedia-titanica.org/sitemap/).

Filby, P.W. and Meyer, M.K., *Passenger and Immigration Lists Index*, (Rq929.373). Guide to published arrival records 1538–1940 to USA and Canada. Gives name, age, place and year of arrival, source of information, list of accompanying passengers.

Liverpool Libraries has also taken out a subscription to ancestry.com for library users, which contains access to emigration records.

On microfilm in Liverpool Record Office

British Emigrant Guides and Pamphlets 1819–1870 (microfilms 7/10, 7/11). Copies of contemporary works that provided information to those planning to emigrate.

Archive collections – the case papers of the Liverpool Catholic Children's Emigration Society, 1880s–1920s (362 CAT).

Liverpool Maritime Museum Archive
www.liverpoolmuseums.org.uk/maritime/archive

The museum has an extensive archive and it is recommended that the helpful and detailed online information leaflets are consulted before visiting or beginning research. The museum also holds an excellent photographic collection. Early images of ships in service from 1839 to 1860 are held, plus engravings and paintings of early emigrant ships.

NUMBERED INFORMATION SHEETS AVAILABLE ON THEIR WEBSITE:

10 – Child Emigration

12 – Emigration to Australia, New Zealand and South Africa

13 – Emigration to USA and Canada

29 – Emigration Mormon Emigration

31 – Emigration Official Records of Passengers

64 – Emigration Liverpool and Emigration in the 19th and 20th Centuries

Moving Here www.movinghere.org.uk

This is a very useful place to start research. There are photos, recordings and documents, where ethnic history can be researched and personal experiences added. Moving Here explores, records and illustrates why people came to England over the last 200 years and what their experiences were and continue to be. It offers free access, for personal and educational use, to an online catalogue of versions of original material related to migration history from local, regional and national archives, libraries and museums. The aims of the site are to overcome barriers to the direct involvement of minority ethnic groups in recording and documenting their own history of migration and to ensure this history is passed on to the next generation through schools. There is also a comprehensive recommended links page. National Museums Liverpool contributed to materials held on the website.

On the net

www.ellisislandrecords.org
This contains information on some passenger lists and a collection of searchable US lists, an online database of 22 million passengers and crew members who passed through Ellis Island (New York), between 1892–1924.

www.immigrantships.net
The Immigrant Ships Transcribers Guild site contains transcriptions of passenger lists.

www.beavis.co.uk
An ongoing project to make databases of the passenger lists held at the National Archives.

www.genuki.org.uk/big/emdesc.html
'The Tide of Emigration to The United States and to The British Colonies' an interesting and detailed extract from an article printed in the *Illustrated London News* on Saturday 6 July 1850. It is a contemporary account of the procedure of emigration from the port of Liverpool to the New World and the Colonies. See also www.genuki.org.uk/big/Emigration.html – the Gen UKI Emigration Page – links to useful sites for genealogists.

www.old-merseytimes.co.uk/Emigrationmain.html
Old Mersey Times – newspaper articles from the nineteenth century on emigration. Includes a very lengthy and detailed letter from an emigrant to America in 1848.

Child Emigration

The idea of sending children to a new and better life in the 'New World', away from deprivation at home (and of course to alleviate the financial burden) was practised for decades, and supported by the Church, Poor Law Guardians and other authorities. Organisations were set up that encouraged or arranged emigration, especially of orphan or pauper children. Some suffered abuse and exploitation, and in the late twentieth century increasing efforts were made to expose the system as an assault on human rights. The Special Collections department of Liverpool University Library has assembled an important collection of books and other material on child migration in the twentieth century: see relevant links under www.liv.ac.uk/library.

Liverpool Record Office holds the case papers of the Liverpool Catholic Children's Emigration Society, 1880s–1920s (362 CAT), which arranged the emigration of children from Liverpool, mainly to Canada.

N.B. A list of the children whose files are deposited at Liverpool Record Office is available, but it should be noted that due to their confidential nature access to these records is only with the permission of the Nugent Care Society. (Contact: The Archivist, Nugent Care Society, 99 Edge Lane, Liverpool, L7 2PT).

Further research

Merseyside Maritime Museum

See the online information leaflet No.10 with detailed advice regarding the variety of institutions involved in Child Emigration.

British Isles Family History Society of Greater Ottowa:
www.bifhsgo.ca/home_children.htm

This society is running a project to collate as much information as possible on the 'Home Children' who emigrated to Canada from Britain. There is a searchable database of children sent to Canada from 1869–1930.

Further reading

Studies of nineteenth-century migration from Liverpool

Stammers, Michael K., *The passage makers: The history of the Black Ball Line of Australian Packets, 1852–1871*, Brighton, 1978. Much material about emigration voyages.

Hollett, Dave, *Fast passage to Australia: The history of the Black Ball, Eagle and White Star Lines of Australian packets*, London, 1986. Contains considerable information about emigrants' voyages to Australia in the second half of the nineteenth century.

––––– *Passage to the new world: Packet ships and Irish famine emigrants 1845–1851*, Abergavenny, 1995. North Atlantic emigration in the sailing ship era.

Busteed, M.A., 'A Liverpool shipping agent and Irish emigration in the 1850s', *THSLC*, Vol.129, 1979, pp145–62.

Scally, Robert, 'Liverpool ships and Irish emigrants in the age of sail', *Journal of Social History*, Vol.17, 1983–84, pp5–30. Critical assessment of the conditions faced by migrants in the mid-nineteenth century.

Gallman, J. Matthew, *Receiving Erin's children: Philadelphia, Liverpool, and the Irish famine migration, 1845–1855*, Chapel Hill, 2000. The most recent major work on the famine migration.

Macdonagh, Oliver, *A pattern of government growth 1800–60: The Passenger Acts and their enforcement*, London, 1961. A classic work of administrative history, with useful material on the problems facing officials who sought to regulate the emigrant business in Liverpool.

Useful addresses

Please note: to avoid a fruitless inquiry it is recommended that any information leaflets or internet sites provided by the institutions listed below are consulted before you make contact.

The National Archives: www.nationalarchives.gov.uk

Ruskin Avenue, Kew, Richmond, Surrey, TW9 4DU. Tel: 020 8392 5200 Email: enquiry@nationalarchives.gov.uk.

Maritime Archivist Library: www.liverpoolmuseums.org.uk/maritime

National Museums Liverpool, Merseyside, Maritime Museum, Albert Dock, Liverpool, L3 4AQ. Tel: 0151 478 4499.

National Archives of Canada: www.archives.ca

395 Wellington Street, Ottawa, Ontario, K1A 0N3. Online genealogy enquiry form.

National Archives and Records Administration, USA: www.nara.gov/genealogy

Attn: NWCTB, 700 Pennsylvania Avenue, NW, Washington DC, 20408-0001. Email: email@nara.gov

National Archives Australia: www.naa.gov.au

Twentieth-century immigration records. For convict records, or records of colonial or nineteenth-century migrants, contact State Government Archives, the National Library of Australia and State Libraries, although advice sheets are available on the above site.

New Zealand National Archives: www.archives.govt.nz

Head Office: 10 Mulgrave Street, Thorndon, Wellington, New Zealand PO Box 12-050 Wellington, New Zealand. Email: enquiries@archives.govt.

Chapter Ten

EDUCATION

In the years before the Education Act, the chief responsibility for providing education lay with the Church, and schools in Liverpool, especially before 1833, were either religious or private. Dame schools or common day schools (fee-paying) provided elementary education, as did charity schools, which were free. In 1833 grants were made available by the Government to build schools for the poor, but applications from large towns were given preference and there had to be support from one of the voluntary education bodies, like the National Society for the Education of the Poor. Educational provision in Liverpool remained extremely patchy and fragmented well into the nineteenth century. A survey in 1835 suggested that only half of Liverpool's 5–15 year-old boys and many fewer girls were likely to be in formal education, and there was no overall system or coordination. It was not until the 1870 Education Act that a national system of elementary education was established which required locally elected school boards to provide elementary schools where existing facilities were inadequate. In 1902 education was placed under local authority control. After the Education Act of 1944, schooling increasingly became the responsibility of local government, which had to provide universal secondary education. By the late 1960s, Liverpool's Education Department was one of the largest in the UK, responsible for 436 establishments, including 280 primary schools, ninety secondaries, forty-three special schools, four colleges of education, ten further education colleges and nine youth and community centres. In the later decades of the century, however, schools once again became a political football, with successive reforms changing the relationships between schools, local and central government.

During the first twenty years of the nineteenth century there were around sixteen schools in Liverpool catering for day pupils. In addition to three schools catering for special needs, there was the Liverpool Workhouse school, the Bluecoat Hospital and the School for the Blind. Two Corporation schools, one in the north of the town, the other in the south, were opened in 1827 for all denominations. The Liverpool Collegiate School (then the Liverpool Collegiate Institution) was founded in 1840 in

Shaw Street as a day school for boys. Here the sons of the middle class were educated in science, commerce and religion. The college was divided into the Upper, Middle (or Modern school) and the Lower (or Commercial) Schools. In 1884 the Upper School moved to Lodge Lane, while the Middle and Commercial schools remained at Shaw Street.

In 1907 the Middle and Commercial Schools merged as the Liverpool Collegiate School, which continued at Shaw Street until its closure in 1985. Meanwhile, the Upper School had split away as the new public school Liverpool College. The Liverpool Record Office holds the records of Liverpool Collegiate School (ref. 373 COL). These include admission registers for 1904–1979, but they do not hold the early records of the school.

The Royal School for the Blind, Liverpool, the first of its kind in the world, was founded by poet and political radical Edward Rushton and his musician friend James Christie in 1791. Both blind, the original purpose was to provide musical instruction to pupils to enable them to be able to support themselves on leaving the institution. A house was rented in Commutation Row until a purpose-built school was erected in London Road. After the redevelopment and extension of Lime Street Station, the school relocated to Hardman Street in 1851. In 1898 a wing for junior pupils was opened at Wavertree, while the Hardman Street School became a technical school for seniors. Hardman Street finally closed in 1957 and education was provided, from then to the present, at Wavertree. There is an excellent archive still held by the school at Wavertree, which has been extensively indexed by this author. The school have resisted all attempts to encourage the relocation of the archive to the local record office where it can be professionally cared for and access given to researchers. Although there are no dedicated registers of admissions in the archive, there is a complete run of minute books which note pupils being admitted or leaving as they occur at the time of the committee meetings. The best start point would be **Royden, M.W.** *A History of the Royal School for the Blind, Liverpool 1791–1991*, Countyvise, 1991.

By the first half of the nineteenth century there were around fifty charity schools in Liverpool. The most well known was the Bluecoat School, founded in 1708 (an excellent example of Queen Anne architecture which still stands today in School Lane, and is a Grade I listed building). It had been a day school until 1716 when it was converted to a hospital and food and lodgings were provided. Established by Bryan Blundell, it was begun in 1708 and completed ten years later. Blundell had been master and owner of a vessel employed in transporting paupers to the New World seeking a better life. So moved was he by their condition that he resolved to give up his life at sea and devote his time to the running of a new school. (Paradoxically, part of his maritime career was an involvement in the slave trade.) The building was opened in School Lane in 1718, but was not fully completed until 1725. In 1906 the school moved to Church Road, Wavertree. The records of the Bluecoat School and Hospital 1709–1962 are held at Liverpool Record Office (ref. 377 BLU). Their holdings comprise

Boys' Applications Books (1862–1922), Girls' Applications Books (1851–1928), Boys' Admission and Dismissal Registers (1743–1962) and Girls' Admission and Dismissal Registers (1889–1943).

The Liverpool Institute School began life as the Liverpool Mechanics' School of Arts in 1825. Early lessons were given in a disused German chapel building in Sir Thomas Street and were confined to evening classes. After ten years in Slater Street, where the Lower Day School was opened in 1832, it then changed its name to the Liverpool Institute School. The High School was opened in 1837 in Mount Street, while the Girls' High School opened in Blackburne House in 1844. In 1856 the boys' school became the Liverpool Institute, which was eventually transferred to the control of the Liverpool City Council in 1905. The records of the Liverpool Institute, 1825–1928, are held in the Liverpool Record Office (ref. 373 INS). These include some records relating to pupils. Blackburne House High School records (ref. 373 BLA) include admission registers (1872–1940), photographs and an evacuation roll of honour (1939–1940).

Workhouses

Local workhouses also had to comply with the 1870 legislation. Prior to this the Liverpool Select Vestry had opened Kirkdale Industrial School in 1845

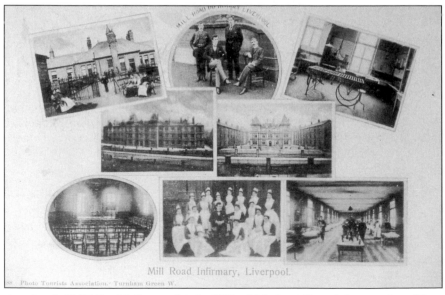

A postcard of Mill Road Infirmary dated c.1905, which shows the only known view of the Workhouse School (top left).

to educate the children of Liverpool Workhouse, although there had been educational provision for some time before this. A school at Mill Road for the West Derby Union Workhouse was also opened to comply with the Education Act of 1870. Kirkdale closed in 1904 and the records were deposited in Liverpool Record Office (ref: 353 SEL). They include admission and discharge registers (1862–1865), classification registers (1845–1897) and religious creed registers (1869–1904).

Colleges and Further Education

There is no single book that traces the history of local colleges and they remain difficult topics to research. The University of Liverpool was founded in 1881 as University College Liverpool. The college opened the following year in 1882 on Brownlow Hill with forty-five students. A brief history is on the university website (www.liv.ac.uk/about/history), while the two volumes documenting its development in much greater depth are listed below. Four colleges – Building, Technology, Commerce and Art – were merged to form Liverpool Polytechnic in 1970, which was later given its own charter as Liverpool John Moores University in 1992. Three Church-run colleges formed the teacher training college of Liverpool Hope University in 2005. Liverpool Community College was formed in 1992 by the amalgamation of four colleges. These in turn had been formed from eight colleges six years previously. Specialist reading on particular colleges has been included in the bibliography.

Charles Wootton College

Established in 1974 the college, which was named after a young black mariner murdered in the 1919 race riots, came into being due to the exclusion of Liverpool's black communities from educational opportunities. Its mission was to raise educational standards locally and confront racism. After the closure of the college some of its staff worked to create Toxteth Community College, founded in 2000.

Training ships

There were four educational ships moored in the Mersey during the latter part of the nineteenth century:

The Indefatigable

This was a charitable institution founded in 1864, set up to provide training for boys in poor circumstances to become merchant seamen. The TS

The Indefatigable.

Indefatigable merged with the Lancashire and National Sea Training Homes in 1945 and records relating to both institutions are held in the Maritime Archives and Library (see sheet No.9), with microfiche copies of the registers for 1865–1995 at the Liverpool Record Office (ref. 387 IND).

HMS Conway

The Merchant Shipping Acts of 1851 and 1854 required those making a career at sea to be trained and educated in academic as well as nautical subjects. The Mercantile Marine Service Associations (MMSA) began to set up institutions and Liverpool was one of the earliest to comply. HMS *Conway*, moored in the Sloyne, off Rock Ferry, was set up in 1859 specifically to train young boys for a life at sea. Their records are held at the Merseyside Maritime Museum. These include annual reports, wage books and registers of cadets. See www.hmsconway.org for history, illustrations and reunions.

The Clarence

This was a reform vessel for Roman Catholic boys who had served prison sentences. They were sent to the *Clarence* to be trained in seamanship in the hope that these skills would enable them to reform their behaviour. Liverpool Record Office holds the records of the Liverpool Catholic Reformatory Association (ref. 364 CAT). These include some records for the *Clarence*: committee minute books (1896–1902), rules and regulations and news-cuttings. Further enquiries should be made to the Nugent Care Society, 99 Edge Lane, Liverpool, L7 2PE.

See also www.mersey-gateway.org – use the search facility for a history of the two vessels of this name.

The Akbar

This was another reform vessel, this time for Protestant boys. The records of the *Akbar* are partly preserved at the Lancashire Record Office, Preston. The records of the Lancashire National Sea Training Homes, Heswall Nautical School and Redbank School, Newton-le-Willows are also held at the Lancashire Record Office. See www.ts2000.royalnavy.co.uk/akbar.htm – an excellent illustrated account of the *Akbar* by Joan Rimmer.
(It should be remembered that documents that contain sensitive personal information are closed for 100 years).

Further research

Admission registers and log books

The most common type of school records that survive are admission registers and log books. Admission registers usually give the name of the child, their date of birth or age, the names of parents/guardians and date of admission into the school. In some cases they contain more information, such as the parent's/guardian's address and occupation. Some discharge registers survive – these usually give the date of withdrawal and reason. Log books give an insight into daily life in the school, with occasional names recorded.

Council schools

A large collection of school records are held at Liverpool Record Office (ref. 352 EDU). Some school records have also been deposited with Church of England parish records (ref. 283). All are available for consultation.

Central government

The National Archives holds the records of the various education departments of central government. It is possible to find information on individual schools scattered among these records. Search the TNA online at www.nationalarchives.gov.uk. See **Anne Morton**, *Education and the State from 1833*, PRO Reader's Guide No.18, Public Record Office, 1997 (ref. H 379.41 MOR), for more detail.

Photographs and plans of schools

As education moves into the twenty-first century, many outdated school buildings are disappearing. Thankfully, there are plenty of local photographers who have been recording local buildings before they disappear for good. Schools feature frequently. For example, see Liverpool Street Gallery www.liverpoolstreetgallery.com (more listed in Appendix Three). For photographs of schools in Liverpool Record Office consult the Index to Photographs and Small Prints under the heading 'Schools and Colleges'. Pictures and views of schools in books can be located by consulting the Local Studies Catalogue. Liverpool Record Office also holds a collection of nineteenth-century plans submitted to central government's Education Department (and its predecessors) in order to obtain grants towards the costs of building a new school or towards improvement (ref. 370 SCH). Background information and about 350 images of Liverpool schools can be found at www.merseygateway .org/pastliverpool. Friends Reunited may be worth a visit as many class and whole school photographs have been added, as well as personal reminiscences and contacts.

Liverpool's Schools and Teachers www.liverpool-schools.co.uk

This is a developing website, which came online in 2006 and is swiftly expanding into a central site for schools in the area. It carries histories, local schools, sources, photographs and weblinks. Liverpool Family History Society holds an online list of Liverpool School Records at www.liverpool-genealogy.org.uk/Liverpool/schools.htm.

Further reading (see Appendix Six for extended bibliography)

Procter, Margaret (Ed.), *Education on Merseyside: A guide to the sources*, 1992. Large listing of archival and printed sources.
Linnell, G., *Education in Liverpool, 1515–1870: A bibliography*, 1958. Guide to older work on the topic.
Transactions of the Historic Society of Lancashire and Cheshire has published many articles on education in Liverpool; see the Index, *1848–2000*, published in 2002.
Midwinter, E. 'The early years of the Liverpool School Board' in *Old Liverpool*, pp.115–130, 1971.
Royden, M.W., *Pioneers and Perseverance: A History of the Royal School for the Blind, Liverpool, 1791–1991*, Countyvise, Birkenhead, 1991.
Heery, Pat, *The history of St Francis Xavier's College, Liverpool 1842–2001*, Liverpool, 2002. Detailed and well-illustrated history of Liverpool's first

Catholic day secondary school, including various phases of its relationship with the local education authorities.

Tiffin, Herbert, *A history of the Liverpool Institute Schools, 1825 to 1935*, Liverpool, 1935. Charts the histories of several Liverpool schools, including Blackburne House Girls' High School.

Gray, T. Cecil and Sheard, Sally, *A brief history of medical education in Liverpool*, Liverpool, 2001.

Power, Helen, *Tropical medicine in the twentieth century: A history of the Liverpool School of Tropical Medicine, 1898–1998*, London, 1999.

Shepherd, John A., *A history of the Liverpool Medical Institution*, Liverpool Medical Institution, 1979.

Ormerod, Henry, *The early history of the Liverpool Medical School from 1834 to 1877*, Liverpool, 1953.

Gemmell, Arthur A., *The Liverpool Medical School, 1834–1934: A brief record*, Liverpool, 1934.

Kelly, Thomas, *For advancement of learning: The University of Liverpool, 1881–1981*, Liverpool, 1981. The official history of the university.

Harrop, Sylvia A., *Decade of change: The University of Liverpool, 1981–1991*, Liverpool, 1994. Sequel to Kelly's official history.

—— *The Merchant Taylor's School for Girls, Crosby: One hundred years of achievement, 1888–1988*, Liverpool, 1988.

Evans, B. *The Training Ships of Liverpool*, Countyvise, 2002.

Chapter Eleven

THE EXPERIENCE OF WAR

Local Regiments in the First World War

At the outbreak of war the British professional army was badly equipped and tiny compared to the conscripted armies on the Continent. It comprised just 450,000 men – including only around 900 trained staff officers – and some 250,000 reservists. While there were confident predictions that the war would be 'over by Christmas', Lord Kitchener, the newly appointed Secretary of State for War, was unconvinced. He warned the Government that the war would be decided by the last million men that Britain could throw into battle. Conscription was still out of the question, so Kitchener decided to raise a new army of volunteers. On 6 August, Parliament sanctioned an increase in Army strength of 500,000 men; days later Kitchener issued his first call to arms. This was for 100,000 volunteers, aged between 19 and 30, at least 1.6m (5ft 3in) tall and with a chest size greater than 86cm (34 inches). General Henry Rawlinson initially suggested that men would be more willing to join up if they could serve with people they already knew – people they worked with, or friends and neighbours. This idea was to develop into the units that became known as Pals Battalions.

Lord Derby was the first to put the idea into practice and announced in late August that he would try to raise a battalion in Liverpool, comprised solely of local men. Within days, Liverpool had enlisted enough men to form four battalions.

King's Liverpool Regiment

The majority of local men were drafted in to the King's Liverpool Regiment (KLR). There were many divisions within the KLR, including the Liverpool Scottish, the Liverpool Rifles, the South Lancashire Regiment, the Cheshire Regiment, the Royal Army Medical Corps and the Pals Regiments of the 17th, 18th, 19th and 20th divisions. The Liverpool Pals Regiments were the first of all the Pals Battalions to be formed in this country and this initial success inspired other towns to follow Liverpool's lead and form their own Pals regiments.

The memorial to the Liverpool Pals on the Somme, France.

Researching Ancestors in the King's Regiment

Liverpool Museum resources: www.liverpoolmuseums.org.uk

A very useful starting point for researching ancestors in the King's. Also includes download on the Movements of Battalions 1914–1918, a full list of copies of Battalion War Diaries held and publications on the King's. The Museum website also hosts a database search facility for soldiers serving in the King's Regiment during the First World War. Searches can be made by surname, initial, first name, number, rank, or a combination of these.

King's Regiment Association, Liverpool:
www.liverpoolkingsregimentassociation.org.uk

Extensive help and advice for research into soldiers of the regiment.

Further reading

Maddocks, Graham, *Liverpool Pals: 17th, 18th, 19th, 20th (Service) Battalions, The King's (Liverpool Regiment)*, Pen & Sword Military. Over 4,000 local men volunteered in 1914 and were formed into the 17th, 18th, 19th and 20th (Service) Battalions of the King's (Liverpool Regiment); they were the first of all the Pals battalions to be raised and they were the last to be stood down. While many believe that the north of England's Pals battalions were wiped out on 1 July 1916, the Liverpool Pals took all their objectives on that day. From then on they fought all through the Battle of the Somme, the Battle of Arras and the muddy hell of Passchendaele in 1917, and the desperate defence against the German offensive of March 1918. This book does justice to the memory of the Liverpool Pals, in a well-researched history, with rolls and places of burial of soldiers who died.
Mileham, P. *Difficulties Be Damned – The King's Regiment 8th, 63rd, 96th, A History of the City Regiment of Manchester and Liverpool.* A well-illustrated, large-format history of the combined regiments, 1685–2000.
Wyrall, E., *The History of the King's Regiment Liverpool 1914–19, 3 vols, 1935, reprinted 2002.* Covers all battalions in quite good detail for specific attacks. Contains maps of the principal operations.
McCartney, Helen B., *Citizen Soldiers. The Liverpool Territorials in the First World War*, Cambridge University Press, 2005. This is an excellent new study on the character and experiences of the Territorials of Liverpool during the First World War. McCartney concentrates on the Liverpool Rifles and the Liverpool Scottish using a wealth of archival material such as letters, diaries, scrapbooks, and memoirs.

Liverpool Scottish: 10th (Scottish) Battalion, The King's (Liverpool Regiment)

The Liverpool Scottish was formed as an infantry battalion in 1900 in response to the crisis of the Boer War. It was raised from among the body of highly educated and professional young Scotsmen in the city as the 8th (Scottish) Volunteer Battalion, The King's (Liverpool Regiment). There was an annual subscription of 10 shillings and an entrance fee of £2. The Battalion was redesignated in 1908 on the establishment of the Territorial Force as the 10th (Scottish) Battalion, The King's (Liverpool Regiment). In 1914 the Liverpool Scottish was mobilised at the outset of war and moved to France on 1/2 November 1914, one of the first Territorial battalions to do so. They sailed to France aboard the SS *Maidan*. During the course of the war over 600 of its soldiers were commissioned (the museum has carefully researched these names to yield a fascinating picture of the social composition of the Liverpool Scottish). See www.liverpoolscottish.org.uk.

Further research

The Liverpool Scottish Regimental Museum c/o Major I.L. Riley TD FSA Scot, The Shambles, 51a Common Lane, Culcheth, Warrington, WA3 4EY,

Soldiers of the Liverpool Scottish enjoying their camp at Denbigh, 1913.

is usually open on Wednesdays 2pm to 7pm or by appointment. Telephone at least a couple of days in advance to avoid a wasted journey. The museum is presently re-establishing its display following relocation to new premises. Research and record facilities are available.

McGilchrist, Colonel A.M., *The Liverpool Scottish 1900–1919.* Detailed First World War history.

Giblin, H., with David Evans and Dennis Reeves *Bravest of Hearts, The Biography of a Battalion, The Liverpool Scottish in the Great War.* Information on hundreds of soldiers including medal citations, biographies and photographs.

Clayton, Ann, *Chavasse: Double VC.* An account of the life and service of Noel Chavasse, VC and Bar.

Cheshire Regiment

The Cheshire Regiment was created in 1881 by the linking of the 22nd (Cheshire) Regiment of Foot and the militia and rifle volunteers of Cheshire. On 24 August 1914 the 1st Battalion suffered 771 casualties at Audregnies in France during the closing stages of the Battle of Mons. The reconstituted battalion served throughout the First World War on the Western Front, winning 35 battle honours. Other battalions served at Gallipoli, in Palestine and on the Western Front. Total losses to the Regiment during 1914–18 were 8,420 dead.

Further research

The most authoritative account is: **Crookenden, A.,** *History of the Cheshire Regiment in the Great War,* Naval & Military Press, 2005. See also **McGreal, Stephen,** *The Cheshire Bantams: 15th, 16th and 17th Battalions of the Cheshire Regiment,* Pen & Sword Military, 2007. The Cheshire Bantams were raised in Birkenhead in 1914, but were unique as the average height of the volunteers was a mere five foot. Initially they had been prevented from enlisting, but seized the chance when the opportunity came. The battalions comprised working-class men from all over Britain: Welsh miners, London dockers, Lancashire mill workers and Merseyside labourers. As part of 35th (Bantam) Division, the Bantams fought on the Somme. Casualties were so severe that by early 1917 the Division effectively ceased to exist. Thereafter reinforcements came from the General Pool. They suffered heavily again at Houlthust Forest. The 35th Division played a key part in stopping the German 1918 offensive. Some 900 members of these battalions lost their lives. An excellent study by local military historian Stephen McGreal.

Barr, Ronald *The Cheshire Regiment,* Images of England, The History Press, 2003. Collected images of the Regiment throughout its history.

*Bombardier Charles
Royden, RFA (1881–1918).*

CHARLES ROYDEN
80135 Bombardier D Battery 18th Brigade Royal Field Artillery
born 1st April 1881 Liverpool-Killed in action 22nd March 1918
buried Ficheux France

McGreal, Stephen *Moreton & Districts Patriots 1914–1919,* Countyvise, 1999. A study of men recorded on the local war memorial, many of whom served in the Cheshire Regiment or the King's.

Cheshire Regiment Military Museum: www.chester.ac.uk

The museum, based at the Castle in Chester, remembers those who fought in the Cheshire Regiment, the Cheshire Yeomanry, the 3rd Carabiniers, the 5th Royal Iniskilling Dragoon Guards, Eaton Hall Officer Cadet School and several other small Cheshire units. Several regiments and periods are featured, and there is also a section of a re-created trench to walk through. There is a programme of temporary exhibitions highlighting topical events and showcasing items from the collection. There are heritage days and educational services directed at the curriculum. For researchers, the archives are open to the public on the first Saturday of each month. There is a charge

Short Service Attestation Record.

456

80135.

<u>To be used for recruits enlisting direct into the Reg...</u>
<u>Army Form B. 178ᴬ to be used for Special Reserve...</u>
<u>and Special Reservists enlisting into the Regular Army.</u>

MEDICAL HISTORY of

Surname *Royden*   Christian Name *Charles*

TABLE I.—GENERAL TABLE.

Birthplace .... Parish *Dingle Lpool* County *Lancs*		
Examined .... {on *20ᵗʰ* day of *Jan* 1915 {at *Seaforth*		
Declared Age	*33* years	*270* days.
Trade or Occupation	*Painter*	
Height	*5* feet,	*7½* inches.
Weight		*123* lbs.
Chest Measurement {Girth when fully Expanded		*3 4 2* inches.
{Range of Expansion		*2½* inches.
Physical Development		
Vaccination Marks {Arm .... {Number	Right	Left *3*
When Vaccinated	*Infant*	
Vision .... {R.E.—V= *6/6* {L.E.—V= *6/6*		

(a) Marks indicating congenital peculiarities or previous disease.... ....   (a)

(b) Slight defects but not sufficient to cause rejection ....   (b)

Approved by .... (Signature)

    (Rank)   Lieut R A M C

     Medical Officer.

Enlisted .... {at *Seaforth* {on day of 191		
Joined on Enlistment	Corps	Regtl. No.
Transferred to		
Became non-effective by		

    on   day of   1

(Signature)

Medical History Record.

to use the facilities and also to use the services of a researcher for those unable to visit. Application forms are available to download on the website. To make an appointment, please contact the museum on 01244 327617.

Researching First World War Ancestors

First World War Soldiers' service records

When new recruits signed on so began their documentary record. Enlistment papers record vital details such as age (not always reliable of course), address, birthplace and civilian occupation. Medical records were also begun, with initial information such as height, weight, eye colour and distinguishing features. Record of service was also included and could show where he was trained and where he served overseas. There may also be a disciplinary record included where relevant. These records can be found at the National Archives under WO 363 (microfilm). However, a large percentage were destroyed by enemy action during the Second World War and what has survived was damaged by fire and water. Consequently, they are known as the 'burnt records'. Ancestry.com are creating an online record and copies can also be obtained from the LDS Family History website. Pension records are also available at the National Archives (WO 364), their website and the Ancestry website.

Fowler, S., *Army Service Records of the First World War*, TNA, 1998.

Spencer, William, *Records of Service of the First World War*, TNA, 2000.

The National Archives has a monthly magazine: www.ancestorsmagazine.co.uk

LIVERPOOL'S FALLEN HEROES.

Official news has just
been received by Mrs.
Royden, of 160, Wellington-road, Dingle,
of the death of her
husband, Bomb Cpl.
Royden, killed in
France on March
22nd. His major and
comrades deeply regret his death. He
was an old scholar of
St. John the Baptist
School, and joined
the forces at the outbreak of the war.

Newspapers

These can be an excellent source of information for detail that cannot be gleaned elsewhere. There were regular reports of local men, and not just in brief lists of casualties. Articles frequently appear with information about the circumstances of death, injury, bravery, service, plus domestic details of family members, home addresses, places of employment or education. This may be the only existing source of a soldiers' photograph.

Both articles were discovered in the pages of the local press.

Refer to local record office holdings for the period. Records are on micro-film.

Army records

Knowledge of a soldier's battalion and his individual Army number will make research easier when trying to identify the correct serviceman. Medal records could be a way to discover this information.

Medal records

British and Commonwealth servicemen and women were awarded a wide variety of orders, medals and decorations for their service in the First World War. These included medals for gallantry, distinguished service and those bestowed by Allied governments. General service during the First

The one we loved so well.   Jessie.
ROYDEN—In loving memory of my dear husband.
Bombardier. Charles Royden, R.F.A., who was
killed in action March 22, 1918, aged 36 years.
(Never forgotten by his sorrowing wife and six
children. 160, Wellington-road; also his mother,
brother Will, and brother-in-law Alan (somewhere
in France); and deeply mourned by all his sisters
and brother-in-law. Respected by all who knew him.)
Rest. my dear husband. but ch. how I'll miss you.
Loving you dearly your memory I'll keep;
Never while life lasts shall I forget you.
Sacred's the spot where you lie asleep.
ROYDEN—March 22, killed in action, aged 36 years.
Bombardier Charles Royden 'our Charlie), R.F.A.
dearly loved youngest brother of Margaret Taylor
and brother-in-law of late Corpl. Jo. Taylor.
396, Mill-street.   (Dearly loved and sadly missed
by his only sister, Maggie, and family.)
Proudly he did his duty,
Nobly he fought and fell;
Our only grief we could not be there
To bid him a last farewell.
Rest peaceful. dear brother, in a hero's grave.
Your life for your country you nobly gave.
Not farewell, dear brother only good-night.
DIED OF WOUNDS.

The only record I have of this generation of my family's voices from the past. We had always called him Charles, but of course to his sister he was 'our Charlie'.

World War was recognised by the issue of the 1914 Star (or the 1914–15 Star), the British War Medal 1914–1920 and the Victory Medal 1914–1919. This trio of awards became popularly known as 'Pip, Squeak and Wilfred' after characters in a *Daily Mail* cartoon of the period.

See the Medal Card Index at www.nationalarchives.gov.uk/documentsonline/medals.asp.

Medal Index Cards (MIC) were compiled by the War Office to keep track of who and what was to be awarded. These records have now gone online and give basic details of the recipient and crucially their regiment and Army number. There are a number of websites that give further information as to what the abbreviations mean (see for example 'The Long, Long Trail' www.1914-1918.net). Colour scans of the original cards can be accessed via Ancestry (pay site) (www.ancestry.co.uk/medals). Medal Rolls (section WO 329) are held at the National Archives at Kew, and these may contain additional detail about overseas service and battalion movements. Brief details about recipients of commendation medals may have been 'gazzetted' and be available online at www.london-gazette.co.uk. The publication *Soldiers Died in the Great War 1914–19 Part 13 The King's (Liverpool Regiment)*, HMSO, 1920, lists men by battalion, including name, place of birth, enlistment and residence, number and rank with nature, date and theatre of death. There is an orders and medal research site at www.omrs.org.uk.

The Next of Kin Memorial Plaque

In 1916 a Government Committee was set up by Secretary of State for War, David Lloyd George, to consider what form of memorial should be made available to the next of kin of those who died 'on active service'. On 7 November 1916, *The Times* informed its readers that the cost of the memorial was to be borne by the State and that the precise form it was to take was a matter for much longer consideration, though the initially accepted idea was that it should be ' . . . a small metal plate recording the man's name and services.' It was not until August 1917, in the midst of the Third Battle of Ypres, that the memorial 'plate' project resurfaced in the General Committee's decision that the commemoration should now take the form of a bronze plaque. The announcement was reported in *The Times* for Monday 13 August 1917 and the public competition for appropriate designs was described in extravagant detail. The first prize of £250, for two model designs, was awarded to 'Pyramus' – Edward Carter Preston of the Sandon Studios Society, Liverpool.

Production of the plaques began in December 1918 and around 1,150,000 were made. The plaques issued commemorated those men and women who died between 4 August 1914 and 10 January 1920 who had been killed on active service.

Memorial Scrolls were also sent to the next of kin and were sent out in seven and a quarter inch long cardboard tubes. The plaques themselves were dispatched under separate cover in stiff card wrapping, enclosed in white envelopes bearing the Royal Arms. Both memorials were accompanied by a letter from King George V, which bore his facsimile signature and read: 'I join with my grateful people in sending you this memorial of a brave life given for others in the Great War. George R.I.' The full story of the Next of Kin Plaque and how it came to be issued is told here: www.iwm.org.uk/collections/exhibits/plaque01.htm.

War Diaries

War Diaries had to be kept by each unit serving abroad, but considering the day-to-day experience of officers they vary considerably. Nevertheless, they are an excellent resource for researchers and can help track down exactly where soldiers were located. However, individual names are infrequently recorded and when they are they usually refer to officers and those who have been cited for bravery or court martial. Again, the National Archives should be your first port of call (WO 95), and they are starting to appear online (www.nationalarchives.gov.uk/documentsonline/war-diaries.asp).

Rolls and Memorials

Memorials and Rolls of Honour appeared in all manner of places after the First World War. In the case of my great-grandfather Charles Royden, his name appeared on his old school memorial, the Liverpool Town Hall Roll of Honour, within the small three-volume memorial books at Liverpool Cathedral, and also in the grander sealed Memorial Book in the Cathedral, of which a page is turned each day.

The are numerous researchers at work who are concentrating on particular village memorials, trying to discover more about the men and women recorded there. Publications are rare, however, but in making contact through the local WFA or on the excellent Long, Long, Trail forum on the internet, the depth of some of this research will come to light. In Halewood, David Irving has carried out excellent research over the last 15 years or so and hopefully this will eventually appear in print, but in the meantime he has made very useful contributions to the Halewood Local History website (www.halewood.org.uk). WFA member and military author Stephen McGreal has produced a good example of what can be done in his *Moreton & Districts Patriots 1914–1919*, Countyvise, Birkenhead, 1999. Vivid accounts of the experiences of local soldiers feature here, plus photos of the men. In Ellesmere Port, the Whitby High School has produced its own website reflecting the ongoing research by Year 9 pupils into the men on the local war memorial. They have also successfully campaigned for a memorial plaque to be erected in the town to remind passers-by that there are also twenty-five Commonwealth War Graves in the graveyard of the former parish church Christchurch. Research continues by some of the pupils, who then go on a battlefields visit where they lead the service at the Menin Gate and also try to find the grave of the serviceman they have been researching. See www.eportwarmemorial.org.uk.

Another excellent website and the best place to start your war memorial research is Carl's Cam: www.carlscam.com. Carl Rogerson has produced a superb site containing a gazetteer of Cheshire memorials, with transcriptions of names, photographs and much more for the family historian.

The Channel 4 website has the 'Lost Generation' website where you can hunt for a name on its evolving list of war memorials.

Navy Records

The service records of 40,000 members of the Royal Naval Volunteer Reserve have now been made available for download on the National Archives website. These records cover ratings – seamen who did not hold a commission – who joined between 1903 and 1919 and officers who signed up between 1914 and 1922. The information provides names, division, date of birth, former occupation, ships and units served in, and periods of service. There are even such personal details as height, hair colour, eye colour and sometimes handwritten remarks about character and ability.

The RNVR was formed in June 1903 when volunteers signed up from all walks of life when there was an increasing threat of war. Seamen agreed to serve either ashore or afloat as required, and were assigned to a division. On the outbreak of war in 1914 they were expected to report to their divisional headquarters. Some went to sea, but most were combined with the Royal Fleet Reserve and the Royal Naval Reserve and were formed into the Royal Naval Division (RND) to fight in the trenches on the Western Front. The RNVR continued until 1958 when it was amalgamated with the Royal Naval Reserve. Today this is still the naval reserve for volunteers.

Medal Records

As with Army records, the best place to start is with the medal rolls at the National Archives. They are indexed in section ADM 171. Unfortunately, at the time of writing they are still not online and a visit to Kew will be necessary.

Officers' Records

Available on microfilm at the TNA under ADM 196, not yet online. The archive is split into two: commissioned and executive officers (from midshipmen to admirals) and warrant officers (eg gunners, cooks, carpenters). Limited information on basic service details is available on the shelves of the TNA in *Navy Lists*. This information can then be used to consult more confidential records under ADM 177. Pension records are available under ADM 22/23.

Ratings Records

Listed alphabetically at the TNA under ADM 188. Now available online.

Operational Records

Once the record and vessel of the rating is known it may be possible to track down where they served at the TNA – see ADM 1, ADM 116 and ADM 137. The logbooks of ships are under ADM 53, although individuals are rarely mentioned by name. Photographs, diaries and oral histories can also be found at the Royal Naval Museum, Portsmouth (www.royalnaval-museum.org) and the Maritime Museum (www.nmm.ac.uk).

Other Naval Services

The various branches of the Navy are also held at the TNA, such as the Royal Marines, the Royal Naval Nursing Service and the Royal Naval Air Service. See listings online.

RFC/RAF records

The Royal Flying Corps and the Royal Naval Air Service began the war under the separate commands of the Army and the Navy, but by April 1918 they had merged to form the Royal Air Force. Service records are not yet online and will entail a visit to TNA. Records are likely to be under AIR 79, although this will depend on whether time was spent in the Army or Navy first. Officers are found in AIR 76.

Medal Records

There are more than 26,000 medal cards for the RFC and 27,000 for the RAF, but it should be noted that many men had an original service life in the infantry and were seconded to the RFC. Sources for medals are as those for the Army. For those making personal visits to TNA, refer to catalogue AIR 1.

War Diaries

The RFC kept regular diaries of movements and action in the same manner as the Army. The squadrons were of a smaller size than army battalions, so there is a greater change of individuals being named. In late 1915 Squadron Record Books were introduced, while wings and brigades continued with the diaries. They can all be consulted at TNA under reference AIR 1.

Other Sources

Other useful records include Unit Histories and Combat Reports, also under AIR 1. Combat Reports provide invaluable and often thrilling descriptions of engagements with German fighter pilots.

Further research

Western Front Association: ww1author.tripod.com/merseysidewfa

The Western Front Association was formed with the aim of furthering interest in the period 1914–1918. The object of the association is to educate the public in the history of the First World War, with particular reference to the Western Front. The Merseyside Branch meets on the first Thursday of each month at the Territorial Army Centre, Harrowby Road [entrance off Whitford Street] Birkenhead, Wirral, Merseyside, CH42 7HT. For security reasons they request that members and visitors arrive between 7.15 and 7.55pm. Membership benefits include occasional branch outings (past trips have included the Imperial War Museum and the National Archives at Kew) and local tours with plenty of related discussions. A week-long minibus tour of the battlefields of France and Belguim has also taken place. A Christmas Social with complimentary food and drinks closes the year. The group regularly has a stall at local history fairs, where on-the-spot research into soldiers killed in the First World War and battalion movements can be offered and general queries answered. Contact Peter Threlfall, 13 Southhill Road, Oxton, Wirral, Merseyside, CH43 5RL. Tel: 0151 653 5311.

Liverpool Town Hall, Hall of Remembrance

The Hall of Remembrance was opened by the Duke of Windsor, then Prince of Wales, in 1921 and contains the City's Roll of Honour. The Roll of Honour carries the names of over 13,000 military men from Liverpool who died during the First World War. This list of war dead began to be compiled during the war, when names of the fallen were posted in a window overlooking Exchange Flags and relatives queued to add names. Because of this, the list is far from complete, but a number of names have been added since 1921, on additional panels. The list is online at www.liverpool.gov.uk/hallofremembrance. Among those whose names are recorded are a number of holders of the Victoria Cross, most famously Captain Noel Chavasse, one of the very few to have earned the distinction twice. The others include Lieut. E.F. Baxter, Captain E.F. Bell, Sergeant

David Bell and Sergeant Thomas Neely. Their lives are recounted, with others, in the two volumes of *Liverpool Heroes*. Others listed include Lord Kitchener of Khartoum, an honorary Freeman of the City, and many who served in the armed forces of Australia, Canada, New Zealand and South Africa and other countries, but had local connections. For more on Captain Noel Godfrey Chavasse, VC and Bar, MC, RAMC, (1884–1917) see www.chavasse.u-net.com/chavasse.html.

Other useful websites

The Long Long Trail: www.1914-1918.net (excellent starting point)
The British Army: www.army.mod.uk
Museums Ogilby Trust: www.armymuseums.org.uk (booklists, museums, ancestral advice)
International Committee of the Red Cross: www.icrc.org – see www.icrc.org/eng/contact-archives for requesting information on a Prisoner of War.
Imperial War Museum: www.iwm.org.uk – no service records but has a reference library.
National Army Museum: www.national-army-museum.ac.uk – holds no records but has an extensive library including Army Lists and *London Gazettes*.
Old Oppos: www.oldoppos.co.uk. Old Comrades site for all Forces since Second World War.

Battlefield visits

A visit to the battlefields of the Western Front is highly recommended. Several specialised organisations offer organised trips, such as Poppy Travel www.poppytravel.org.uk (through the British Legion) and others which can be found through a simple internet search or in the back pages of family history magazines. Local branches of societies and the WFA also organise trips for members.

Commonwealth War Graves Commission: www.cwgc.org

For grave location and information on unit and date of death, contact: The Commonwealth War Graves Commission, 2 Marlow Road, Maidenhead, Berkshire, SL6 7DX. Tel. 01628 34221, ask for Register enquiries. A searchable database is available on the Commission's website.

Second World War

Liverpool endured a harrowing time as a major target for the enemy, suffering great devastation both in communities and infrastructure. In the

After years of research I was finally able to visit the grave of my great-grandfather, Charles Royden, near Arras in France, pictured here with my two sons, Lewis and Liam.

first week of May 1941 alone, Liverpool suffered the heaviest bombing of the war in Britain outside London. The docks were the main target, but 3,000 people were killed and 11,000 homes completely destroyed. As the most important port outside London, Liverpool became a crucial route for military equipment and supplies to the country, and consequently the 'Western Approaches Command' headquarters, based in Plymouth, was transferred to Liverpool in February 1941. The purpose of the Command was to co-ordinate intelligence information from the Admiralty and the Air Ministry, and to protect supply ships on their approach to the Mersey. This move was instigated by Winston Churchill, and an underground complex was constructed, known locally as the 'Citadel' or 'Fortress'. Located underneath Derby House in Exchange Flags (to the rear of the Town Hall), it was designed to be bomb-proof and gas-proof, with a 7ft thick roof and 3ft walls, and 100 rooms covering an area of 50,000 square feet. The decoding room was home to the Enigma decoding machine, which had been recovered from a sinking U-Boat. Today the headquarters have been reopened to the public as the Liverpool War Museum (see On the net, p.180). In the docks were sited important munitions factories, while naval U-Boat hunters were stationed at Bootle. As the German campaign to immobilise London's docks became more intense and the Mersey became more important to the British war effort, it was inevitable that Merseyside would soon become a target for the Luftwaffe. Evacuation would be essential.

Evacuation

When war broke out in September 1939, 95,000 people were evacuated to escape the threat of bombing. 57,000 of these were school children, and 31,000 were mothers and children under five years of age. Yet as the 'Phoney War' convinced many that the threat was minimal, around 40 percent of the children were returned home by January 1940. Lancashire, Cheshire, Shropshire and Herefordshire received a total of 51,000 Liverpool evacuees, while another 44,000 were sent to live in Wales. A second programme of evacuation began following the 'Christmas raids' of 1940, when 1,399 children were rushed out of Liverpool between 20–22 December. Yet more children were evacuated during the 'May Blitz' of 1941.

During the summer of 1941, the threat of bombing seemed to lessen, and increasing numbers of children began to return home. More came back to the city in late 1944. But in many cases the upheaval changed the destiny of families forever. Some of the evacuated children did not stay in Merseyside when they were returned. There were cases of some children returning with their foster parents to live together in Liverpool. In other instances family bonds had been irreparably broken, or parents felt their child would have better prospects if they grew up with their foster parents in their place of evacuation. Other foster parents were known to have funded their evacuees' education even after they had returned to their Merseyside homes.

Paradoxically, by January 1942, Liverpool had taken in more evacuees from other parts of the country than it had children staying elsewhere.

Further research

It may be possible to find precise dates of an individual's evacuation and return by consulting admission registers and log books of the school the child attended. If a child was evacuated during the Second World War it may be recorded in the withdrawal register. Details of discharge can sometimes be found in the admission register.

Boyce, Joan, *Pillowslips and gasmasks: Liverpool's Wartime Evacuation*, Liver Press, 1989. According to Joan, 'The main reasons that prompted me to write this account were, first I was an evacuee myself, and secondly it troubled me deeply that despite the fact that it was the worst hit city outside of London, suffering many losses, Liverpool's wartime experiences were rarely ever mentioned in any books or magazines. I wanted in a small way to redress the balance'.

Wallis, Jill, *A Welcome in the Hillsides? The Merseyside and North Wales Experience of Evacuation 1939–1945,* 2000. This is a thoroughly researched account and contains a great deal of original material.

In the archive of the School for the Blind was a diary of the evacuation to Rhyl 1939–41, kept by the staff and senior girls in a small black exercise book. Numerous extracts have been reprinted in **Royden, Michael W.,** *Pioneers and Perseverance: A History of the Royal School for the Blind, Liverpool, 1791–1991,* Countyvise, 1991, pp.190–202.

Personal recollections of evacuation can be found on the BBC Peoples' War website (more in On the net, p.180).

Breck Road sidings

Not all children left Liverpool, as this story reveals. During the May Blitz a munitions train arrived in Liverpool late in the evening of 3 May – too late to be accepted at the docks. It was then shunted back to the nearest available sidings, which was a compromise between being safely away from the docks, but near enough to get on with the job of unloading in the morning. The Breck Road sidings, about three miles away, were deemed most suitable. What happened next was not a directed or precise attack on the sidings, but was generally accepted as being a stray plane offloading bombs as it flew away from the targeted dock area. It was an unlucky hit in a relatively quiet residential area, around midnight. The bomb landed on the track next to the munitions trucks, but soon set them alight, and then the trucks began to explode one by one. Meanwhile adjacent houses (Worcester Drive, Pennsylvania Road) were suffering fire damage and they were evacuated, as well as their Anderson shelters. Several emergency teams of signalmen, ARPs and firemen tried to manhandle the trucks away, but had to call for the help of a locomotive. The men who went off for the engine fetched a shunter from Edge Hill, two miles to the south on that line. On the way they met a goods train and took that instead. However, as they approached they came across a crater in the line and realised they could not get near the sidings. One of the men fell in the crater and had to be rescued. They had to settle for saving other trucks, mostly containing Spam and corned beef. The situation had not improved by dawn and the fires raged throughout the next day (4 May). The munitions trucks continued to explode at regular intervals during the day, leaving a 250-yard trench gouged out along the main line. The nearby houses were uninhabitable for some time afterward. Three men received the BEM and one the George Medal – amazingly, no one was killed.

My mother, Hazel Royden (née Wiggins), lived nearby in Daneville Road:

It was an horrific night, there were blasts going off everywhere – we were in the Anderson shelter throughout the continuous bombing. In the morning, we emerged to find our house damaged – the windows were blown in, but then my father said 'Look at this – it's not even part of a bomb, its like iron plate off a train'. He had found a big piece of iron or steel – it had sliced straight through our front door and taken it clean off the hinges – it was the only real damage our house sustained in the war. It had been blown over from the sidings. We were always up between 5–6am to collect shrapnel out of gutters to take in to school for recycling. I remember there were loads more that morning. That same day my father and I walked to the siding – we didn't know what had happened – there were rumours abounding, so we went to see. It felt a long way for my little legs, but in reality it was a short distance. Many land mines had dropped – there were huge holes cordoned off in the roads. I can remember hoping the Clubmoor Picture House where we went to hadn't been bombed, but luckily it was unscathed. As we approached the siding we were not allowed near, there were big white tapes and we were stopped by the ARPs from going any further. Later there was a great fuss over why the train was there in the first place – I remember heated discussions

Hazel Royden being interviewed for the BBC Radio 4 programme Making History *by producer Nick Patrick.*

between the adults. But then, the bombs could have hit the Royal Ordnance Factory at Stopgate Lane near Aintree – only a mile away. They did hit a munitions ship (*Malakand*) in the docks that night, which was the greatest explosion ever heard in the area. Captain Kinley, whose ship it was, became a close friend of our family and we often visited him in his retirement in Port Erin on the Isle of Man. (This incident and interview was first aired as a featured story on the BBC Radio 4 programme *Making History* in 2001.)

That is a story very personal to my own family history, but the opportunities to record similar incidents are still with us and should not be lost. As the experience of the Second World War is still a vivid memory to many of those who lived through it, great strides have been taken to capture those recollections. Liverpool Libraries have an extensive archive and the BBC Peoples' War project also features dozens of local contributions. (See On the net, p.180).

The story of the heroics surrounding the *Malakand* incident and many others are told in *Port in a Storm* by John Hughes – a recommended starting point for any research on this topic.

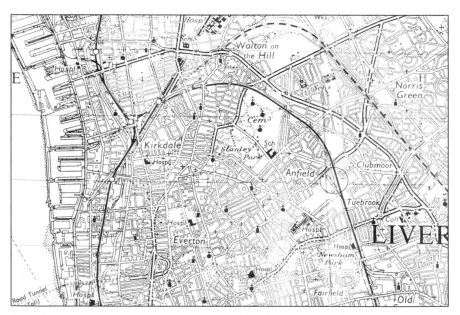

Map of Liverpool showing rail access to the north docks and the Breck Road sidings (circled), where the munitions train was backed up.

The Blitz

The first German bombs landed on Merseyside on 9 August 1940 at Prenton, Birkenhead. In the following sixteen months, German bombs killed 2,716 people in Liverpool, 442 people in Birkenhead, 409 people in Bootle and 332 people in Wallasey. The worst periods of bombing were the 'Christmas Raids' of December 1940, and the 'May Blitz' of 1941. The final bombs to be dropped on Merseyside during the war landed on 10 January 1942. Coverage of these events is very good and the following are recommended:

Whittington-Egan, Richard, *The Great Liverpool Blitz*, The Gallery Press, 1987.

Hughes, John, *Port in a Storm – The air attacks on Liverpool and its shipping in the Second World War*, National Museums and Galleries on Merseyside, 1993.

Whitworth, Rodney, *Merseyside at War – A day-to-day diary of the 1940–41 Bombing*, Scouse Press, 1988.

Wade, Beryl, *Storm over the Mersey*, 1990.

Liverpool Daily Post & Echo, *Bombers Over Merseyside*, 1943. A facsimile edition of this work was issued as:

Spiegl, Fritz (Ed.), *Bombers Over Merseyside: The Authoritative Record of the Blitz, 1940–1941*, Scouse Press, 1984.

Merseyside May Blitz: news-cuttings, Liverpool Record Office.

The May Blitz, 1941, S.E.A.R.C.H. Pack No.8, Liverpool Record Office.

Johnson, Arthur, *Merseyside's secret Blitz diary: A remarkable personal account of Liverpool at war*, Liverpool, 2005. An intriguing original diary interspersed with photographs and commentary.

Royden, Michael W., *A History of Mill Road Hospital*, Liverpool, 1993. Chapter 6 'The May Blitz' contains a harrowing account of the direct hit on the hospital and maternity wards with numerous personal recollections.

Ayers, Pat, *Liverpool Docklands*, Liver Press, 1999.

Collard, Ian, *Mersey Ports: Liverpool and Birkenhead*, Tempus Publishing, 2001.

Dunn, C.L. (Ed.), 'The Emergency Medical Services Vol.II' from the series *A History of the Second World War – United Kingdom Medical Series*, 1953. Official records of the roles played by the emergency services, specific details regarding incidents, damage and casualties.

Kemp, Paul, *Liverpool and the Battle of the Atlantic 1939–1945*, 1993. A collection of over 100 photographs.

Horton, Max, *Liverpool and the Western Approaches*, 1954.

Mersey Docks and Harbour Board, *Port at War: The Story of the Port of Liverpool, its ordeals and achievements during the World War 1939–1945*, 1946.

Marsh, B.J. & Almond, S., *The Home Port: Bootle, the Blitz and the Battle of the Atlantic*, 1993.

Battle of the Atlantic: An anthology of personal memories from those involved with the Battle of the Atlantic, Birkenhead, 1993.

The battle of the Atlantic: The official account of the fight against the U-Boats 1939–1945, London, 1946; also *British coaster, 1939–1945: The official story*, London, 1947. Accounts compiled by government departments in the aftermath of the war; now revealing historical texts in their own right.

Laskier, Frank, *My name is Frank: A merchant seaman talks*, 1941. Transcripts of radio broadcasts aimed at seamen.

Wemyss, David, *Walker's Groups in the Western Approaches*, Liverpool, 1949. An immediate post-war account of one of the best-known aspects of Liverpool's war effort.

Van der Vat, Dan, *The Atlantic campaign: The great struggle at sea, 1939–1945*, London, 1988. Good general text.

Lane, Tony *The merchant seamen's war*, Manchester, 1990. A major study, with an extensive bibliography for further reading.

Liverpool Record Office, *Liverpool at war, 1939–45*, 2002.

The Maritime Archives and Library, Merseyside Maritime Museum, has an information sheet on the Battle of the Atlantic, with a useful reading list. Many individual histories of Liverpool shipping companies contain chapters about the companies' experiences in wartime; search the catalogue for particular firms.

Perrett, Bryan, *Liverpool: A City at War*, 1990.

Liverpool women at war: An anthology of personal memories, Birkenhead, 1991. First-hand testimony and some rare photographs.

Accounts of the activities of the battalions during the Second World War are found in **J.J. Burke-Gaffney**, *The Story of the King's Regiment (Liverpool) 1914–45*, 1954.

On the net

The People's War: www.bbc.co.uk/ww2peopleswar/categories/c1141/
A superb collection of web links of Merseyside wartime memories on the BBC website. The local web listings occupy fifteen pages alone.

Port Cities: www.mersey-gateway.org
Numerous pages dedicated to the Merseyside experience of war, such as defending the port, the Blitz, morale, and so on.

World War Two Memories: www.liverpool.gov.uk (select leisure & culture, then archive collection, then local history & heritage, enter archive ref. 940 PWP into search engine – full listings will result).
Memories of the Second World War collected by Liverpool Libraries in 2004, consisting of transcripts of recordings and DVD footage titled 'Liverpool 1941: the effects of German bombing raids on Liverpool and the docks'. Also included are video recordings of interviews undertaken in the library.

Liverpool Blitz: www.liverpoolmuseums.org.uk/nof/blitz/index.html
This website reveals the Second World War memories of the people of Liverpool. The stories are set over 24 hours during the May Blitz of 1941. While the particular day presented is fictional, all of the events happened over the course of the bombing campaign, many during those seven horrific days in May.

The Spirit of the Blitz: Merseyside Maritime Museum
Record of a past exhibition, plus useful links: www.liverpoolmuseums .org.uk/maritime/exhibitions/blitz/home.asp

Liverpool War Museum: www.liverpoolwarmuseum.co.uk
See Appendix Five for more details regarding visiting the museum.

Appendices

RESEARCH GUIDE

Appendix One

RESEARCH ADVICE

Useful books on family history

It may be convenient to read up on tracing family and local history before leaving the comfort of your armchair. There are several general books available, some of which may be in your local library. The first guide I purchased was *Discovering Your Family History* by Don Steel who, well before *Who Do You Think You Are?*, was the pioneer behind the 1979 BBC TV series *Family History*, narrated by Gordon Honeycombe and based on Gordon's own researches. The book may be out of print and a little dated now, but the basics haven't changed and I still refer to it. *Tracing Your Family Tree: The Comprehensive Guide to Discovering Your Family History* by Jean A. Cole and Michael Armstrong is highly recommended, as is *Explore Your Family's Past: Trace Your Roots and Create a Family Tree*, produced by various authors for the *Reader's Digest*.

Oral history

The family should be the first port of call if at all possible. Are there are older members of your family, or local residents who have personal memories of the subject of your researches? A great deal of time could be saved here. They could provide information such as dates, addresses, occupations and religious denomination, and may also have useful documents. These could include birth, marriage or death certificates, entries in family bibles, copies of wills and old photographs. Take along a camera, a notebook and a small recorder if your interviewee does not mind. Always prepare before your visit and try to think of relevant questions. However, remember that personal recollections often need to be corroborated or verified by other evidence. Many oral studies have been carried out in recent years, on topics such as the history of particular streets (*Athol Street Oral History Project* at the University of Liverpool Dept of History) to football memories (*Three Sides of the Mersey: Oral History of Everton, Liverpool and Tranmere Rovers* by Rogan Taylor). The *BBC Voices* pages at www.bbc.co.uk/liverpool/voices provide many links to web-based memories on subjects such as community history and memories of the Blitz.

Site visits

Your family history is not just about tracing the names of each generation. Try to discover more about the community in which they lived to give yourself an insight into what their lives were like: their housing conditions, the workplace, church and education, how they spent their leisure time. A site visit is often essential. New questions will arise too. Again, be prepared. Take recording equipment, including cameras and notebooks. Take along early photographs and maps if you can, to help you understand the development of the site. 'Then and now' type photographs are always useful and interesting to study.

Join a society

There are family and local history societies throughout the area. Some local history societies are linked to university History or Archaeology departments and have an academic emphasis, but this does not preclude beginners from joining. There are also many efficiently organised societies run by enthusiastic locals. New members, including beginners, are always welcomed. There are usually monthly meetings, which include local news bulletins and a lecture by a visiting speaker. Many societies undertake research projects and journals, and sometimes publications on aspects of the history of the area.

Useful magazines

There are currently several family history monthly magazines available, which gives some idea of their popularity in such a competitive market. The BBC publishes *Who Do You Think You Are?* throughout the year in conjunction with the television programme. *Ancestors* magazine is produced by the National Archives, and *Your Family Tree*, *Family History Monthly* and *Practical Family History* all offer practical advice, written by experts, on all areas of family history research. Issues carry an array of old documents, answer readers' questions, and put family historians in touch with one another. All are worthy publications and give excellent help and advice.

Enrol on a course

There are regular courses available across Liverpool and Wirral, which are held in a variety of local venues such as libraries and community centres. See the local listings circulated by the education authority and relevant groups such as family history societies. Again, beginners are always made very welcome. Details of courses may also be found on the government's LearnDirect website. For those who can afford the time and money and are prepared to travel, there are regular residential courses available for beginners and experts alike. See www.ancestor-search.info.

Family trees already researched – has it been done before?

This may take some of the fun away, but it is worth checking whether there is an existing tree. There are single-name websites on the internet that can be checked simply by carrying out Google searches. The *British Isles Genealogical Register* lists more than 155,000 surnames, recording the places and dates of families currently being researched along with the names and addresses of the researchers. This is available on CD-ROM or microfiche from the Federation of Family History Societies. Your local family history society will probably have a directory of members' interests. The Liverpool and South West Lancashire Family History Society compile an annual list, which is published on microfiche. The *Genealogical Research Directory* is published annually and contains lists of names being researched. The Guild of One Name Studies (GOONS) and the Society of Genealogists also maintain lists.

Certain family tree computer programmes, such as Family Tree Maker, encourage the researcher to automatically share their findings by uploading their records to their website (for free), which they then charge others to consult. Whatever the ethics of this, there is a wealth of material out there. In my own case I was contacted by someone who was just beginning their research and wanted to know if we were related. I referred him to the full tree on my own website. He downloaded the information, then uploaded the lot a few days later to Genes Reunited without my permission. His name was alongside this as the 'researcher' and 'contact' on the website. It had taken me over 30 years of solid research to produce a very extensive one-name study containing over 2,000 related names, most of which was done before the advent of the internet and thus involved a great deal of travel and expense, including numerous trips back and forth to the records in London. With the click of a button he effectively claimed it as his own. I may have been prepared to share the information for free with anyone who wanted it, as most researchers do, but there are clearly drawbacks on the information super highway.

Help on the web

There are hundreds of websites concerning family and local history on the web, some of which will be highlighted throughout this book, but the Family History section of the BBC History website (www.bbc.co.uk/familyhistory) provides an excellent introduction to researching your family history, complete with video guide, case studies and links. Visiting this site will provide you with a sound understanding of what is involved in tracing your ancestors in an entertaining and easy-to-understand form.

Visiting the Record Office

Preparing yourself

If you have never visited before, why not just go along to browse the catalogues, indexes and books? Staff will be happy to help you find your way around, and you will be better prepared for your next visit. Gather as much information as possible before a visit and bring copies of relevant documents to help staff advise you. Think about the questions you want to ask – this can save a lot of time. Leave plenty of time for your visit, as identifying the records you need and searching for the required information usually takes longer than you think. Ensure you take along proof of your identity if you have not visited a record office before, to register for a CARN reader's ticket. This needs to be proof of name and current address, so a driving licence, or a utility bill and bank card would be ideal.

Liverpool Record Office Archive Leaflets

These very useful leaflets are frequently referred to here. See here for full listings:
www.liverpool.gov.uk/Leisure_and_culture/Local_history_and_heritage/Reading_guides/Archive_sources/index.asp.

(The advice below refers largely to Liverpool Record Office, but for those researching in the Wirral, most records are held in Cheshire Record Office in Chester, although certain local libraries hold copies – see Appendix Two for further details).

Indexes of Births, Marriages, Deaths

Civil registration of Births, Marriages and Deaths started in England and Wales in 1837. Liverpool Record Office holds microfiche copies of the indexes to births, marriages and deaths from 1837 to 2002 (also referred to as the General Register Office (GRO) Index). These indexes include most births, marriages and deaths, giving you sufficient information to purchase a certificate with full details from a Register Office. Refer to LRO online leaflet No.1. Indexes are also available at www.bmdindex.co.uk and www.ancestry.com.

Parish records

Parish registers
Parish registers are the main source of information for family historians before the start of civil registration. They give information about christenings/baptisms, marriages and (sometimes) burials. Liverpool Record Office holds many of the records of Liverpool's Church of England, Roman Catholic and Non-conformist churches, as well as some Jewish synagogue registers. Visitors can consult the handlist guides before searching and records are held under catalogue reference 282 and 283. Parish maps showing the area covered (essential for finding out which church your ancestor would have attended) and the location of churches are also available for consultation.

Church of England
Registers of baptisms, marriages and burials were first ordered to be kept on 5 September 1538. The earliest register in the Record Office is for St Mary, Walton-on-the-Hill, which starts in 1586/87. Early registers were often poorly maintained and there are frequent gaps, especially in times of political upheaval, such as during the Civil War.

Early registers
Standardisation did not take place until 1754 (marriages) and 1813 (baptisms and burials). Prior to that, the detail recorded is largely down to the incumbent or the parish clerk. Basic details usually included were date; name(s); street location; occupation (where relevant).

Baptisms
From 1 January 1813 baptism registers record the following details: date of baptism; child's Christian name; parents' Christian and surnames; abode; quality, trade or profession (of father); by whom the ceremony was performed. It became customary to add the child's date, or alleged date, of birth.

Marriages
From 25 March 1754 marriage registers record the following details: name of male party; parish from which he comes; occupation; name of female party; parish from which she comes; status, e.g. spinster, widow; whether married by banns or licence; date; by whom the ceremony was performed; signatures of parties and witnesses. From July 1837 marriage registers gave the following information: date; names (of both parties); age (of both parties); condition (e.g. bachelor, widow) of both parties; rank or profession of male; residence at time of marriage (of both parties); fathers' names

(of both parties); rank or profession of (both) fathers; whether married by banns or licence; signatures of parties and witnesses; by whom ceremony was performed.

Burials
From 1 January 1813 burial registers record the following information: name; abode; date of burial; age; by whom the ceremony was performed. See: *Handlist of Church of England Parish Records, Map of Church of England parishes, Liverpool and district, 1900.*

Roman Catholic
The registers of over thirty Roman Catholic churches are kept in the Record Office. Many can only be consulted on microfilm. A detailed handlist is available for purchase. See *Handlist of Roman Catholic Parish Records.* Although some early registers give simple information in English, the standard details given in Roman Catholic parish registers, on Latinised printed form, is as follows. Baptisms: date of birth; date of baptism; name of child; name of child's father; name of child's mother [and whether married to child's father]; mother's name before marriage; signature of priest; name of godfather; name of godmother. Marriages: date; name of priest; name of bridegroom; address of bridegroom; name of bridegroom's father; name of bride; address of bride; name of bride's father; names and addresses of witnesses; signature of priest. Deaths: date of death; name of deceased; address; age; date of burial; name of cemetery; signature of priest.

Non-conformist records
A number of Non-conformist churches have deposited their records and copies of local registers deposited at the National Archives are also available on microfilm. Denominations include Methodist, Unitarian, Baptist, Presbyterian and Congregational. See: *Handlist of Non-conformist records* to check what type of records are available.

Jewish registers
The earliest Liverpool Jewish births, deaths and marriages (1722–1816) are recorded in the Register Book of the Jews in the records of the Old Hebrew Congregation (LRO ref. 296 OHC). Other synagogue registers survive, some of which are closed under section 40 of the Data Protection Act 1998. More information can be found in the catalogues in the search room and in the Merseyside Jewish Community Archives leaflet.

Burial records
Liverpool Record Office holds the records of Liverpool churchyards and cemeteries. These include private cemeteries and, from the mid-nineteenth century, those maintained by the City Council. Burial records often include details of the deceased's last address, age and occupation. Gravestones often give biographical information about the deceased and other family

members and Liverpool Record Office holds the records of copies of inscriptions from gravestones. When visiting refer to *Handlist of Cemetery and Burial records*. Online refer to leaflet No.6. Also online: St James Cemetery: www.stjamescemetery.co.uk – a partial index. Anfield cemetery and St Peter's, Woolton memorial transcripts: liverpoolcemetery.co.uk and liverpool-ancestors.co.uk. St Nicholas, Halewood, graveyard project: www.halewood.org.uk.

International genealogical index

The International Genealogical Index, commonly known as the IGI, is a vast collection of transcribed birth/christening, marriage and death/burial records from many countries, compiled by the Church of Jesus Christ of Latter-day Saints (Mormon Church). Although vast, it is not comprehensive. It includes only entries supplied by members of the Church of Jesus Christ of Latter-day Saints for their religious purposes. The section of the IGI that covers the British Isles includes mainly birth/baptism and marriage records, with just a few death/burial records, from parish and Non-conformist registers from around 1500 to around 1880. For further information about how the IGI is compiled, see the International Genealogical Index page on the Genuki web site: www.genuki.org.uk/big/eng/LIN/igi.html. LRO has a 1992 edition of the IGI, on microfiche, for the British Isles. The information is now also available on the church website www.familysearch.org.

L DIRECTORY. [GORE'S

Royden John painter 29 Nuttall st. Wavertree road, E
———— Joseph coal dealer Dickens st. S
———— Joseph farmer 54 Prenton road East, Hr. Tranmere
———— Joseph painter 114 Park st. S
———— Joseph shipwright 159 Northumberland st. S
———— Joseph B. shipbuilder (*T. R. and Co.*) The Hollies' Sefton near Liverpool
———— Joseph J. cashier 27 Wendover avenue, S
———— Mrs. Mary, Yew Tree farm, Bidston village Cheshire
———— Richard carter 20 Miranda road, N
———— Thomas farmer Greasby, Birkenhead
———— Thos. shipbuilder (*T. R. & Co.*) High Carrs, Roby road Roby. W
———— Thomas Bland, Esq., J.P. shipowner Frankby hall Frankby, Birkenhead & the Constitutional Club Northumberland av. London—office 13 Castle st.W
———— Thomas and Co. shipbuilders Queen's pierhead works Jordan st. W
———— Thomas H. shipwright 3 Brock st. N
———— William 39 Jenkinson st. E
———— William book keeper 6 Redgrave st. E

Gore's Directory, *1900*, *extract*

Birth certificate of an unusual resident (see www.roydenhistory.co.uk for the story of the Hitlers in Liverpool.)

Maps

The local record offices have excellent coverage of maps. Bear in mind that urbanisation in some areas was a twentieth-century phenomenon and the area you are concerned with may have been covered by earlier maps such as enclosure and tithe. Liverpool Record Office in particular has a large collection of all types of maps and plans in a variety of scales and dates. The first properly surveyed map of the town was produced in 1725 by Chadwick, although there are plans before that date. Once maps begin to record street names, they can be used effectively in conjunction with the census or parish records to pinpoint where your ancestor lived or worked. Liverpool Record Office has a *Handlist of Liverpool Street Maps* for consultation. There are also excellent online guides on their website, see leaflets Nos 3, 4 and 5. A self-service selection of facsimile street maps of Liverpool is now available. Facsimile reproductions of several old Liverpool maps are for sale in the Record Office. Alan Godfrey has also produced old editions (www.alangodfreymap.co.uk). Cassini Maps have produced an excellent boxed set of five Historical Liverpool maps based on the Ordnance Survey of 1840/43, 1850/51, 1902/3, 1923/24 and 1947. They are also available individually. Of particular use is the six inch to one mile map of 1850/51, which includes *Liverpool in the 1850s* by Mike Royden and covers Liverpool from Bootle in the north to Otterspool in the south, with street names throughout. (www.cassinimaps.co.uk)

Street Directories

It is essential you know where your ancestor lived if you are to recover relevant parish records such as baptism, marriage and burial entries in church archives. Liverpool's first Street Directory was published in 1766 and contained 'an alphabetical list of the merchants, tradesmen and principal inhabitants of the town of Liverpool, with their respective addresses.' Before the telephone directory, street directories were essential and continued to be published annually until the advent of the Yellow Pages. Information given has varied, but usually an alphabetical list of householders' names is included. This gives the name of the head of household, with their occupation and address. Once an address is discovered, parish records and census records can then be narrowed down. Copies are held in local record offices, usually on microfilm. Liverpool Record Office provides a guide sheet online – see leaflet No.8. Digital images for certain directories (national coverage) can be accessed online at www.historicaldirectories .org. Gore's 1900 Directory is on the site and a good starting point.

Census

Census returns give the details of all the members of individual households, including children, servants, visitors and so on, who were present on the night the census was taken. Family groups and relationships can be discovered as well as addresses, ages, occupations and places of birth. The first national census giving details about individuals was taken in 1841. A census has been taken at ten-year intervals, except in 1941, ever since. As with many other archives holding personal information, data is not released until it is 100 years old. Liverpool Record Office holds microfilm copies of the Liverpool census returns from 1841 onwards, although it has become very easy to access records through other media such as boxed sets of CDs and internet sites. Regarding CDs, Liverpool and the surrounding area is stored within the sets for Lancashire, while Wirral is under Cheshire. Copies are held in record offices, by local societies or they can be purchased online (see S & N Genealogy www.genealogysupplies.com). Online access is at: www.familysearch.org, www.ukcensusonline.com, www.ancestry.com and Liverpool Record Office online leaflet No.2. There is useful guidance in **Christian, Peter & Annal, David**, *Census: The Expert Guide*, TNA, 2008.

Electoral registers

Using the street directories may not reveal names being researched, so the electoral registers may prove useful. LRO holds Electoral or Voters' Registers, for Liverpool only, from 1832 to the present. Although they show who was entitled to vote in elections, most people could not vote before 1918. See LRO online leaflet No.7. Online access: www.findmypast .com/electoral-roll.

Wills

Wills can reveal much about wealth, possessions and how ancestors lived, plus they may give precious information about links with named relatives. Indexes of wills from 1458 to 1837 are published by the Record Society of Lancashire and Cheshire, with the originals available at the Lancashire or Cheshire Record Offices. National indexes of wills from 1858 to the 1950s are kept in the Record Office. There is currently no online access, but there is online help with Liverpool Record Office leaflet No.13 and on the TNA website.

Newspapers

Newspapers can be useful when tracing articles about family or local events, but indexes do not exist in Liverpool Record Office. Nevertheless, they have a vast collection, from the first continuous newspaper, begun in 1756, called *Williamson's Liverpool Advertiser*. Most newspapers have been microfilmed and can only be viewed in this format because the originals are too fragile.

Eighteenth-century newspapers
Williamson's Liverpool Advertiser starting in 1756, (later *Billinge's Liverpool Advertiser* and then the *Liverpool Times* (lasted until 1856)). *Liverpool General Advertiser* (from 1765 until 1875). Both were weekly and mainly featured shipping movements.

Nineteenth-century newspapers
Daily Post 1855 to date (merged with the *Liverpool Mercury* in 1904.) *Evening Express*, 1870 to 1958. *Liverpool Daily Courier*, 1808 to 1929 (name changed to just *Daily Courier* and then back again.) *Liverpool Echo*, started 1879 to date. *Liverpool Mercury*, started 1811 to 1904 (merged with the *Daily Post* above), indexed half yearly to 1824/5.

Twentieth-century newspapers
By 1940 there were only three main Liverpool newspapers left: *Daily Post*, *Liverpool Echo*, both still published, and the *Evening Express* (ceased publication 1958).

Suburban newspapers
There were numerous local papers covering Bootle, Crosby, Garston, Woolton, Prescot and Huyton, Walton and West Derby. Refer to LRO online leaflet No.16. Visitors to the LRO refer to **Gibson, J.**, *Local newspapers 1750–1920: a select location list*, 1987, and **LRO**, *List of Liverpool newspapers 1756 to date*, (both kept at Enquiry Desk).

Record keeping

It is essential to have an efficient system of record keeping from the outset as your files will soon expand and become chaotic if you are not organised. Ensure you keep a record of all your searches, even if they have drawn a blank. You may find yourself duplicating searches later if you do not. Manual methods such as charts, ring binders and notebooks may be your preference, but many researchers now computerise their records and input information directly to laptops in the Record Office. There are a variety of Family Tree programmes available such as Family Tree Maker, RootsMagic and Family Historian. As well as providing a database for your research, photographs, documents and all types of digitised media can be stored and attached to relevant individuals. Charts can also be customised and printed.

Dead web links

It is inevitable, given the transient nature of the internet, that over time some web links will no longer work. This does not mean the web site has disappeared.

The Queen and Mike Royden in deep discussion about local archives.

*Harry and Joyce Culling
man the Liverpool and SW
Lancs Family History
Society stall at a local fair.*

1. Try searching for the title of the site on Google, being prepared for a redesigned and possibly renamed site.

2. Copy some of the front page text or any other phrases you can remember into Google.

3. The site may have been removed completely – but you may be surprised to learn that millions of such web pages haven't actually disappeared, but have been archived. True, they may not be updated, but Wayback Machine at www.archive.org can give you access to several pages of the final updates of the site you are looking for. It may also be able to take you back to earlier versions of the site. An example of this is the sad demise of Toxteth.net – an excellent site no longer online. So, access Wayback Machine, type Toxteth.net into the search engine and click the latest update to at least access the final appearance of the site.

Appendix Two

ARCHIVES, LIBRARIES AND LOCAL STUDY CENTRES

LOCAL ARCHIVES

Liverpool Record Office (www.liverpool.gov.uk/Leisure_and_
culture/Local_history_and_heritage/index.asp)

A vast resource of information covering the fascinating history of the city
from the 13th century to the present. These include archives of the City
Council and its predecessors, schools, churches, families, businesses and
societies, books, maps, watercolours and unique photographs to help you
find out about the history of your family, house, street, district, famous
Liverpool people, landmarks and events. Visitors are welcome to bring
their own camera to obtain copies of documents for personal use only.
Anyone intending to publish images from the collections must obtain
permission from the manager.

    Address: 4th Floor, Central Library, William Brown Street, Liverpool
L3 8EW.

    General enquiries: 0151 233 5817

    Microfilm/microfiche bookings: 0151 233 5811

    Fax: (Central Library) 0151 233 5886

    E-mail: recoffice.central.library@liverpool.gov.uk

    The Record Office is just a few minutes walk from Lime Street railway
station and many bus routes. Parking on William Brown Street itself is very
limited but there are city centre car parks nearby.

    Opening hours: Monday to Friday 9am to 6pm, Saturday 9am to 5pm,
Sunday 12pm to 4pm. Appointments are not necessary for viewing sources
on microfilm/fiche, but they are recommended if you require reader
printers. A reader's ticket is needed to request archives, books, maps,
photographs and watercolours. Please bring proof of name and address.
You will be asked to leave any bags in lockers before consulting original
material. There is an annual closure for stock-taking and special projects
during the third and fourth weeks in June. Online catalogue available to
search on the above website.

Copying documents: Photocopying self-service for permitted documents, A4/A3. No professional photographic service provided. Own photos permitted, use of flash not allowed, use of tripod at discretion of staff. Self-service microform reader printer available, A4 printout, no A3.

Records: Local Authority archives from 1207 (minute books from 1550). Ecclesiastical archives: Anglican parishes from 1586, Roman Catholic parishes from 1741, Non-conformist from 1787, Liverpool Diocesan Registry, Jewish archives from 1804. Board of Guardians and other statutory bodies. Hospitals. Family, estate (including manorial) and personal papers include Moore of Bank Hall, Plumbe-Tempest, Marquess of Salisbury, Norris of Speke Hall, William Roscoe, Earls of Derby (see also Lancashire Record Office) and others. Business, trade union, charity, association and society archives. Literary manuscripts. Other material held includes newspapers from 1756, street directories from 1766, census returns, slides, photographs, engravings, prints, watercolours, maps. Sound material includes the library of BBC Radio Merseyside. The reference library of the Historic Society of Lancashire and Cheshire is housed in the department. Sources for family history, including St Catherine's House Index of births, marriages and deaths 1837–1940, national probate indexes 1858–1946, and 1881 census index for England and Wales. *Please Note: no passenger lists or other records of immigration and emigration are held.*

Finding aids and publications: Lists, catalogues and indexes. General information sheet, Brief Guide for Family Historians, Handlist of Church of England Parish Records, Map of Church of England Parishes, Liverpool and District, c.1900 etc., Handlist of Roman Catholic Parish Records, others in preparation. Authorised Reader's Ticket is needed to consult archives, rare books and audio-visual material. These are available only by personal application with proof of identity.

See website for excellent set of pdf guides to the record office's holdings.

Maritime Archives and Library at the Merseyside Maritime Museum (www.liverpoolmuseums.org.uk/maritime)

The museum houses a fine collection of maritime books and documents spanning three centuries. These include one of the finest collections of merchant shipping records in the UK. Every aspect of Liverpool's maritime history from the early eighteenth century is covered, and while the emphasis is on Liverpool, the coverage is national and international. The museum website is excellent and gives plenty of advice and information about its collections.

Access: Open Tuesday to Thursday, 10.30am–4.30pm (2nd floor of the Merseyside Maritime Museum). Entry to and use of the archives and library is free. You will need to collect a free ticket from the archives enquiry desk. The tickets will be either an annual reader's ticket (for which proof of identity will be required), or by temporary daily ticket valid only on day of issue.

They request that visitors use one of the provided lockers for storing coats and bags. There is a £1 refundable charge. You will need a lead (graphite) pencil and paper for making notes. You may want to take photocopies of some documents, in which case you'll need change to pay for them.

Laptops must be run on batteries only as the library cannot provide mains charging.

Facilities: Microfilm/fiche reader printers (Maritime Archives and Library only, please book in advance where possible), photocopier, photographic/plan reprographic service.

Before you visit: It is recommended that you consult the 'Start your search' and 'Frequently Asked Questions' sections on the website. It is advisable that you also consult the helpful (and downloadable) Information sheets. There is a large selection of these sheets covering all aspects of Liverpool's maritime past and general maritime history. They describe the records held (and those not held) and the information they contain. The keyword facility on the webpage enables effective searching. They can be viewed on the site or downloaded in Adobe Acrobat PDF or Rich Text Format. Direct link to the index page: www.liverpoolmuseums .org.uk/maritime/archive/listGuides.aspx

Merseyside Record Office (Records held at Liverpool Record Office)

Address: Local Studies and Family History Services, 4th Floor, Central Library, William Brown Street, Liverpool L3 8EW.

Tel: 0151 233 5817

Fax: 0151 233 5886

E-mail: recoffice.central.library@liverpool.gov.uk

Opening hours: Monday–Thursday 9am–7.30pm; Friday 9am–5pm, Saturday 10am–4pm. No car parking.

Archives held: Merseyside County Council, Merseyside Residuary Body. Liverpool, Southport, Wirral coroners. Merseyside Passenger Transport Executive, Merseyside Fire Service (from mid-nineteenth century). Hospital archives. Methodist and United Reform churches. Social agencies, e.g. Child Welfare Association, League of Well-doers. Business archives. Some family and estate archives.

Finding aids: Lists and indexes, information sheet, *Brief List of Holdings*, handlist of genealogical sources.

Knowsley Local Studies and Archives Library
(www.knowsley.gov.uk/leisure/libraries)

Address: Huyton Library, Civic Way, Huyton, Knowsley, L36 9GD.
  Tel: 0151 443 3738
  Fax: 0151 443 3739
  Opening hours: Monday–Friday 9.15am–7pm, Saturday 10am–4pm,
Sunday 12pm–4pm.
  Records: Their libraries have a wide range of local history materials
including books, archives, maps and photographs to help you find out the
history of life in your area.
  Holdings include: Local Authority and predecessor authorities. Prescot
Grammar School sixteenth to twentieth century. Prescot Cooperative
Society. Court Registers for Huyton, Kirkby and Liverpool (Islington
Division) as well as some of the earlier records from Prescot, St Helens and
Childwall Petty Sessional Divisions.
  Other material includes: Local census returns, parish registers and
Bishop's Transcripts, Prescot records fifteenth to nineteenth century,
Halewood and Huyton courts leet seventeenth to nineteenth century.
Maps, plans and photographs.
  Advance booking system: Researchers wishing to consult material on
microfilm, microfiche or CD-ROM are advised to book a microform
machine in advance. Machines may be booked for a maximum two-hour
period per customer, per day. Bookings will be accepted by telephone or by
personal visit. Printouts from reader printers and IGI machines are charged
at 10p per page.
  Finding aids: Majority of archive collections listed. Card index to printed
local studies collections and photographs.
  Location of collections: Main collection at Huyton Library, smaller
collections at other branches.
  Archive service: Archive store at Kirkby Library, historic records of
Knowsley Council and predecessor authorities, archives viewed by
appointment, please call 0151 443 3738.
  Publications: *Huyton* (Archive Photographs series), *Kirkby & Knowsley*
(Archive Photographs series), *Huyton & Roby, Inns of Prescot & Whiston,
Prescot Records* (court rolls), *From Slacky Brow to Hope Street: a Century of
Prescot Football*, maps, postcards.

Wirral Archives (www.wirral.gov.uk, under 'Leisure and
culture/Local History)

Address: Wirral Archives Service, Lower Ground Floor, Cheshire Lines
Building, Canning Street, Birkenhead, Wirral, CH41 1ND. Access to the
Lower Ground Floor is via Shore Road.
  Tel: 0151 606 2929

Fax: 0151 606 2928
E-mail: archives@wirral.gov.uk
Opening hours: Monday to Friday 9.30am–4.30pm, Saturdays 10am–1pm.

Wirral Archives Service cares for and offers public access to thousands of historical records relating to the history of the Wirral. Researchers are welcome to consult original documents and other sources free of charge. The service provides records for those interested in family history, local history and maritime and industrial history. The new premises feature a spacious, attractive search room, with microfilm and microfiche readers as well as new computers to help people with their research. Wirral Archives Service is running free Saturday-morning workshops aimed at everyone from schoolchildren to family and local history groups. The sessions will be brought alive with original documents and cover topics including family history, the history of Wirral, schools and education, and Wirral at war.

Holdings: Wirral Archives Service holds documents dating back to the fifteenth century, with most dating from the nineteenth and twentieth centuries. These documents include:

- Records of Wirral local government (i.e. borough and district councils), including minutes, building plans and rate books

- Records of the Poor Law and of local workhouses

- School records

- Hospital records

- Court records, including Quarter Sessions and County Court

- Business records, including the extensive collection of Cammell Laird Shipbuilders Ltd

- Records of local clubs, societies, organisations and individuals

- Solicitors' records, including title deeds

- Maps and plans, including tithe maps, Ordnance Survey maps and marine maps of the Wirral Coastline

- Local newspapers

In addition to these original documents, they also hold on microfilm or microfiche a number of sources of particular use to family historians, including:

- Census returns for Wirral 1841–1901

- Electoral registers for Wirral 1842–1900

- Records of burials in municipal cemeteries

Researchers requiring parish registers of baptisms, marriages and burials should contact Cheshire Record Office or Birkenhead Reference Library, and those requiring birth, marriage and death certificates should contact the Superintendent Registrar's Office, Wirral Register Office, Town Hall, Mortimer Street, Birkenhead, CH41 5EU. **Tel:** 0151 606 2020.

Birkenhead Reference Library

Address: Borough Road, Birkenhead, Wirral, CH41 2XB.
   Tel: 0151 652 6106 Ext. 7
   Fax: 0151 653 7320.
   Opening times: Monday 9am–8pm, Tuesday 9am–8pm, closed Wednesday, Thursday 9am–8pm, Friday 9am–5pm, Saturday 9am–1pm, 2–5pm.
   E-mail: birkenhead.ref@wirral-library.net
   Family and local history resources: Census returns (1841–1901), parish registers, historical maps, street directories, electoral registers (1862 to date), IGI (Mormon Index), GRO Index (births, marriages and deaths), newspaper archives including *Birkenhead News* (1860 to date), cemetery records for Wirral.
   Photographic collection: A copying service is available: photocopies, laser copies and photography options available, details of scale of charges available on request.
   Group visits/talks can be catered for. Please contact a member of staff for details. As many records are on film or fiche, it is essential to book in advance a microfilm/fiche reader/printer to avoid disappointment. Micro prints are available at nominal charges. Research (to a reasonable extent) undertaken by staff in response to telephone, e-mail and postal enquiries. Charges include up to four microfilm/fiche prints or photocopies, and postage.

Sefton Council Local Archives (www.sefton.gov.uk under Libraries/Local History)

A Local History Library Service that operates from two main units: Southport Library (covering North Sefton) and Crosby Library (covering South Sefton). Sefton Metropolitan Borough is in the historic county of Lancashire.
   Southport Library: Lord Street, Southport, PR8 1DJ.
   Tel: 0151 934 2119
   Fax: 0151 934 2115
   E-mail: local-history.north@leisure.sefton.gov.uk
   Local History Librarian: Andrew Farthing
   Assistant Librarian: Matthew Tinker

Crosby Library: Crosby Road North, Waterloo, L22 0LQ.
Tel: 0151 257 6401
Fax: 0151 934 5770
E-mail: local-history.south@leisure.sefton.gov.uk
More details regarding holdings and opening hours can be found on the website.

Lancashire Record Office (www.lancashire.gov.uk/education/record_office)

Address: Lancashire Record Office, Bow Lane, Preston, Lancashire, PR1 2RE
Tel: 01772 533039
E-mail: record.office@ed.lancscc.gov.uk
Opening hours: see Opening Times within the Planning a Visit page on the record office's website.
Entry access: member of CARN readers ticket scheme.
Visiting guide: see Search Room Rules within the record office's website.
Directions: see Location page within the record office's website for street map.
Fee-based research service provided, see Enquiry Service within the Enquiries and Research page on the record office's website.
Sources held: Records of local government: including Lancashire County Council and district and parish councils, and their predecessors, including Quarter Sessions, Poor Law unions and turnpike trusts.

- Probate records of the Archdeaconries of Chester and Richmond

- Records of Anglican, Roman Catholic and Non-conformist churches, including registers of baptisms, marriages and burials

- School records, including logbooks and admissions registers

- Private records, including manorial and estate records, family papers, and the records of businesses and societies

- Maps and plans, including tithe, enclosure and estate plans, Ordnance Survey and other printed maps

- Copies of some national sources: including census returns for the whole County Palatine

Online Catalogue: see Records Search on the website.
Copying documents: Photocopying: staff only for permitted documents, see Copying page for charges. Photographic reproduction service available. Own photos permitted, use of flash not allowed, tripods allowed. Photography only allowed in lecture room which must be booked, charge

£20 per hour. Microform token-operated microform reader-printer available, see Copying page for charges.

Cheshire and Chester Archives and Local Studies Service
(www.cheshire.gov.uk/recoff)

Address: Cheshire and Chester Archives and Local Studies Service, Duke Street, Chester, Cheshire, CH1 1RL.
   Tel: 01244 972574
   E-Mail: recordoffice@cheshire.gov.uk
   Opening hours: Monday 1pm–5pm, Tue–Fri 9am–5pm, third Saturday in the month 9am–4pm. (Please note: closed Monday am)
   Entry access: member of CARN readers ticket scheme.
   Visiting guide: see Planning a Visit within the record office's website.
   Sources held: see Family History page within the record office's website. Wills: see the record office's Wills Database Online covering probate documents proved at Chester for the years 1492 to 1940 and containing over 130,000 entries (name, residence, occupation, date of probate).
   Online catalogue: see Search the Archives page within the record office's website, see National Archives Access to Archives website.

Last orders for documents 45 minutes before closing; there is no lunchtime production 12.30pm–1.30pm. (It is helpful if document requests are presented by 12.15pm to allow enough time for production). Advance bookings can be made by telephoning the searchroom on 01244 602574.

- Parish registers from the sixteenth century (for more information on Cheshire parishes and their registers, see 'Cheshire Towns and Parishes' on the Family History Society of Cheshire website)

- Wills and probate records. Details of Cheshire wills for the period 1492–1940 are on our wills database (www.cheshire.gov.uk/Recordoffice/Wills/Home.htm) from which copies can be ordered online.

- Census returns 1841–1901.

- Poor Law records

- Diocesan records

- Electoral records

- Non-conformist records

- Tithe maps and apportionments (online at http://maps.cheshire.gov.uk/tithemaps)

- Deeds

- Estate papers

Also the records of societies, businesses, hospitals, schools, courts, local authorities, collections of local newspapers from the eighteenth century onwards, photographs and other illustrations.

Local Studies library: located in Cheshire Record Office, the major collection of books, pamphlets, printed maps, trade directories and other local studies material relating to Cheshire. For details of local studies material such as books, maps, census returns and electoral registers, which are available in libraries across the county, visit www.cheshire.gov.uk/library.

Post and e-mail enquiries: For those unable to visit in person, staff will answer, free of charge, postal and email enquiries on the availability of documents and suggest appropriate types of record for particular research topics. Searches for information in records or other sources held by the Record Office can be undertaken, for a fee, by their Research Consultant.

Copying documents: Photocopying: staff only for permitted documents, small charges apply per copy from original documents, microfilm and the self-service microfilm reader printer in the record office search room. Photographic reproduction service available. Own photos permitted with permission from Duty Archivist, use of flash not allowed, tripods allowed, normally no charge but may charge for use of tripods and large cameras. Microform coin-operated microform printer provided, again, small charges apply per printout.

Liverpool Register Office (www.liverpool.gov.uk/Registrars_office)

Here you can obtain copies of birth, marriage or death certificates from the period 1837 to the present day or by post. The Register Office has been present in Liverpool since 1837, when the first legal requirement to register births, stillbirths, deaths and marriages was introduced. They hold all the original Liverpool birth, marriage and death registers from 1837 to the present day.

Address: Liverpool Register Office, The Cotton Exchange, Old Hall Street, Liverpool, L3 9UF.

Opening times: Monday–Thursday: 9am–5pm, Friday: 9am–3.45pm, Saturday: 9am–noon.

Lancashire BMD and Cheshire BMD (www.lancashirebmd.org.uk, www.cheshirebmd.org.uk)

Register Offices in Lancashire and Cheshire hold records of local births, marriages and deaths back to the start of civil registration in 1837. The county's Family History Societies are collaborating with local Registration Services to make indexes to these records freely searchable via the internet. Although the indexes are not yet complete for all years and districts, the database will eventually cover births, marriages and deaths for the years 1837 to the present day. There are weblinks to local family history societies and similar BMD sites across the country.

University of Liverpool Special Collections and Archives
(http://sca.lib.liv.ac.uk/collections)

The materials held in the Special Collections and Archives Division have their foundation in the gifts and bequests made to the University by diligent and generous collectors for more than a century. The collections include manuscripts, medieval to modern; incunabula, early and finely printed books, and archival collections.

Address: Dr Maureen Watry, Head of Special Collections & Archives, Sydney Jones Library, The University of Liverpool, PO Box 123, Liverpool, L69 3DA.

Tel: 0151 794 2696

Fax: 0151 794 2681

E-mail: mwatry@liv.ac.uk

Holdings: Too extensive to list here, comprehensive list of university holdings on their web page.

North-West Regional Archives (www.northwestarchives.org.uk)

The NWRAC represents the interests of the archive community in Cumbria, Lancashire, Merseyside, Greater Manchester and Cheshire. There are over forty major archive services in the region with another hundred smaller services and many more archival collections in museums, libraries and other organisations. These archive services are managed by a variety of organisations including local authorities, businesses and academic institutions. This site contains a comprehensive list of local archive services.

CARN Readers Ticket Scheme

CARN, which stands for County Archives Research Network, is a group of record offices that provides a uniform readers ticket that is used to gain admission to any local authority archive within the scheme – the vast majority of record offices are members of the CARN readers ticket scheme.

CARN reader's ticket.

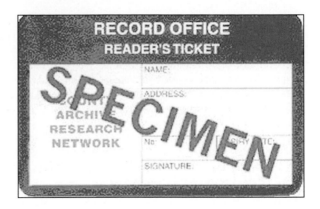

They are free, valid for four years and issued on your first visit to any record office that is a member of the scheme.

Application: You must apply in person, bringing official proof of identity validating your name with permanent address and signature. You may also be asked to provide two passport-sized photographs. Examples of documents that could contain the details required include (you may have to bring a combination of two to show name, permanent address and signature): driving licence (name, address and signature); foreign passport (name and signature); bank statement (name and address); building society passbook (only if the address is included); pension/benefit book (name and address); NHS medical card (the address is not always included); disabled person's registration (name and address); own vehicle registration documents (name and address); National Archives' readers ticket (but need second ID proof); Credit/debit/cheque guarantee cards (name and signature). NB: UK passports do not provide proof of address. Please also bring something with your current address.

National Records

The National Archives (TNA) (www.nationalarchives.gov.uk)

Address: The National Archives, Kew, Richmond, Surrey, TW9 4DU.
Tel: +44 (0) 20 8876 3444
Opening hours: Monday, Wednesday, Friday, Saturday 8am–5pm; Tuesday, Thursday 8am–7pm.
The National Archives of England, Wales and the United Kingdom has one of the largest archival collections in the world, spanning 1,000 years of British history from the Domesday Book of 1086 to government papers recently released to the public. You can see this collection at Kew, West London, or view certain documents online. Documents are opened for

public inspection thirty years after the file was closed, except in a few cases where the closure period is longer. The National Archives also acts as a clearing-house for information about the location of non-public records and manuscripts relating to British history kept elsewhere in the UK and overseas. Many documents can be accessed online; visit the site for latest news. For family historians, it is the central guide for births, marriages and deaths, census, citizenship and naturalisation, divorce, passenger lists, wills.

Research guides: Extensive guides available online covering all aspects of historical research. An excellent place to start, even if records are not held in the TNA.

Access to Archives (www.nationalarchives.gov.uk/a2a)

A2A allows you to search and browse for information about archives in England, dating from the 900s to the present day. These archives are cared for in local record offices and libraries, universities, museums and national and specialist institutions across England, where they are made available to the public. To find out whether archives are of interest to you, it is necessary to consult a catalogue or other finding aid. A2A allows you to search across detailed catalogues from over 340 repositories in England beyond the National Archives at Kew, so you may arrange to see or to obtain copies of specific, useful, real archive documents with a few mouse clicks. The database is regularly updated, so revisit often for newly-included catalogues.

Archives Hub (www.archiveshub.ac.uk)

The Archives Hub provides a single point of access to 18,917 descriptions of archives held in more than 90 UK universities and colleges. At present these are primarily at collection-level, although complete catalogue descriptions are provided where they are available. The Archives Hub forms one part of the UK's National Archives Network, alongside related networking projects. The service is hosted at MIMAS on behalf of the Consortium of University Research Libraries (CURL) and is funded by the Joint Information Systems Committee (JISC). Systems development work is undertaken at the University of Liverpool.

Commonwealth War Graves Commission – Debt of Honour Register

(www.cwgc.org)

This Register provides personal and service details and places of commemoration for the 1.7 million members of the Commonwealth forces who died in the First or Second World Wars. (A record of some 60,000 civilian casualties of the Second World War is provided without details of burial location.) The cemeteries and memorials where these names are commemorated, in perpetuity, are located in around 150 countries This database makes it possible to identify the exact location, by cemetery plot or memorial panel, where any given name is commemorated.

Family History Societies

Liverpool & South-West Lancashire FHS (www.liverpool-genealogy. org.uk)

The original and main society for the Merseyside area. Founded by Joyce and Harry Culling and others in May 1976. The Liverpool & South West Lancashire Family History Society (L&SWLFHS) was originally founded as the Liverpool Family History Society. The inaugural meeting, held in the Liverpool Central Library, was attended by thirty people with common interests in tracing their own ancestry through personal research and exchange of information. Liaison with the Record Office was established to seek advice on the locality and use of local archives. As the membership of the Society grew, other branches were set up by members residing outside Liverpool, but within the Liverpool Diocese and the historic area of the West Derby Hundred. These were St Helens, Southport, Skelmersdale, Leigh, Warrington and Widnes and a special interest group for those with Anglo-Irish ancestry. The Society changed its name to accommodate the groups, first to Liverpool and District FHS, then to its present name, to reflect the area within the Hundred. In 1981 it was realized that members based in and around Liverpool itself were the only group unrepresented in the Society, and the Liverpool branch was set up with its own local committee. They continue to meet each month, with several founder members still attending regularly. Half of the regulars travel from the Wirral, North Wales and all parts of Lancashire and they frequently welcome overseas members to the meetings or visitors who have arrived via the weekly Help Desk. The Society aims to encourage the study of Family History and Genealogy in the area and to provide a forum for those interested, to meet and help each other.

Members' benefits: Regular journal, lecture programme at monthly meetings, visits and other activities connected with subjects of interest to the Society. Membership of the Federation of Family History Societies

Projects: constant and ongoing – transcribing and indexing records and whenever possible publishing material relevant to the interests of the Society.

Meetings: Friends Meeting House, 22 School Lane, Liverpool, L1 3BT. Open 6.15pm. Meetings start at 7pm, open to non-members. Nearest Merseyrail stations: Central Station (Bold St) Buses: Gyratory (walk to Church Street, across to School Lane, turn left, Meeting House on right-

hand side). There is some parking in the area and streets nearby, all free after 6pm.
Membership: Application form and fees available online.

Skelmersdale and Up Holland Family History Group (www.liverpool -genealogy.org.uk/SkemGrp/Skem.htm)

Meetings: Fourth Tuesday of the month except December, July and August at the Hall Green Community Centre, Up Holland, at 7.30pm. (Project work may well carry on in July and August but not in the meeting room). Beginners and more experienced family historians are always very welcome. For further details contact our Secretary, Sue Hesketh, tel: 01942 212940, suehesketh@blueyonder.co.uk.

Widnes Family History Group (www.liverpool-genealogy.org.uk/Widnes /Widnes%20Welcome.htm)

Aims: to copy, transcribe and index any record that will help those people researching their family trees. They also provide speakers every month on a variety of subjects and trips out twice a year to record offices.
  Meetings: on the last Wednesday of the month at Our Lady's Church Hall, Mayfield Avenue, off Royal Avenue, Ditton, Widnes. For 7pm.
  Programme information: online or contact John Humphreys on 07979 616795.
  Secretary: John Cosgrove, 130 Alder Ave, Widnes, WA8 6QS.
  Helpline: operated by Steve Holt. E-mail: busby455@hotmail.com.

Leigh and District Family History Society (www.liverpool-genealogy. org.uk/LeighGrp/Leigh%20Family%20History/index.htm)

Contact: leighfhs@blueyonder.co.uk
  Meetings: 7.30pm in the Derby Room at Leigh Library on the third Tuesday of each month except June and July. The winter session starts in August and usually takes the form of a Beginners' Evening when members and newcomers are able to use the group's microfiche viewers and library facilities to carry out their own research. Other meetings usually have a family history speaker, but members are always able to browse and borrow books from the group's library.
  Projects: Members have been involved in many projects over the years. The first project was a compilation of the whereabouts of all church records for the whole of the area covered by Leigh & District and surrounding areas. Monumental inscriptions recording is carried out regularly by members and the following churchyards and cemeteries have been recorded: Abram St John's, Golborne St Thomas's, Westleigh St Paul's, Lowton St Mary's, Ashton-in-Makerfield St Thomas's, Heath Road (Non-conformist), Leigh Cemetery.

St Helens Townships Family History Society (www.sthelenstownshipsfhs
.org.uk)

Membership: Current fees and application form available on the website.
    Contact: contactus@sthelenstownshipsfhs.org.uk
    Meetings: Monthly meetings are held at St Helens Town Hall, 6.45pm
for a 7.15pm start. Non-members welcome.
    Workshops: 'Help and workshop' evenings are held on the second
Monday of each month at the Local History and Archive Library, 1st Floor,
Central Library, Victoria Square, St Helens (5.30pm–8pm).

Southport Family History Group (www.liverpool-genealogy.org.uk/
SthportGrp/Southport.htm)

Projects: The group have carried out several research projects in the past,
including an index of memorial inscriptions of St Cuthbert's Church,
Halsall, and are currently involved in compiling an index of births,
marriages and deaths from the *Southport Visitor* newspaper from its
commencement in 1844, a history of the Southport Flower Show, an
extended family tree of the Rimmers (a popular local name) of North
Meols, Circus biographies, especially of Henglers Circus and several other
personal indexes.
    Activities: Occasional visits to local record offices and libraries.
Members make occasional visits to the Public Records Office at Kew and
are very happy to help beginners in their research. They also maintain a
Group and Society library, where members have access for research
purposes.
    Meetings: Held at Birkdale Library, Liverpool Road, Birkdale,
Southport, at 7.30pm on the second Friday of each month except where
noted. Lecture programme on the website. New members and visitors are
welcome.
    Contact: Hilary Ambrose, 2 Chelsea Court, 12 Lulworth Road,
Southport, PR8 2AT. Tel: 01704 562792.

Warrington Family History Group (www.liverpool-genealogy
.org.uk/Warrington/Warrington.htm)

Membership: Current fees and application form available on the Liverpool
website.
    Meetings: see website for current monthly lecture programme. Non-
members welcome.
    Projects: transcription work has included Burials for St Paul's, Bewsey
St, Warrington 1832–1856. Warrington Cemeteries Records.

Ormskirk and District FHS (www.odfhs.org.uk)

Coverage: The Society covers the ancient parishes and townships of western Lancashire including: Aughton, Bickerstaffe, Burscough, Downholland, Halsall, Hesketh with Becconsall, Lathom, Lydiate, Maghull, Melling, Ormskirk, Rufford, Scarisbrick, Simonswood, Skelmersdale and Tarleton.

Meetings: on the fourth Wednesday of each month (excluding December when there is no meeting) at the Guide HQ, Moorgate, Ormskirk at 8pm, with various speakers and topics (see the meetings page on the website). Non-members can attend for a fee of £1.

Research library: located at the Scout Hall, Wigan Road, Ormskirk.

Membership: application information on the website. Three journals published per year.

Contact: secretary@odfhs.org.uk

North-West Group of Family History Societies (www.nwgfhs.org.uk)

A non-profit making concern established in 1980 to provide education services for the furtherance of research into genealogy and family history and to support the work of the region's societies, libraries and record offices.

Contact: webmaster@nwgfhs.org.uk.

The Family History Society of Cheshire (www.fhsc.org.uk)

The Family History Society of Cheshire (FHSC) was founded in 1969 to advance the study of family history and genealogy, and they now have around 3,000 members worldwide. As well as helping people with ancestors in Cheshire, they also assist members living locally whose ancestors originated elsewhere.

Local groups: West Kirkby, Birkenhead, Wallasey, Bebington, Chester.

Members' benefits: There are now seventeen groups based throughout the county. Each group arranges its own programme of meetings and activities, and members of the Society are welcome to attend the meetings of any group. Open days are held for all members at various venues throughout Cheshire. Computer Club offers help to members with all levels of experience in family history and computing. Members have use of the Research Centre, based at Alderley Edge near Macclesfield, where members may use a range of research materials, including an extensive book collection, microfiche libraries and computer facilities. The main Library is housed at Alderley Edge and contains over a thousand books and exchange journals from other societies. A selection of books is often available at society conferences and general meetings, and most of the groups have smaller libraries of their own, which often contain books relating to their own areas. Some items from the Microfiche Library may be loaned to members by post. The group produces a large number of publications relating to Cheshire family history, including marriage census indexes, monumental inscriptions and parish register transcripts. A quarterly Journal, the *Cheshire Ancestor*, includes articles of general genealogical interest, as well as articles relevant to Cheshire genealogy. Society notices, new members' interests, news of forthcoming events, group reports and programmes complete the contents. Members' Interests can be submitted for publication in the *Cheshire Ancestor*, and in the annual register, which is published on microfiche every summer. Members are also invited to participate in the society's numerous projects, which include indexing of parish registers, transcribing gravestone inscriptions and inputting data for publication.

Membership: on-line membership form available on the website. Members may choose to affiliate themselves to one of the local groups, or remain unattached. Although society members are free to attend any of the group meetings throughout Cheshire, most of the groups operate additional activities and facilities just for their own members.

Affiliation: Member of Federation of Family History Societies

E-mail: info@fhsc.org.uk

Contact: Mr M.H.C. Craig, 10 Dunns Lane, Ashton Hayes, Chester, CH3 8BU.

LDS Family History Centres (www.familysearch.org)

The Church of Jesus Christ of Latter-day Saints (more commonly known as the Mormons) operate over 4,000 Family History Centres worldwide, including over eighty centres spread across England and Wales. All family historians of whatever belief are welcome to use these centres. These local centres are effectively branches of the Family History Library in Salt Lake City, Utah. As such they provide access to most of the microfilms and microfiches held at this extensive genealogical library, with copies being loaned out on request to your local centre. Although the volunteer staff at these centres cannot do any research for you, you will find them very helpful in answering any general queries you might have and in ordering microfilm/fiche copies from the central Family History Library in Utah. To find out where the Family History Centre nearest to you is located and what its opening hours are, simply go on to the Latter-day Saints website and use their Family History Centre search facility.

Address: 4 Mill Bank, West Derby, Merseyside, England.

Tel: 0151-252 0614

Opening hours: Tuesday 9am–4pm, 7pm–9pm; Wednesday, Thursday 10am–4pm.

Resources:

• Microfiche copy of the complete Family History Library catalogue

- Computer access to the International Genealogical Index (IGI) Access to microfilm copies of the source documents (e.g. parish registers, etc.) on which the International Genealogical Index is based. The relevant microfilm is ordered from Utah for viewing at your local centre for a modest fee.

- Computer access to the British Isles Vital Records Index

- Microfiche copies of the General Register Office master indexes of Births, Marriages and Deaths in England and Wales since 1837

- Computer access to the 1881 Census Index

- Access to microfilm/fiche copies of all census records from 1841 to 1901. Following an online catalogue search for its reference number, the relevant microfilm reel can be ordered and subsequently viewed at your local centre for a modest fee

- Microfiche copies of the National Probate Indexes from 1858 to 1957

- Microfilmed copies of the Death Duties Registers from 1796 to 1857

Appendix Three

WEB RESOURCES

Local History links

LIVERPOOL 2007 www.liverpool2007.org.uk
An online history of Liverpool, celebrating the 800th anniversary of the city of Liverpool. This site hosts an evolving portal or doorway to other independent but linked local history sites, acting to index and catalogue websites.

MERSEY GATEWAY (Port Cities Liverpool)
www.mersey-gateway.org
An online history of the port and its people. 20,000 images drawn from local museums, libraries and archives tell the fascinating story of the individuals, events and communities that shaped the port, the city and the wider Merseyside region.

MIKE ROYDEN'S LOCAL HISTORY PAGES
www.roydenhistory.co.uk
A site covering aspects of the local history of Liverpool, Wirral, South-West Lancashire and Cheshire. Numerous history articles, downloads, and a 'how to research local history' guide. Comprehensive links and forums.

HALEWOOD PARISH LOCAL HISTORY PAGES
www.halewood.org.uk
A website created by Mike Royden. Halewood lies to the south-east of Liverpool and was once a township in the large parish of Childwall. This website covers various aspects of Halewood's history, including articles, documents, image store and then and now photographs.

KNOWSLEY LOCAL HISTORY PAGES http://history.knowsley.gov.uk
Compiled by Knowsley Record Office covering all local areas in the Borough of Knowsley (Cronton, Kirkby, Huyton, Roby, Halewood, Knowley, Prescot, Tarbock, Whiston).

TOXTETH.NET www.toxteth.net

An excellent site covering the history of the former area of the Royal Park. Includes street directories, maps, list of churches and a variety of illustrations, plenty for the local and family historian. Authored by Paul Christian. NB: removed in 2008. However, visit Wayback Machine on www.archive.org/web/web.php, type in Toxteth.net and archive pages for this site can still be accessed. It is hoped the site will return sometime in the future.

HISTORY OF ST JAMES'S CEMETERY, Liverpool www.stjamescemetery.co.uk

Located at the rear of the Anglican Cathedral, it occupies ten acres of ground which were once the final resting place of nearly 58,000 souls. From an American sea captain, stabbed to death, to children who died within hours of their birth. From a midget artist who painted England's nobility, to a simple serving girl. They all found their way into this Liverpool cemetery. Mike Faulkner shows why this small corner of Liverpool fascinates, and what stories are hidden in the past.

TOXTETH PARK CEMETERY www.toxtethparkcemetery.co.uk

Transcription site, with useful links.

LIVERPOOL'S HISTORIC CANNING STREET AREA
http://canning.merseyworld.com

In 1800, the Corporation Surveyor John Foster Senior drew up plans for an area known as Mosslake Fields. Situated on top of St James's Mount, away from the grime of the city centre, the area offered an opportunity to live in spacious comfort. Over the next 100 years a succession of developers built a large number of imposing and elegant town houses, mostly in the Georgian style. Read much more on Andrew O'Hare's excellent site.

OLD LIVERPOOL www.old-liverpool.co.uk

Liverpool snippets from old Liverpool newspapers and other sources. This site came into being when Caryl Williams purchased a large collection of old *Liverpool Mercury* newspapers and started putting marriages, obituaries and snippets from them online. Since then the site has grown and grown. Caryl has also added Liverpool snippets from old books, other old newspapers and theatre programmes from her collection. Regularly updated.

SCOTTIE PRESS www.scottiepress.org.uk

The *Scottie Press* is Britain's longest running and award-winning community newspaper, serving the Scotland Road and Vauxhall Road areas of Liverpool for twenty-nine successful years. In that time they have presented the news and views of the local community, together with a regular nostalgia page featuring old photographs, memories and stories from the Scotland Road area.

LIVERPOOL TALES FROM THE MERSEY MOUTH
www.liverpooltales.com
By John Williams: an excellent collection of essays and anecdotes covering every aspect of Liverpool life.

WILLIAMSON'S TUNNELS www.williamsontunnels.com
Find out all about these amazing and mysterious tunnels, built beneath the Edge Hill area of Liverpool around the turn of the nineteenth century.

LIVERPOOL MURDERS
www.geocities.com/stevenhortonuk/liverpoolmurders.html
'Some gruesome tales of Liverpool's past': Steven Horton's excellent pages on gruesome crimes.

LITERARY LIVERPOOL
www.geocities.com/stevenhortonuk/literaryliverpool.html
Another Steven Horton site looking at famous writers connected with Liverpool.

LIVERPOOL HISTORY ONLINE www.lmu.livjm.ac.uk/lhol
The Liverpool History Online project (formerly ETMS) has been funded by the European Regional Development Fund. The project has also received funding from the *Liverpool Daily Post and Echo*, Liverpool Central Library and John Moore's University. There is a lot of information on this site, plus many images donated from various sources, including Liverpool Record Office.

LEVERPOOLE.CO.UK www.leverpoole.co.uk
Local books, maps, images, photographs, architecture and transcriptions on this expanding site by Tony Swarbrick.

BBC LEGACIES: LOCAL HISTORY
www.bbc.co.uk/legacies/myths_legends/england/liverpool/user.shtml
From buildings to legends and from myths to people, discover our local history through tales of our ancestors from all around the UK.

BBC MERSEYSIDE LOCAL HISTORY PAGES
www.bbc.co.uk/liverpool/localhistory
People, places, local memories, resources and opportunities to contribute stories to the site.

PORT SUNLIGHT VILLAGE COMMUNITY ONLINE
www.portsunlight.org.uk

NEW BRIGHTON HISTORY SITE www.merseyside.net/newbrighton

A HISTORY OF CHILDWALL www.childwall.info
A history of Childwall and much more by local resident Jonathan Wild.

SPEKE LOCAL HISTORY PAGES www.spekeliverpool.co.uk
Local pages based around All Saints Church, Speke.

HALE VILLAGE ONLINE www.halevillageonline.co.uk

Local photography sites

LIVERPOOL DAYS www.liverpooldays.com
Liverpool photographs of places, people, and everyday Liverpool life:
Gerard Fleming's photos of the city, with a large collection of Beatles-
related pics.

LIVERPOOL STREET GALLERY www.liverpoolstreetgallery.com
Created by Dave Wood – a major project to photograph every street in
Liverpool, over 4,000 photos online.

LIVERPOOLPICTORIAL www.liverpoolpictorial.co.uk
Dave Wood's commercial site for Liverpool images, views, photographs,
photos, videos.

INACITYLIVING www.inacityliving.piczo.com
Ged Fagan's collection of over 5,000 photographs of the Gerard Gardens,
Vauxhall area of Liverpool and much more.

Forums and Message Boards

YO LIVERPOOL www.yoliverpool.com
Over the last few years, Yo! Liverpool has grown into an independent
popular online forum community, a result of the positive contributions
made by an increasing army of registered users.
     Created and moderated by Kev, a virtual learning experience.

**MERSEYSIDE GENEALOGY AND HISTORY FORUM http://genchat-
friends.proboards39.com/index.cgi**
An excellent local forum site covering a variety of categorised message and
discussion boards.

MIKE ROYDEN'S LOCAL HISTORY PAGES
www.btinternet.com/~m.royden/mrlhp/forum/forum.htm
Local History forums.

LIVERPOOL EX-PATS http://icliverpool.icnetwork.co.uk/expats
Forum and message board for Liverpudlians worldwide hosted by the
Liverpool Daily Post & Echo website.

LIVERPOOL STADIUM - The Rock Years
www.liverpoolstadium-rockyears.com/index.html
Ah, sweet nostalgia . . . Led Zeppelin playing a three-hour set in 1971 . . .
Hawkwind, Free... Family . . . Jethro Tull . . . Traffic . . . Gong . . . working
as a stagehand at the Stadium and watching Frank Zappa rehearse all afternoon . . . Gentle Giant . . . Can . . . The Groundhogs . . . Captain Beefheart . . .
The Last Trumpet . . . Roger Eagle...

Appendix Four

OTHER USEFUL ORGANISATIONS AND RESOURCES

Liverpool Local History Society (www.liverpoolhistorysociety .org.uk)

Information: Anyone interested in learning more, or helping others to learn more about the history of the fascinating City of Liverpool is warmly invited to attend any of these meetings. Guests are always most welcome, but after their first free visit they are invited to make a contribution towards expenses.

Meetings: See website for dates and lectures. All meetings start at 2pm (doors open 1.30pm), Room C114, 1st floor Cornerstone Building, 'Hope at Everton', Shaw Street, Liverpool.

Journal: Issued free to members, copies £3.50, available for purchase by the public from a number of commercial outlets in Liverpool and area, or by post from the Secretary of the Society (address below).

Membership details: Individual £10 per year; Joint, for any two persons living together at the same address £15 per year; Student, for anyone 12–18 years of age, or of any age undergoing a course of full-time education, £5 per year; Life at ten times the annual rates shown above (not available to students).

Contact: The Secretary, LHS, 46 Stanley Avenue, Rainford, WA11 8HU. **E-mail:** liverpoolhistsoc@merseymail.com.

Historic Society of Lancashire and Cheshire (www.hslc.org.uk)

Information: The Society is a charity which exists for educational purposes to promote the study of any aspect of the history of the Palatine counties of Lancashire and Cheshire and successor local authorities. The aims of the Society are achieved principally through public lectures and the publication of an annual volume of *Transactions*.

Meetings: All meetings are free. Members and non-members are welcome. Please note different times and venues. See website for dates and lectures. The Roscoe Room is on the fifth floor of Liverpool Central Libraries, William Brown Street, Liverpool.

Journal: Articles published in the annual *Transactions*, a peer-reviewed journal, reflect recent high-quality research and scholarship on the two counties.

Membership: Individual membership (UK residents) £16. To join the Society, please complete the membership form on the Society website and return to: Dr. D.E. Ascott, School of History, University of Liverpool, 9 Abercromby Square, Liverpool, L69 7WZ.

E-mail: liverpoolhistsoc@merseymail.com

West Derby Society

The West Derby Society, Liverpool, was founded in 1977 and holds regular monthly meetings at Lowlands, a beautiful Grade II-listed 1846 merchant's mansion set in a rare Victorian city woodland garden. Registered with the Civic Trust, the Society seeks to protect and promote the history and heritage of West Derby, an ancient community older than Liverpool. The Society is as also actively involved in planning and environmental issues in the area.

Meetings: 7.30pm on the third Wednesday of each month except during the summer. All are welcome. Evening outing in June and a day trip in July. No meetings in August.

Membership: The annual subscription is £8, which includes a free quarterly newsletter. Under-18s have free membership. Meetings are lively and include a discussion and update on West Derby issues followed by a guest speaker. Recent topics have ranged from Liverpool John Lennon Airport and taxidermy to the Mole of Edge Hill and protecting wildlife!

The Wavertree Society (www.wavertreesociety.org)

The Wavertree Society aims to improve local amenities and to protect the local environment and architectural heritage, especially within the Wavertree Village and Wavertree Garden Suburb Conservation Areas.

Membership: please apply to 338 Wavertree Nook Road, Liverpool L15 7LJ.

Note that payment of the first subscription ensures delivery of newsletters for at least twelve months.

The Gateacre Society (www.liverpool.ndo.co.uk/gatsoc)

Gateacre is a Liverpool village which has kept its character more than most. Within a quarter-mile radius there are over 100 listed buildings, some of them dating back to the seventeenth century. Aims are to improve local amenities, protect the environment and conserve the architectural heritage of the Gateacre district of Liverpool, research local history, issue newsletters to members to keep them informed, hold meetings, outings and illustrated talks.

Membership secretary: 6 Hayles Grove, Liverpool L25 4SL.

The Birkdale and Ainsdale Historical Research Society
(www.harrop.co.uk/bandahrs/index.html)

The Society's purpose is to carry out and publish research into these two historic communities on the south-west coast of Lancashire, England and their surrounding area. Since its foundation in 1985 the Society has published eight books and a historic map.

The Formby Civic Society (www.formbycivicsociety.org.uk)

The Formby Civic Society aims to make learning about Formby more accessible and appealing to a wider audience. The website contains information about the Society, Formby's history and latest news and events within the area.

Meetings: first Thursday of each month, commence at 8pm and finish at approximately 10pm, held in the Ravenmeols Community Centre, Park Road, Formby.

Contact: Hon. Secretary Mr David Willis, 5 Phillips Close, Formby. Tel: 01704 878994

E-mail: secretary@formbycivicsociety.org.uk.

All Historical (Local History) enquiries to the History Group Secretary: Barbara Yorke, Briardale, 3 Wicks Lane, Formby, L37 3JE. Tel: 01704 872187. Email: yorke@formbycivicsociety.org.uk.

Birkenhead Historic Society (www.birkenheadhistorysociety.org.uk)

Over the last thirty years, the society has successfully raised the awareness of Birkenhead's history through the following activities by individual members and the Society as a whole:

- The publication of *Sidelights on Tranmere* by J.E. Allison.
- The restoration of Tam O'Shanter's Cottage on Bidston Hill as a Visitors' Centre and Urban Farm.

- Through the help of Mr W. Hunt, the saving of the Knox Bell, which was presented to the town. It is now displayed in the restored tower of St Mary's, by Birkenhead Priory.

- The purchase of the Presentation Deed Box of the Borough Hospital.

- A Library Exhibition of Birkenhead in the Second World War.

- The creation of the central Birkenhead Historical Town Trail.

- Involvement in other local interest groups including 'Friends of the Ferries', 'Friends of Flaybrick Memorial Gardens', 'Friends of Birkenhead Park', and Greasby Oral History Project (by Friends of Greasby Library).

- Publication of a Wilfred Owen information leaflet and trail.

- Saving the Woodside Ferry Terminal building from demolition in partnership with the Merseyside Industrial Heritage Society.

- Active participation in the Bidston Conservation Area Advisory Committee of Wirral Borough Council.

- Listing and retention of the 'Alabama' dock and lock-gates at Cammell Laird.

- Taking a leading role in the revival of 'Old Time Music Hall' performances, assisted by the Hamilton Quarter.

- Assemby and cataloguing of Birkenhead and Mersey Ferry plans and artefacts in conjunction with Wirral Library Services.

New members welcomed. See membership page on website. Regular series of talks and visits throughout the year, on a variety of local history topics, meeting on the third Thursday of every month at the Williamson Art Gallery in Birkenhead. More details can be found on the relevant pages on the rest of the site.

Lancashire Local History Federation (www.lancashirehistory.co.uk)

Formed in 1973, this is the official coordinating body for local history in the County Palatine of Lancaster. Whether you are interested in Local History, Family History, Archaeology or Industrial Archaeology, if there is a bearing on Lancashire in your field of research, one or more of their member societies will be able to help. Membership of the Lancashire Local History Federation is open to all societies with an interest in local and/or family history within the County Palatine of Lancaster (that is, Lancashire within its pre-1974 borders). Individual local historians, whether resident or not within Lancashire, are equally welcome.

Journal: *Lancashire Local Historian* (Annual, £2.50)

Membership details: If you have a query about membership of the Federation, please contact Simon Martin, Membership Secretary, by email at members@lancashirehistory.org. Please send membership applications to Simon at: 21 Petticoat Lane, Higher Ince, Wigan, Lancashire, WN2 2LH.

Contact: Mark Pearson, Hon. Secretary, 101 Todmorden Road, Littleborough, OL15 9EB. Tel: 01706 379949.

E-mail: secretary@lancashirehistory.co.uk

There is an extensive list of Lancashire Local History Societies and their websites on the Lancashire Local History Federation web pages.

Cheshire Local History Association (www.cheshirehistory.org.uk)

'Promoting the study of, and interest in, local history within the ancient County Palatine of Chester'. The Association is an independent body whose membership includes organisations and individuals alike. It encourages Local History Societies by offering help and advice on how they may be run. It meets every three months at locations around the county. It publishes the much-respected journal *Cheshire History* in December each year. It organises the Cheshire History Day held on the last Saturday in October.

Meetings: See website for dates and lectures.

Journal: Around 130 pages, various local articles and reviews with black and white illustrations plus one colour plate and available for £5 plus 75p post and packing.

Membership details: Personal membership is available for an individual or couple living at the same address at a subscription of £8 or £10 if overseas. It entitles the member to a complimentary copy of *Cheshire History*, to attend the quarterly meetings and ensures that they are well informed on Cheshire local history matters by being on the Association's mailing list. It is hoped that in time further benefits of membership will be introduced. Use the application form to apply for individual membership.

Contact: Bruce Thompson, Membership Secretary, c/o Cheshire County Record Office, Duke Street, Chester, CH1 1RL. Tel: 01270 760810

E-mail: brucet@netcentral.co.uk

There is an extensive list of Cheshire Local History Societies and their websites on the Cheshire Local History Association web pages.

Chester Society for Landscape History (www.chesterlandscape history.org.uk)

The object of the society is to promote interest in the study of landscape history, to encourage a deeper enjoyment of and respect for our landscape, to hold lectures and field visits, to organise study groups with a view to the recording and, where appropriate, the publication of their findings. Landscape history involves elements of History, Archaeology, Geography, Botany and Geology. The Society has a thriving membership drawn from a wide area and includes professionals, students, local and family historians and those simply wanting to know more about how their surroundings evolved. Although based in Chester, the Society's interests stretch well beyond Cheshire. Counties such as Shropshire, Staffordshire, Lancashire, Merseyside, Yorkshire and Flintshire have all been sourced.

Meetings: monthly lectures held in the Lecture Theatre at the Grosvenor Museum, Chester at 7.30pm. Our lecture programme is very popular and attracts well-known speakers in the field of landscape history. Professor Mick Aston (of *Time Team*) has spoken to the Society twice in recent years and Richard Muir (of *Landscape Detective* fame) has also appeared. Members can attend the lectures free of charge. A charge of £2 per lecture is made for non-members.

Field trips: The Society organises field visits for its members each year. These are held on Saturdays, usually during the summer months. Recent visits have included Ludlow, Mold, Denbigh Moors, Bolsover, NW Wirral, Mellor Archaeological Project and Chester Geological Trail. Members of the Society have the opportunity to enjoy a weekend away studying the landscape of a particular area. Scotland and South Wales are two examples of places visited in the past. The weekend is held during September each year and is led by experts in the area concerned. Aspects of the surrounding landscape are studied, interspersed with ample opportunities to socialise.

Other benefits: Members have a private area on the website, where the library catalogue can be searched and items ordered. The Committee meets once a month, and regularly discusses and reviews the service offered to the members, in line with the Society's objectives. They welcome comments and feedback about all aspects of the Society's work.

Contact: Honorary membership secretary: Miss A. Rowe, 5 Nicholson Close, Mickle Trafford, Chester, CH2 4QN.

Merseyside Archaeological Society (www.merseyside archaeologicalsociety.pwp.blueyonder.co.uk)

The Society holds a monthly programme of lectures and several full-day field trips to archaeological sites during the summer. Weekend trips to visit areas further afield are also arranged. Through a regular newsletter members receive information about local fieldwork and excavations in which they can participate. Reports on archaeological work in the region appear in the Society's Journal.

Meetings: held on the second floor at the new Friends'Meeting House at 22 School Lane, off Hanover Street, near the Bluecoat Centre. All our evening lectures begin at 7.30pm and finish at around 9pm.

Chester Archaeological Society (www.chesterarchaeolsoc.org.uk)

Programme of lectures and excursions. Collaboration with Chester Archaeology and Liverpool University in field projects and excavations. Special programme of lectures, conferences and other events.

Meetings: See website for dates and lectures.

Journal: The Society has published a journal since 1850. It contains reports on local excavations, discussion articles by distinguished scholars and conference proceedings. Members are entitled to a copy of the current journal free of charge and to discounts on back numbers.

Benefits: Ordinary and Associate Members are entitled to attend lectures organised by the Society free of charge, to take part in the Society's excursions at preferential rates, to borrow books from the Society's library and receive copies of the Society's twice-yearly newsletter, the *Chester Antiquary*. Ordinary and Institutional Members also receive copies of the Society's Journal.

Contact: Chester Archaeology, 27 Grosvenor Street, Chester, CH1 2DD. Tel: 01244 402023. Fax: 01244 347522.

Merseyside Industrial Heritage Society (www.mihs.org.uk)

A friendly amateur society whose members share a common desire to find out more about local Industrial Heritage, particularly that of Merseyside, its products, remains, and the people who shaped it. Originally formed in 1964 as the North Western Society for Industrial Archaeology and History, MIHS is amongst the oldest societies of its kind in the country. Affiliated to both the Council for British Archaeology and the Association for Industrial Archaeology. From the outset MIHS has provided a winter programme of lecture meetings and a short programme of field visits in the summer. The May Study Weekend was first held in 1977 and has continued ever since, visiting a wide variety of venues all around Britain.

Meetings: 7.15pm on Monday evenings at Merseyside Maritime Museum, Albert Dock, Liverpool.

Enquiries from intending new members are very welcome. Details are given on the Contacts page or, alternatively, just turn up at any of the meetings shown on the programme and make yourself known to a member of the committee.

Membership: Membership form available for download on the website.

Benefits: A monthly Bulletin is sent to all members.

Society aims are: to further interest in our Industrial Heritage; to study and record by written, photographic or other means the physical evidence and the techniques of past industries; to encourage active involvement in community archaeology projects.

Contact: Malcolm Verity: 01928 724804, e-mail: mv@malcolmverity.com, or Roy Forshaw: 0151 708 5939.

Jewish Historical Society of England, Liverpool Branch
(http://jhse.org)

All lectures commence at 8pm at the Liverpool Jewish Community Centre, Harold House, Dunbabin Road, Liverpool, L15 6XL. Admission free for JHSE members, otherwise £2.50. Refreshments after the lectures.

Contact: Arnold Lewis, Tel: 0151 722 5021.

E-mail: liverpool@jhse.org

Appendix Five

MUSEUMS AND HERITAGE CENTRES

NATIONAL MUSEUMS LIVERPOOL www.liverpoolmuseums.org.uk
The eight venues in the National Museums Liverpool group are the World
Museum Liverpool, the Walker Art Gallery, Merseyside Maritime
Museum, the International Slavery Museum, the National Conservation
Centre, Lady Lever Art Gallery, Sudley House and the Museum of
Liverpool.
    Web links to each of the museums can be found on the website, which
gives details of locations, opening times, admission charges and site facili-
ties.

WORLD MUSEUM LIVERPOOL www.worldmuseumliverpool.org.uk
World Museum Liverpool, William Brown Street, Liverpool, L3 8EN. Tel:
0151 478 4393.
World Museum Liverpool combines historic treasures from across the
globe with the latest interactive technology to make an unbeatable family
day out. Our internationally important collections include archaeology,
ethnology and the natural and physical sciences as well as Britain's only
free Planetarium. With everything from real live bugs to Egyptian
mummies, prehistoric pottery to space exploration, as well as lots of hands-
on fun, there's something for everyone inside.

WALKER ART GALLERY www.liverpoolmuseums.org.uk/walker
William Brown Street, Liverpool, L3 8EL. Tel: 0151 478 4199.
The national gallery of the North, housing outstanding collections of
British and European art from 1300 to the present day. Well-known works
include stunning Renaissance masterpieces and one of the best collections
of Victorian and Pre-Raphaelite art in the country. Visitors are also bound
to recognise many other much-loved works on our walls such as *'And when
did you last see your father?'* and the famous Tudor portraits.

**MERSEYSIDE MARITIME MUSEUM www.liverpoolmuseums.org.uk
/maritime**
Albert Dock, Liverpool, L3 4AQ. Tel: 0151 478 4499.
The Merseyside Maritime Museum in the historic Albert Dock tells the
story of one of the world's greatest ports. Discover Liverpool's central role

in centuries at sea as the gateway to the new world, how the *Titanic*, *Lusitania* and *Empress of Ireland* tragedies affected the city and how merchant navy ships operating out of the port have provided a lifeline in times of war and peace. The museum now also includes Seized! Revenue and Customs uncovered – the museum of the HM Revenue and Customs collections.

INTERNATIONAL SLAVERY MUSEUM www.internationalslavery-museum.org.uk

Albert Dock, Liverpool, L3 4AQ. Tel: 0151 478 4499.
This exciting new museum explores both the historical and contemporary aspects of slavery, addressing the many legacies of the slave trade and telling stories of bravery and rebellion among the enslaved people.

NATIONAL CONSERVATION CENTRE www.nationalconservation-centre.org.uk

Whitechapel, Liverpool, L1 6HZ. Tel: 0151 478 4999.
Science meets art in this award-winning venue that reveals the important behind-the-scenes work of museum conservators to the public. Everything in National Museums Liverpool's diverse collections, from Roman sculpture to fabulous Vivienne Westwood outfits, comes here to be preserved and restored. Find out how our conservators use the latest scientific techniques to investigate these objects and unlock their secrets.

LADY LEVER ART GALLERY ww.liverpoolmuseums.org.uk/ladylever

The Lady Lever Art Gallery is the beautiful legacy of soap magnate and discerning art collector William Hesketh Lever, the first Lord Leverhulme. The gallery is famous for its Pre-Raphaelite paintings, but also has outstanding collections of Wedgwood, Chinese porcelain and eighteenth-century furniture among the treasures on show. Named in memory of Lever's wife, the gallery forms the centrepiece of Port Sunlight, the garden village built for his workforce.

SUDLEY HOUSE www.sudleyhouse.org.uk

Mossley Hill Road, Aigburth, Liverpool, L18 8BX. Tel: 0151 724 3245.
Open: Sudley House is now open after major refurbishments. Open 10am–5pm daily. Closed: from 2pm on 24 December, all day 25 and 26 December and 1 January.

Sudley House has the only Victorian merchant's art collection still held in its original setting – the former family home of the Liverpool ship owner George Holt. Works on show are drawn mainly from his fine collection of British paintings, including works by Landseer and Turner, major Pre-Raphaelite pictures and eighteenth-century portraits by Gainsborough, Reynolds and Romney.

MUSEUM OF LIVERPOOL www.liverpoolmuseums.org.uk/wml

The new Museum of Liverpool will be one of the world's leading city history museums. Building on the success of the former Museum of Liverpool Life, which closed in 2006, the new museum will demonstrate Liverpool's unique contribution to the world and showcase popular culture while tackling social, historical and contemporary issues. It will be housed in a new landmark building at the Pier Head, at the core of the World Heritage Site on Liverpool's famous waterfront.

National Trust

SPEKE HALL, GARDEN AND ESTATE
www.nationaltrust.org.uk/main/w-spekehall

The Walk, Liverpool L24 1XD. Tel: 0844 800 4799 (Infoline), 0151 427 7231.

One of the most famous Tudor manors in Britain, with rich interiors, fine gardens and an estate. Intriguing period interior: discover the secret priest's hole and 'thunderbox' toilet. Countryside walks, with panoramic views over the Mersey Basin towards North Wales. E-mail: spekehall@nationaltrust.org.uk.

20 FORTHLIN ROAD, ALLERTON www.nationaltrust.org.uk/main/w-20forthlinroadallerton

20 Forthlin Road, Allerton, Liverpool L24 1YP. Tel: 0844 800 4791 (Infoline). The childhood home of music icon Sir Paul McCartney and his brother Michael. One of the most important houses in the history of popular music. The Beatles composed and rehearsed some of their earliest songs here. Authentically furnished as it would have appeared during the 1950s and early 60s when Paul and his family lived here. Houses display of family photographs taken by Michael McCartney. Email: 20forthlinroad@nationaltrust.org.uk.

MENDIPS

Woolton, Liverpool. Tel: 0844 800 4791 (Infoline).
Childhood home of 20th-century icon John Lennon, where some of the earliest Beatles' hits were first composed. A unique insight into the life and times of John Lennon as a boy through photographs, documents and other fascinating memorabilia.

E-mail: mendips@nationaltrust.org.uk.

MR HARDMAN'S PHOTOGRAPHIC STUDIO
www.nationaltrust.org.uk/main/w-59rodneystreet

59 Rodney Street, Liverpool L1 9EX. Tel: 0151 709 6261.
A beautiful Georgian terraced house – the former studio and home of the renowned local photographer E. Chambré Hardman and a unique time capsule of Liverpool life in the mid-twentieth century. There is a small exhibition space devoted to a selection of Hardman's work and his

amazing techniques for photographing people and landscapes. Email: 59rodneystreet@nationaltrust.org.uk.

LIVERPOOL WAR MUSEUM: THE WESTERN APPROACHES
www.liverpoolwarmuseum.co.uk
Tel: 0151 227 2008. Set beneath Derby House/Exchange Flags, behind the town hall, the visitor can relive the times of 1940s Britain with an insight into the life and work of the Wrens and WAAFs working under constant pressure in the original area command headquarters for the Battle of the Atlantic. Now open to the public, you can visit the reconstruction of the 50,000sq ft labyrinth of original rooms, which brings a dramatic period of history vividly to life. Among the rooms you can visit are the main operations room, the Admiral's office, the teleprinter station and also a reconstructed educational centre, with Anderson shelter and bombed-out room. Visitors can see and handle genuine artefacts, such as gas masks and ration books, from the Second World War. The museum shop holds an extensive range of Western Approaches souvenirs. Also available to buy are videos and memorabilia of the Second World War.

WILLIAMSON TUNNELS HERITAGE CENTRE
www.williamsontunnels.co.uk
The Old Stableyard, Smithdown Lane, Liverpool, L7 3EE. Tel: (0151) 709 6868.
The Williamson Tunnels are a labyrinth of tunnels and underground caverns under the Edge Hill district of Liverpool. They were built in the first few decades of the 1800s under the control of a retired tobacco merchant called Joseph Williamson. The purpose of their construction is not known with any certainty. Theories range from pure philanthropy, offering work to the unemployed of the district, to religious extremism, the tunnels being an underground haven from a predicted Armageddon. Although some of the tunnels have been lost over the years, a lot of them still exist under what is now a residential area. One section of the tunnels has been cleared and renovated and is open to the public. The remaining parts of the labyrinth are closed, with many suspected tunnels yet to be rediscovered. Friends of Williamson's Tunnels is a voluntary organisation which is trying to find and excavate the whole of the system. It is a rectangle of land bordered by Mason Street, Grinfield Street, Smithdown Lane and Paddington. This is a few hundred metres from the city's land-mark Metropolitan Cathedral. E-mail: enquiries@williamsontunnels.co.uk.

WIRRAL MUSEUM www.wirral.gov.uk/ed/wirral_museum.htm
Birkenhead Town Hall, Hamilton Street, Birkenhead, L41 5BR. Tel: 0151 666 4010.
Open: Open all year Tuesday–Sunday 10am–5pm (includes all Bank Holidays). Closed Mondays.

WIRRAL TRANSPORT MUSEUM & BIRKENHEAD TRAMWAY
www.wirraltransportmuseum.org
1 Taylor Street, Birkenhead, CH41 1BG. Tel: 0151 647 2128.
Birkenhead is a town packed with transport heritage. It is the home of
Cammell Laird's shipyard and the European tramway. George Francis
Train chose Birkenhead for the first European tramway back in 1860. He
agreed that if the tramway was unsuccessful, he would return
Birkenhead's streets to their original state with his own money. Luckily the
tramway was a success and operated until 1937, when the petrol motor bus
took hold. The Starbuck factory on Cleveland Street built approximately
3,000 trams between 1862 and 1913. Trams were made for the UK market
and for export. The Manx Electric Railway and Snaefell Mountain Railway
are both still using vehicles built in Birkenhead. Trams still operate on the
streets of Birkenhead; the main service trams were built in Hong Kong in
1992 to a 1948 pattern. However, a genuine 1901 Birkenhead Tramways
tram of the Merseyside Tramway Preservation Society can be seen in
service on special days. The Merseyside Tramway Preservation Society has
a number of local trams, both electric and horse-drawn. Pictures of the electric trams at Taylor Street tram depot are included under the 'vehicles'
page, while further information about the group and its trams can be found
on their webpage.

Wirral Museums Historic Vehicle Collection is housed at Wirral
Transport Museum, showing a selection of vintage buses representing a
variety of local operators. There is also a display of cars and motorcycles
and a 1930s garage scene. The 26-foot model railway layout is always the
centre of attention. As well as operating trams, Wirral Museums are also a
bus operator. Using a London Routemaster they provide transport for
school children to visit the various historic sites on the Wirral peninsula.
Operations increase when special events require additional public transport. The museum's resident vintage buses may be seen providing a free
service connecting the tramway at Woodside Ferry terminal and Egerton
Bridge, Seacombe Ferry terminal and Seacombe Aquarium.

Key artists and exhibits: Wirral Heritage Transport Collection; Taylor
Street Model Railway; Baxter Collection; George Francis Train; Starbuck
factory; Merseyside Tramway Preservation Society; 201 Bus Group; Wirral
Transport Library and Archives. Open: Sat–Sun 1pm–5pm; Easter, Whit
and Summer school holidays, open all week 1pm–5pm. Group visits
welcome by arrangement, outside of normal opening hours. Closed:
Mondays and Tuesdays. E-mail: birkenheadtram@tiscali.co.uk.

THE NATIONAL WATERWAYS MUSEUM ELLESMERE PORT
www.nwm.org.uk/ellesmere
South Pier Road, Ellesmere Port, Cheshire, CH65 4FW. Tel: 0151 355 5017.
Making the most of its canal-port origins, at Ellesmere Port you can see
many items from the inland waterways collection as they would have been
originally placed and used. Examples from the historic boat collection are

available to view in the canal, Porters' Row details what the dock worker's cottages would have been like from 1833 to the 1950s, equipment in the blacksmith's forge is still used to create ironwork and the engines in the Power Hall reveal what was needed to make the canal port function. Within the main gallery, the Island Warehouse, patterns and tools illustrate how boats used to be constructed and on the upper floor you can see the type of material which used to be transported on our waterways and hear stories of people who lived and worked on the canals. E-mail: ellesmere-port@thewaterwaystrust.org.uk.

BIRKENHEAD PRIORY & ST MARY'S TOWER
www.wirral.gov.uk/ed/birkenhead_priory.htm
Birkenhead Priory & St Mary's Tower, Priory Street, Birkenhead, L41 5JH. Tel: 0151 666 1249. Open: summer: Wednesday–Friday 1pm–5pm, Saturday and Sunday 10am–5pm; winter: Wednesday–Friday 12noon–4pm, Saturday and Sunday 10am–4pm. Also open Bank Holidays Other times by appointment only.

CROXTETH HALL & COUNTRY PARK www.croxteth.co.uk
Croxteth Hall & Country Park, Croxteth Hall Lane, Liverpool, L12 0HB. Tel: 0151 228 5311.
Open: From Easter daily 10.30am–5pm. Closed: October–Easter.

University of Liverpool

VICTORIA GALLERY AND MUSEUM www.liv.ac.uk/vgm
Ashton Street, off Brownlow Hill, University of Liverpool, Liverpool, L69 3DR. Tel: 0151 794 2348. Open: Monday–Saturday, 10am–5pm.
The Tate Hall Museum, a large Gothic-style hall on the second floor, show-cases material from wide-ranging university museum collections. Highlighting the innovation and excitement of academic discovery and the history of teaching, the collection includes a number of objects relating to innovation and research in areas such as anaesthesia, dentistry, archae-ology, zoology, engineering and oceanography. Exhibits include sea creatures and animal skeletons from an early twentieth-century zoology museum, fossils of footprints from extinct dinosaur ancestors, a display of calculators from the nineteenth century to the present day and X-rays from the beginning of X-ray technology.

UNIVERSITY OF LIVERPOOL, MUSEUM OF ARCHAEOLOGY, CLASSICS AND EGYPTOLOGY
www.liv.ac.uk/sacos/facilities/museum.html
14 Abercromby Square, Liverpool, L69 3BX. Tel: 0151 794 2467.
The Garstang Museum of Archaeology, in the School of Archaeology, Classics and Egyptology is named in honour of Professor John Garstang, whose excavations in Egypt, Sudan and the Levant produced the majority

of the archaeological collections. From 1904–1914 Garstang's work at the cemeteries of Beni Hassan, Esna and Abydos in Upper Egypt produced a wealth of objects from burials of all periods of Egyptian civilisation, while his work at Nagada and Hierakonpolis, also in Upper Egypt, is critical for our understanding of the earliest phase of Egyptian history. The Garstang Museum also contains objects which came from his work outside Egypt, from Meroe in the Sudan, Jericho in the Levant, and Sakje Geuzi in Anatolia. The museum displays some of the key objects in the collection, which also indicate the key areas of strength in teaching and research in the School – Egyptology, Classical Studies and Prehistoric and Near Eastern Archaeology. The Garstang Museum can be found on the first floor of the school at 14 Abercromby Square, Liverpool. The museum is normally open on Wednesday afternoons (1.30pm–4pm) in term time, and all day (9.30am–5pm) on the first Friday of every month. Other times by appointment. The entrance is at the rear of the building through a wrought-iron gate from Chatham Street. E-mail: winkerpa@liv.ac.uk.

CATALYST SCIENCE CENTRE AND MUSEUM, WIDNES www.catalyst.org.uk
Mersey Road, Widnes, Cheshire, WA8 0DF. Tel: 0151 420 1121. Fax: 0151 495 2030.
This is the only science centre (and museum) solely devoted to chemistry and how the products of chemistry are used in every day life – from medicines to Meccano. The key aim is to inform people of all ages about chemistry, industry and its role in our lives, past, present and future. Holdings include an extensive collection of (mostly local) photographs, the Peter Spence archive, the entire ICI General Chemicals Division research archive and much research done by the original Museum Project regarding the chemical industry in the North-West. There are also several ad hoc documents prepared for various enquiries over the years, plus the J.W. Towers and Co. Ltd archive, which is in the process of being catalogued.

THE BEATLES STORY www.beatlesstory.com
The Beatles Story, Britannia Vaults, Albert Dock, Liverpool, L3 4AD. Tel: 0151 709 1963.
Located within Liverpool's historic Albert Dock, the Beatles Story is a unique visitor attraction covering an atmospheric journey into the life, times, culture and music of the Beatles. E-mail: info@beatlesstory.com.

PRESCOT MUSEUM www.prescotmuseum.org.uk
34 Church Street, Prescot, Knowsley, L34 3LA. Tel: 0151 430 7787.
Open: Mondays by appointment, Tues–Sat 10am–1pm, 2pm–5pm, Sun 2pm–5pm. Closed on public holidays.

ST HELENS LIBRARY & INFORMATION SERVICE
www.sthelens.gov.uk
St Helens Central Library, The Gamble Building, Victoria Square, St Helens, WA10 1DY. Tel: 01744 456954.
Open: Mon and Wed 9.30am–8pm, Tues, Thurs, Fri 9.30am–5pm, Sat 10am–1pm. Closed: Sat after 1pm, Sun, Christmas and New Year.

NORTH WEST MUSEUM OF ROAD TRANSPORT
www.hallstreetdepot.info
The Old Bus Depot, Hall Street, St.Helens, WA10 1DU. Tel: 01744 451681.
A unique and extensive collection of vintage buses, British trolleybuses and classic cars in the UK are the centrepiece of this regional transport museum formerly known as St Helens Transport Museum. Following its extensive and comprehensive refurbishment the North West Museum of Road Transport has joined the ranks of the top North West attractions and is open to the public every Saturday and Sunday. E-mail: information@hall-streetdepot.info.

WORLD OF GLASS www.worldofglass.com
World of Glass, Chalon Way East, St Helens, WA10 1BX. Tel:01744 22766.
Open: For visitors the centre is open Tuesday to Sunday, 10am–5pm and Bank Holidays. Group bookings for evening visits are available on request.

Field Trips/Heritage Walks

SLAVERY HISTORY TRAIL
www.liverpoolmuseums.org.uk/maritime/trail/trail_accessible.asp
From around 1740 and until abolition, Liverpool was Britain's main slaving power. Thousands of ships travelled to Africa, where they loaded up with slaves and transported them to the Americas. There they were sold and luxury goods such as cotton, sugar, coffee and rum were bought with the proceeds, for sale on return to Britain. The fortunes of many Liverpool-based merchants and investors were effectively made by the trade, and the legacy can still be seen today around the city centre, whether in street names, in the carving on buildings, or in the existence of the buildings themselves. This map tours some of the more visible examples you can see as you walk around the city.

ALBERT DOCK HISTORY TRAIL
www.diduknow.info/docks/trail2.html
Printable sheets that enable you to explore this historic area.

HISTORY OF PUBLIC HEALTH
Morris, Maggi & Ashton, J. *The Pool of Life: A public health walk in Liverpool*, 1997. The history of public health told through key buildings and people, arranged in a number of guided walks.

MERSEYGUIDES www.showmeliverpool.co.uk

Highly trained tourist guides are ready to walk, talk, and tour to make your visit even more enjoyable and fascinating. Walks: there are regular walking tours taken by Blue and Green badge guides to suit many interests. For a full list call at the Tourist Information Centres at John Lennon airport, Anchor Court at the Albert Dock, or in the city centre at the 08 Place in Whitechapel, opposite the Met Quarter shopping mall. On the Bus: there is an open-top bus service around the city with live commentary by a guide. Private tours: Some guides have their own vehicles licensed and insured to carry small groups. Those who are qualified are shown in the Guides List. Contact: discuss your plans and requirements, they can build a tour or walk to suit your party. E-mail: welcome@showmeliverpool.co.uk or phone 01928 566969.

DUCK TOURS: THE WACKER QUACKER

These are two Second World War DUKW amphibious landing craft that the Yellow Duckmarine company has rebuilt, updated and turned into 30-seat sightseeing vehicles. Wacker Quacker 1 and Wacker Quacker 2, as they are named, have been operating tours from the Albert Dock since April 2001 and between them they provide up to 11 tour departures most days from 11am. This unique road and water adventure provides knowledge, excitement and interest for all ages. On the road, Ducks travel a circular route along Liverpool's historic waterfront and through the city, taking in the major sights including the Pier Head, Royal Liver Building, St George's Hall, the cathedrals, Chinatown and many other places of interest. On returning to the Albert Dock the vehicles dramatically drive straight from the road down the main slipway and into the Salthouse Dock – the famous Duck Splashdown! On the water the tour continues through the nineteenth-century south docks, via Wapping and Queens Docks to Coburg Dock and then back to circle the Albert Dock itself before returning to the start point. There is a live tour commentary throughout each tour, which is delivered by very knowledgeable crews. DUKWs were built in the USA by General Motors and started life in the mid-1940s as military ship-to-shore transports. Many were used in the D-Day landings and in other wartime theatres. They remained in service with the British and other armies into the 1960s. Liverpool's DUKWs have been extensively rebuilt, fitted with new diesel engines and updated where necessary to meet current road and water regulations. On the road they are considered to be a 30-seat bus, and on the water a Class V passenger vessel. The company is therefore heavily regulated, by both the road transport and maritime agencies. Tickets are on sale to individuals from the ticket office in Anchor Courtyard, Albert Dock, and by telephone on 0151 708 7799. Pre-booking is advised to avoid disappointment. The ticket office and shop is at: 32 Anchor Courtyard, Albert Dock, Liverpool L3 4AS. Open: 10am–5pm.

MAGICAL MYSTERY TOURS www.cavern-liverpool.co.uk

The magical mystery tour is one of the most popular tours around Liverpool. Stopping off at many of the Beatles' homes, schools and birth-places it shows you round famous spots. Strawberry Fields, Penny Lane and many other landmarks made famous by the Fab Four are all stop-off points. At the end of the two-hour tour you are dropped at the famous Cavern Club. The tour goes daily and starts at the famous Beatles Story. The price of the tour is £10.95 per person. For further information please call 0871 222 1963.

Appendix Six

RECOMMENDED READING

Main histories of Liverpool

Belcham, J. (Ed.), *Liverpool 800: Culture, Character & History*, Liverpool University Press, 2006.

Chandler, G., *Liverpool*, Batsford, London, 1957.

Aughton, P., *Liverpool – A People's History*, Carnegie, 1991.

Belcham, J., *Merseypride: Essays in Liverpool Exceptionalism*, second ed., Liverpool University Press, 2006.

Eighteenth/nineteenth-century works on the history of Liverpool

Enfield, W., *An Essay towards the History of Liverpool*, 1773.

James Wallace, *A History of the Ancient and Present State of Liverpool*, 1795.

—— *Liverpool and Its Environs*, **(A Liverpool Guide Book), 1795.**

—— *Stranger in Liverpool*, **(Visitors' guide book, several editions), 1800–1840.**

Troughton, T., *History of Liverpool*, 1810.

Baines, E., *History, Directory, and Gazetteer of the County Palatine of Lancaster*, 1825.

Gregson, M., *Portfolio of Fragments of Lancashire*, ed. Harland, J., 1869.

Smithers, H., *Liverpool – its Commerce, Statistics & Institutions*, London, 1825.

Herdman, W.G., *Pictorial Relics of Ancient Liverpool*, 1847.

Aspinall, Rev. James, *'Liverpool a Few Years Since' by An Old Stager*, Liverpool, 1852.

Baines, T., *History of Liverpool*, 1852.

Brooke, R., *Liverpool During the Last Quarter of the 18th Century*, 1853.

Stonehouse, *Recollections of Old Liverpool by a Nonagenarian*, Liverpool, 1863.

Picton, Sir J.A., *Memorials of Liverpool*, Vol. I & II, 1875.

—— *City of Liverpool Municipal Archives*, Vol. I, 1883, Vol. II, 1886.

Peet, H., *Two Centuries' Records of Liverpool Parish: Our Poor Law History*, Liverpool, 1898.
Irvine, W.F., *Liverpool in Charles I's Time*, 1899.

Twentieth century

Hope, E.W. (Ed.), *City of Liverpool; Handbook compiled for the Congress of the Royal Institute of Public Health 1903*, Liverpool, 1903.
Farrer, W. & Brownbill, J., *Victoria County History of Lancashire*, 1906.
Muir, R. & Platt, E.M., *A History of Municipal Government in Liverpool*, 1906.
Peet, H., *Liverpool in the Reign of Queen Anne*, 1908.
Touzeau, J., *The Rise and Progress of Liverpool from 1551 to 1835*, 1910.
Pike, W.T., *Liverpool and Birkenhead in the 20th Century*, Brighton, 1911.
Young, H.S. & H.E., *Bygone Liverpool*, 1913.
Twemlow, J.A., *Liverpool Town Books*, Vol. I, 1918, Vol. II, 1935.
Bickerton, T.H., *A Medical History of Liverpool*, Liverpool, 1936.
Lumby, J., 'The Norris Deeds', Chetham Society Vol. 9, 1939.
Chandler G. & Saxton, E.B., *Liverpool under James I*, 1960.
Chandler, G. & Wilson, E.K., *Liverpool under Charles I*, 1965.
Millington, R., *The House in the Park*, Liverpool C.C., 1957.
Jackson, W.C.M., *Herdman's Liverpool*, 1968.
Harris, J.R. (Ed.), *Liverpool and Merseyside: Essays in the Economic and Social of the Port and its Hinterland*, Cass, 1969.
Hyde, F.E. (Ed.), *Liverpool and the Mersey: an Economic History of a Port 1700–1970*, David & Charles, 1971.
Bagley, J.J., *A History of Lancashire*, Phillimore, 1972.
Channon, Howard, *Portrait of Liverpool*, Hale, London, 1970.
Midwinter, E., *Old Liverpool*, London, 1971.
Liverpool Heritage Bureau (Ed.), *Buildings of Liverpool*, Liverpool, 1978.
Liverpool Heritage Bureau (Ed.), *Liverpool Conservation Areas*, 1982.
Waller, P.J., *Democracy & Sectarianism – A Political and Social History of Liverpool 1868–1939*, Liverpool University Press, 1981.
Pye, Ken, *Discover Liverpool*, Trinity, 2007.
McIntyre-Brown, Arabella & Woodland, Guy, *Liverpool, the First 1,000 Years*, Garlic Press, 2001.

Local areas

Hatton, P., *The History of Hale*, second ed., 1978.
Hollinshead, J., 'Halewood Township: A Community in the Early Eighteenth Century' in *Transactions of the Historic Society of Lancashire and Cheshire*, Vol. 130, 1981.
King, A., *Huyton & Roby – A History of Two Townships*, Knowsley Libraries, 1984.

Lally, J. & Gnosspelius, J., *History of Much Woolton*, Woolton Society, 1975.

Nicholson, S., 'Farming on a South Lancashire Estate 1066–1795: evidence from Speke Hall' in *Journal of the Merseyside Archaeological Society*, Vol 3., 1979.

Stewart-Brown, R., *A History of the Manor and Township of Allerton, Liverpool*, 1911.

Archaeological Survey of Merseyside, *The Changing Face of Liverpool*, University of Liverpool, 1981.

Cooper, J.G. & Power, A.D., *A History of West Derby*, Ormskirk, 1982.

—— *The People of West Derby*, Liverpool, 1985.

Whale, D., *The Lost Villages of Liverpool Vols 1–3*, Liverpool, 1984.

Wilkinson, C., *The Streets of Liverpool, & More Streets of Liverpool*, Liverpool, 1989.

Griffiths, R., *The History of the Royal and Ancient Park of Toxteth*, 1907.

Saunders-Jones, *Leaves from My Note Book: Interesting Items concerning the Ancient Historic District of Garston*, Liverpool, 1926.

Stonor, J., *Liverpool's Hidden Story*, Liverpool, 1957.

Swift, J.M., *The Story of Garston and its Church*, Liverpool, 1937.

Pinnington, J., *Photographs of Aigburth 1873–1906*, Liverpool Record Office. (102 photographs including extensive coverage of Stanlawe Grange taken by this former occupant.)

Waite, J., *Historic Houses of Liverpool 1888–1921*, Liverpool Record Office. (3 volumes of photographs – Vol.1 covers Aigburth.)

Philpott, R.A., *Historic Towns of the Merseyside Area*, Liverpool Museum Occasional Papers No. 3, 1988.

Horton, Steven, *Street Names of the City of Liverpool*, Countyvise, 2002.

Work and economy

Rise of the nineteenth-century port: salt

Ashton, T. & Sykes, J., *The Coal Industry of the Eighteenth Century*, 1959.

Barker, T.C., 'The Sankey Navigation – The First Lancashire Canal' in *THSLC*, Vol. 100, 1948.

—— 'Lancashire Coal, Cheshire Salt and the Rise of Liverpool' in *THSLC*, Vol.103, 1951.

Calvert, A.F., *Salt in Cheshire*, London, 1915.

Chaloner, W., 'Salt in Cheshire 1600–1870' in *Transactions of the Lancashire and Cheshire Antiquarian Society*, 1961.

Crump, W.B., 'Saltways From the Cheshire Wiches' in *Transactions of the Lancashire and Cheshire Antiquarian Society*, Vol.54, 1939.

Langton, R., *Geographical Change and the Industrial Revolution: Coal-Mining in South West Lancashire 1590–1799*, Cambridge University Press, 1979.

Nef, J., *The Rise of the British Coal Industry*, 1932.

Wallwork, K., 'The Mid-Cheshire Salt Industry' in *Geography*, 1959.

Rochester, M. (compiler), *Salt in Cheshire*, Cheshire Libraries and Museum Education Resources Library.

Raistrick, A., *Industrial Archaeology*, London, reprinted 1986.

Willan, T.S., 'The Navigation of the River Weaver in the Eighteenth Century', *Chetham Society Transactions*, Vol.3, third series, 1951.

Forshaw, R. (Ed.), 'Hale Cliff Wharf', *North Western Society for Industrial Archaeology and History – Interim Survey and Excavation Report*, Liverpool, February 1990.

Slave trade and West Indian immigration

Liverpool History

Cameron G. & Cooke S., *'Liverpool – Capital of the Slave Trade'*, Picton Press, 1992.

Anstey, P. & Hair, P.E.H., *'Liverpool, the African Slave Trade and Abolition'*, Historical Society of Lancashire and Cheshire, 1976.

Richardson, D., Schwarz, S. and Tibbles, A. (Eds.), *Liverpool and Transatlantic Slavery*, 2007.

Midgley, Clare, *Women Against Slavery: The British Campaigns, 1780–1870*, Routledge, 1995.

Murphy, Andrea, *From the Empire to the Rialto: Racism and reaction in Liverpool, 1918–1948*, Birkenhead, 1995.

Nassy Brown, Jacqueline, *Dropping anchor, setting sail: Geographies of race in Black Liverpool*, Princeton, 2004.

Phillips, Caryl, *The Atlantic sound*, London, 2000.

Frost, Diane, *Work and community among West African migrant workers since the nineteenth century*, Liverpool, 1999.

Lord Gifford, Wally Brown and Bundey, Ruth, *Loosen the shackles: First report of the Liverpool 8 inquiry into race relations in Liverpool*, London, 1989.

Costello, Raymond, *Black Liverpool: The early history of Britain's oldest black community, 1730–1918*, Liverpool, 2001.

Contextual history

Fryer, Peter, *Staying Power: The History of Black People in Britain: Black People in Britain Since 1504*, 1984.

Dabydeen, David (Ed.), Gilmore, John, Jones, Cecily, *The Oxford Companion to Black British History*, Oxford University Press, 2008.

Phillips, Trevor & Phillips, Mike, *Windrush: The Irresistible Rise of Multiracial Britain*, Harper Collins, London, 1999.

Walvin, James, *Black Ivory: Slavery in the British Empire*, 2001.

Morgan, Kenneth, *Slavery, Atlantic trade and the British economy, 1660–1800*, Cambridge, 2000.

Walvin, James, *Making the Black Atlantic: Britain and the African diaspora*, London, 2000.

Industry/Manufacturing

Anderton, B.L. & Stoney, P. (Eds.), *Commerce, Industry and Transport: Studies in Economic Change on Merseyside*, Liverpool University Press, 1983.

Ashmore, O., *The Industrial Archaeology of Lancashire*, David & Charles, 1970.

Barker, T.C. & Harris, J.R., *A Merseyside Town in the Industrial Revolution: St Helens 1750–1900*, Liverpool University Press, 1954.

Hardie, D.W., *A History of the Chemical Industry in Widnes*, 1950.

Harris, J.R. (Ed.), *Liverpool and Merseyside: Essays in the Economic and Social of the Port and its Hinterland*, Cass, 1969.

Hyde, F.E. (Ed.), *Liverpool and the Mersey: an Economic History of a Port 1700–1970*, David & Charles, 1971.

Millward, R., *Lancashire, an Illustrated History of the Landscape*, Hodder & Stoughton, 1955.

Musson, A.E., *Enterprise in Soap and Chemicals: Joseph Crossfield and Sons Ltd 1815–1965*, Manchester University Press, 1965.

Parkinson, C.N., *The Rise of the Port of Liverpool*, 1952.

Starkey, H.F., *Schooner Port: Two Centuries of Upper Mersey Sail*, W. & A. Hesketh, Ormskirk, 1983.

Wadsworth, A.P. and De Lacy Mann, J., *The Cotton Trade and Industrial Lancashire 1600-1780*, Manchester University Press, reprinted 1965.

Shipbuilding

Warren, Kenneth, *Steel, ships and men: Cammell Laird, 1824–1993*, Liverpool, 1998.

Roberts, David, *Life at Lairds: Memories of working shipyard men*, Wirral, 1992.

General

Burton, A., *The Rise and Fall of British Shipbuilding*, London, 1994.

Ritchie, L.A., *The Shipbuilding Industry – A Guide to Historical Records*, Manchester University Press, 1992.

Ville, S. (Ed.), *Shipbuilding in the United Kingdom in the 19th Century: A Regional Approach*, Research in Maritime History, No.4., IMEHA/National Museums Liverpool, 1993.

Moss, Michael & Hume, John R., *Shipbuilder to the world: 125 years of Harland and Wolff, Belfast 1861–1986*, Belfast, 1986.

Pollard, Sidney & Robertson, Paul, *The British shipbuilding industry, 1870–1914*, Cambridge, MA, 1979.

Johnman, Lewis & Murphy, Hugh, *British shipbuilding and the state since 1918: A political economy of decline*, Exeter.

Shipping Lines and Seamen

Chandler, G., *Liverpool Shipping*, Liverpool, 1960.

McCarron, K. & Jarvis, A., *Give a Dock a Good Name?*, Countyvise, 1992.

Burton, V., *Liverpool Shipping, Trade & Industry*, National Museums and Galleries on Merseyside, 1989.

Jarvis, A., *Prince's Dock*, Countyvise, 1991.

Richie-Noakes, N., *Liverpool's Historic Waterfront*.

Stewart-Brown, R., *Liverpool Ships in the Eighteenth Century*, 1932.

Whale, Derek, *The Liners of Liverpool*, Countyvise, 1986.

Lane, Tony, *Liverpool: City of the Sea*, Liverpool University Press, 1997. (N.B. an update and revision of *Liverpool: Gateway of Empire*, Lawrence and Wishart, 1987.)

Milne, Graeme J., *Trade and Traders in Mid-Victorian Liverpool: Mercantile Business and the Making of a World Port*, Liverpool University Press, 2000.

Cubbin, Graeme, *Harrisons of Liverpool: A Chronicle of Ships and Men 1830–2002*, The World Ship Society, 2003.

Hyde, F.E., *A History of Blue Funnel*.

Behrend, A., *Portrait of a Family Firm*, Bahr Behrend, Shipping Agent.

Ayers, Pat, *The Liverpool Docklands: Life and work in Athol Street*, Birkenhead, 1999.

The Bibby Line, *The Bibby Line; 175 years of achievement*, (company publication), 1982.

Heaton, Paul, *Lamport & Holt Line*, 2004.

Estate and agriculture

Farrer, W. (Ed.), *Victoria County History of Lancashire Vol.III*, 1907.

Royden, M.W., *The Effects of Enclosure: Halewood Township by the Mid Nineteenth Century*, Liverpool University B.A. thesis – unpublished, 1989. (Held in Knowsley RO and Halewood Library.)

Lewis, J.M., *The Medieval Earthworks of the Hundred of West Derby*, PhD thesis, University of Nottingham, 1991. (Copy held at Liverpool University.)

Royden, M.W., *The Moated Sites of Halewood*. (See www.roydenhistory.co.uk.)

Stewart-Brown, R., 'The Townfield of Liverpool' in *THSLC*, Vol.68, 1916.

Hollinshead, J., *The People of S.W. Lancashire During the Second Half of the Sixteenth Century*, unpublished PhD thesis, Sydney Jones Library University of Liverpool, 1986.

—— *Halewood Township during the first quarter of the eighteenth century*, M.Phil thesis, Liverpool University, 1980.

Cowell, R., *Knowsley Rural Fringes Survey (Field Archaeology, Nat Museums on Merseyside)*

Hoult, J., *Early Highways and Byways of West Derby Hundred*, 1923.

Lumby, J., 'The Norris Deeds' in *Chetham Society*, Vol. 93, 1939.

Booth, P., 'From Medieval Park to Puritan Republic' in Crosby.A. (ed.) 'Lancashire Local Studies', 1993.

—— 'The Background, People and Place' in *Sefton Park*, 1984.

Lewis, J., 'Medieval Landscapes and Estates' in *JMAS*, Vol. 7, 1991. (For 1986/7.)

Cunliffe-Shaw, R., *A History of the Royal Forest of Lancaster*, 1956.

Gregson, M., *Portfolio of Fragments of Lancashire*, (ed. Harland, J. 1869)

Saunders-Jones, R., *Ancient Liverpool (Old Liverpool Industries)*, 1924.

Boult, J., 'The Historical Topography of Aigburth and Garston' in *THSLC*, Vol.20, 1868.

King, A., *Huyton & Roby - A History of Two Townships*, Liverpool, 1984.

Lally, J.E. & Gnosspelius, J.B., *History of Much Woolton*, Liverpool, 1975.

Cox, E.W., 'Some Account of Garston, and of the Ancient Chapel of St. Michael formerly existing there' in *THSLC*, Vol.40, 1888. (New Series Vol.4.)

Youd, G., 'The Common Fields of Lancashire' in *THSLC*, Vol.113.

Stewart-Brown, R., *A History of the Manor and Township of Allerton*, 1911.

Griffiths, R., *A History of the Royal and Ancient Park of Toxteth*, 1907.

Walker, F., *Historical Geography of S.W. Lancashire before the Industrial Revolution*, Vol.103, Chetham Society new series, Manchester, 1939.

Davis, C.S., *Agricultural History of Cheshire 1750–1850*, Manchester, Chetham Society, 1960.

Transport

Roads

Harrison, W., 'The Development of the Turnpike System in Lancashire and Cheshire' in *Transactions of the Lancashire and Cheshire Antiquarian Society*, Vol.IV, 1886.

—— 'Pre-Turnpike Highways in Lancashire and Cheshire' in *Transactions of the Lancashire and Cheshire Antiquarian Society*, Vol.IX, 1891.

Bailey, F.,'The Minutes of the Trustees of the Turnpike Roads from Liverpool to Prescot, St. Helens, Warrington, Ashton-in-Makerfield, 1726–89' in *THSLC*, Vol.88, 1936 and Vol.89, 1937.

Hoult, J., *Early Highways and Byways of West Derby Hundred*, St Helens & Prescot Reporter Booklet, 1923. (From article in *THSLC*.)

Tupling, G.H., 'The Turnpike Trusts of Lancashire' in *Memoirs and Proceedings of the Manchester Literary and Philosophical Society*, Vol.94, 1952–3.

Horses and carters

Wooding, Harry, *Liverpool's working horses*, Liverpool, 1991.

Clark, Edward N., *The carthorse and the quay: The story of the Liverpool cart horses*, Garstang, 1989.

Smith, Paul, 'A proud Liverpool union – The Liverpool and District Carters and Motormen's Union, 1889–1946' in *Historical Studies in Industrial Relations*, Vol.16, 2003, pp.1–38.

Dampier, A. J., *Kingdom of the horse*, 1987.

Canals

Barker, T.C., 'The Sankey Navigation – The First Lancashire Canal' in *THSLC*, Vol.100, 1948.

Clarke, Mike, *The Leeds and Liverpool Canal: A History and Guide*, Carnegie, 1990.

McIntyre, W., 'The First Scheme for Docks at Birkenhead and the Proposed Canal Across Wirral' in *THSLC*, Vol.124, 1972.

Willan, T.S., 'The Navigation of the River Weaver in the Eighteenth Century' in *Chetham Society Transactions*, Vol. 3, third series, 1951.

Canals – general

Hadfield, C., *The Canal Age*, David & Charles, 1968.

—— *British Canals, an Illustrated History*, 5th edition, 1974.

Mullineux, F., *The Duke of Bridgewater's Canal*, 1959.

Porteous, J.D., *Canal Ports: the Urban Achievement of the Canal Age*, Academic Press, 1977.

Smith, P., *Discovering Canals in Britain*, Shire, 1981.

Willan, T.S., *River Navigation in England 1600–1750*, Cass, 1964.

Railways

Bankes, J.M., 'A Nineteenth-Century Colliery Railway' in *THSLC*, Vol.114, 1962.

Bolger, P., *Illustrated History of The Cheshire Lines Committee*, 1984.

Carlson, R.E., *The Liverpool and Manchester Railway Project*, 1972.

Clarke, J. & Patmore, J.A., *Railway History in Pictures: North West England*, 1968.

Donaghy, T.J., *Liverpool and Manchester Railway Operations*, 1973.

Dendy Marshall, D., *Centenary History of the Liverpool and Manchester Railway*, 1930.

Greville, M.D., 'Chronological List of the Railways of Cheshire' in *THSLC*, Vol.105, 1954.

Holt, G., *A Short History of the Liverpool and Manchester Railway*, Railway & Canal Historical Society, 1965.

—— *Regional History of the railways of Great Britain*, Vol.10.

Nock, O.S., The North Western, 1968.

Prys Griffiths, R., *The Cheshire Lines Railway*, 1947.

Royden, M.W., *The Impact of the Coming of the Railway on 19th Century Halewood*, B.A.(Hons.) dissertation Liverpool University, 1989. (Copies lodged at Halewood, Huyton and Liverpool Central Libraries.)

Singleton, D., *Liverpool and Manchester Railway*, Dalesman, 1975.

Smith, L.J., 'The Impact of the Liverpool and Manchester Railway on a South Lancashire Township: Newton-le-Willows 1821–1851' in *THSLC*, Vol.129, 1979.

Steel, W., *A History of the L.N.W.R.*, 1914.

Thomas, R.H.G., *The Liverpool and Manchester Railway*, Batsford, 1980.

Veitch, G.S., *The Struggle for The Liverpool & Manchester Railway*, 1930.

Ferneyhough, F., *Liverpool and Manchester Railway 1830–1980*, 1980.

Walker, J.S., 'Accurate Description of the Liverpool and Manchester Railway' in *TLCAS*, 1968.

Spiegl, F., *A Picture History of The Liverpool and Manchester Railway*, Scouse Press, Liverpool Packet No.4, 1971.

Anderson, Paul, *An Illustrated History of Liverpool's Railways*, 1996.

Tramways

Horne, J.B. and Maund, T.B., *Liverpool transport*, four volumes, London, 1975–89.

Passenger Transport Department, *Liverpool Corporation electric tramways*, 1904.

Jarvis, Adrian, *Transport in Liverpool*, Ian Allan Publishing, 2001.

Overhead railway

Gahan, John W., *Seventeen Stations to Dingle: Liverpool Overhead Railway Remembered*, Countyvise, 1982.

Bolger, Paul, *Docker's Umbrella: History of Liverpool Overhead Railway*, The Bluecoat Press, 1992.

Local airport/airfields

Butler, Phil, *Liverpool Airport: An illustrated history*, Stroud, 2004.

Bowdler, Roger et al, *Berlin-Tempelhof, Liverpool-Speke, Paris-Le Bourget*, Paris, 2000.

Black Spot on the Mersey/The House in the Park

Urban development

Belchem, J (Ed.), 'Living in Liverpool' and 'City of change and challenge' in *Liverpool 800*, Liverpool, 2006.

Burnett, J., *A social history of housing, 1815–1985*, London, 1986.

Tarn, J., *Five percent philanthropy: An account of housing in urban areas between 1840 and 1914*, Cambridge, 1973.

Sharples, J., *Liverpool*, New Haven, 2004.

—— *Merchant Palaces: Liverpool and Wirral Mansions*, Bluecoat Press, 2007. (Photographed by Bedford Lemere.)

Couch, Chris, *City of change and challenge: Urban planning and regeneration in Liverpool*, Aldershot, 2003.

Kerr, Madeline, *The people of Ship Street*, London, 1958.

Muchnick, D., *Urban renewal in Liverpool*, London, 1970.

Munck, Ronaldo (Ed.), *Reinventing the city? Liverpool in comparative perspective*, Liverpool, 2003.

Taylor, I., 'The court and cellar dwelling: The eighteenth-century origin of the Liverpool slum' in *THSLC*, Vol.122, 1970, pp.67–90.

Vereker, Charles and Barron Mays, John, *Urban redevelopment and social change: A study of social conditions in central Liverpool, 1955–56*, Liverpool, 1961.

Cormack, Margaret, Cook, Kathleen and Morley, Deirdre, *Liverpool housing: Facts and figures*, Liverpool, 1981.

Liverpool Corporation Housing Department, *City of Liverpool housing, 1937*, Liverpool, 1937.

City of Liverpool, *Artizans' and labourers' dwellings*, Liverpool, 1908.

Stewart-Brown, R., *A History of the Manor and Township of Allerton*, Liverpool, 1911.

Barker, E., *In and Around Broadgreen*, 1991.

Millington, R., *The House in the Park*, Liverpool Corporation, 1957.

Hope, E.W., *City of Liverpool; Handbook compiled for the Congress of the Royal Institute of Public Health 1903*, Liverpool, 1903.

Harris, J.R. (Ed.), *Liverpool and Merseyside: Essays in the Economic and Social of the Port and its Hinterland*, Cass, 1969.

Hyde, F.E. (Ed.), *Liverpool and the Mersey: an Economic History of a Port 1700–1970*, David & Charles, 1971.

George, S., *Liverpool Park Estates: Their Legal Basis, Creation and Early Management*, Vol.17, Liverpool Historical Studies, Liverpool University Press, 1999.

Lewis, David, *Walks Through History: Liverpool*, Breedon Books, 2007.

Architecture and buildings

Liverpool Heritage Bureau, *Buildings of Liverpool*, Liverpool, 1978.

—— *Liverpool Conservation Areas*, 1982.

—— 'Liverpool: Work in progress' in a special issue of the *Architectural Review*, Vol.1331, January 2008.

De Figueiredo, Peter, 'Symbols of empire: The buildings of the Liverpool waterfront' in *Architectural History*, Vol.46, 2003, pp.229–54.

Stenhouse, D.K., 'Liverpool's office district, 1875–1905' in *THSLC*, Vol.133, 1984, pp.71–87.

Hughes, Quentin, *Seaport: Architecture and townscape in Liverpool*,1993.

Cottrell, David, *The Little Book of Liver Birds*, Breedon Books, Derby, 2006.

Hemm, Gordon, *St George's Hall, Liverpool*, Liverpool, 1949.

Parrott, Kay, *Portrait of Liverpool*, Bluecoat Press.

Giles, Colum and Hawkins, Bob, *Storehouses of Empire: Liverpool's historic warehouses*, 2004.

Giles, Colum and Goodall, Ian, *Building a Better Society: Liverpool's historic institutional buildings*, 2008.

Sharples, Joseph and Stonard, John, *Built on Commerce: Liverpool's central business district*, 2008.

Brown, Sarah, *Religion and Place: Liverpool's historic places of worship*, 2008. **Menuge, Adam**, *Ordinary Landscapes, Special Places: Anfield, Breckfield and the growth of Liverpool's suburbs*, 2008.

Parks

Twist, Colin, *A history of the Liverpool Parks*, Southport, 2000.

McInniss, Jean, *Birkenhead Park*, Birkenhead, 1984.

Channon, Howard, *A pride of parks*, Liverpool, 1974.

Crompton, John, 'The role of the proximate principle in the emergence of urban parks in the United Kingdom and in the United States' in *Leisure Studies*, Vol.26, 2007, pp.213–34.

Layton-Jones, Katy and Lee, Robert, *Places of Health and Amusement: Liverpool's Historic Parks and Gardens (Informed Conservation)*, English Heritage.

George, Susan, *Liverpool Park Estates: Their Legal Basis, Creation and Early Management*,Vol.16, Liverpool Historical Studies, 1999.

Photographic record

Wilkinson, Colin, *Liverpool from the Air*, Bluecoat Press.

—— *The Streets of Liverpool A Photographic Record*, The Bluecoat Press, 1993.

Fagan, Ged, *In a City Living – The Story of the Tenements Vols 1–3*, 2007.

Cooke, Terry, *Scotland Road 'The Old Neighbourhood'*.

O'Connor, Freddy, *It all Came Tumbling Down*.

—— *Liverpool— Our City Our Heritage*.

—— *A Pub on Every Corner*.

Hughes, Quentin, *Liverpool – City of Architecture*, Bluecoat Press.

Fallon, Bernard, *Bernard Fallon's Liverpool*, Bluecoat Press.

Poverty and the labouring poor

Blease, W.L., 'The Poor Law in Liverpool' in *THSLC*, Vol.61, 1908.
—— *The Poor Law and the Parochial Government in Liverpool 1681–1834* in **H. Peet (Ed.)**, *Liverpool Vestry Books Vol.1 1681–1799*, University of Liverpool, 1912.

Royden, Michael, W., *A History of Mill Road Hospital*, Liverpool, 1993. (West Derby Union Workhouse history, copy deposited in LRO)
—— *The 19th Century Poor Law in Liverpool and its Hinterland: Towards the Origins of the Workhouse Infirmary*, Vol. 11, Journal of the Liverpool Medical History Society, 2000.

Oxley, G.W., 'The Permanent Poor in South West Lancashire under the Old Poor Law' in *Liverpool and Merseyside*, ed. Harris, J.R., Frank Cass, London, 1969, pp.16–49.
—— 'The Administration of the Poor Law in the West Derby Hundred of Lancashire 1601–1837', M.A. thesis, University of Liverpool, 1966.

Midwinter, E.C., 'Liverpool and the New Poor Law' in *Old Liverpool*, David and Charles, 1971.

Gibson, Jeremy and Rogers, Colin, *Poor Law Union Record 2.The Midlands and Northern England*, Federation of Family History Societies, 1997.
—— *Poor Law Union Record 4. Gazetteer of England and Wales*, Federation of Family History Societies, 1997.

Taylor, I., 'The court and cellar dwelling: The eighteenth-century origin of the Liverpool slum' in *THSLC*, Vol.122, 1970, pp.67–90.

Health and Charity

Pooley, C., 'Living in Liverpool' in Belchem, J. Ed., *Liverpool 800*, Liverpool, 2006.

Porter, D., *Health, civilization, and the state: A history of public health from ancient to modern times*, London, 1999.

Procter, Margaret (Ed.), *Public health on Merseyside*, 1991. (Listing of archive and printed material.)

Allan, A., 'Caring for Records? – Records of Health Care on Merseyside as untapped resources for the historian' in *Medical Historian – Bulletin of Liverpool Medical History Society*, No.4, July 1991.

Royden, Michael W., 'The Roots of the New Liverpool Women's Hospital: The early medical care of women and babies in the late 18th/early 19th century' *Journal of the Liverpool Medical History Society*, Vol.10, 1999.
—— 'A History of Liverpool Maternity Hospital and the Women's Hospital', Liverpool, 1995.
—— 'A History of Mill Road Hospital', Liverpool, 1993.
—— *Pioneers and Perseverance: A History of the Royal School for the Blind, Liverpool, 1791–1991*, Countyvise, Birkenhead, 1991.

Morris, Maggi and Ashton, J., *The pool of life: A public health walk in Liverpool,* 1997.

Ashton, J. & Seymour, H., *The new public health: The Liverpool experience,* Milton Keynes, 1988.

Ashton, John, *The changing health of Mersey, 1948–1994,* Liverpool, 1994.

Hope, E.W., *Health at the gateway: Problems and international obligations of a seaport city,* Cambridge, 1931.

Hope, E.W. (Ed.), *City of Liverpool; Handbook compiled for the Congress of the Royal Institute of Public Health 1903,* Liverpool, 1903.

Moss, William, *A Familiar Medical Survey of Liverpool,* 1784.

Bickerton, T.H., Collected papers concerning research into a medical history of Liverpool, LRO.

—— 'A Medical History of Liverpool', Liverpool, 1936.

Simey, Margaret, 'Charity Rediscovered: A Study of Charitable Effort in Nineteenth Century Liverpool', Liverpool University Press, reprinted 1992.

Jones, Rev John, (congregational minister, Kirkdale) *'The Slain in Liverpool during 1864 by Drink (including Social, Medical and Criminal Statistics of Drunkenness)',* reprinted from *Liverpool Mercury,* 1865.

Liverpool City Council, *The Handbook of Merseyside Social Services,* (also known as the Social Worker's Yearbook, which carried hugely detailed listings of government and voluntary agencies, often with descriptions, officers and contact details; several editions are in the Local Studies Catalogue).

Miller, Anthony, *Poverty deserved? Relieving the poor in Victorian Liverpool,* Birkenhead, 1998.

Belchem, J., 'Charity, ethnicity and the Catholic parish' in Belchem, Merseypride, Liverpool, 2000/2006.

Jordan, Jane, *Josephine Butler,* London, 2001.

Pedersen, Susan, *Eleanor Rathbone and the politics of conscience,* New Haven, 2004.

Shepherd, J.A., *A History of the Liverpool Medical Institution,* Liverpool, 1979.

Murray, R.W., *Edward Alanson and His Times,* Liverpool, 1914.

Ross, Dr. J. (Ed.), Collected papers concerning Liverpool Medical History, LMI, 1976.

Ross, Dr J., 'History of the Liverpool teaching Hospitals Until 1907' in *Medical Historian,* Vol.16, 1972, p.369.

Fletcher, F.D., 'A Sketch of the Medical History of Liverpool' in *Liverpool Med-Chir Journal,* Vol.1, 1857, pp.1–147.

Dunn, C.L. (Ed.), *The Emergency Medical Services Vol II,* from the series 'A History of the Second World War – United Kingdom Medical Series', 1953.

Francis, H.H., 'A History of Obstetrics and Gynaecology in Liverpool' in *Sphincter,* Vol.17, 1955, pp.114–120.

Starkey, P. (Ed.), *Nursing Memories,* NMGM, 1994.

Mersey Regional Director of Public Health, *The Changing Health of Mersey 1948-1994*, 1994.

Miller, Patricia J., 'Malaria, Liverpool' in *An illustrated history of the Liverpool School of Tropical Medicine*, Liverpool School of Tropical Medicine, 1998.

Knowles, Lorraine, *Public health: The Liverpool School of Hygiene Museum collection*, Liverpool, 2003.

Porter, Dorothy, *Health, civilization, and the state: A history of public health from ancient to modern times*, London, 1999.

Religion and Migration: The World in One City

Belchem, J. & MacRaild, D., 'Cosmopolitan Liverpool', in **Belchem, J. Ed.**, *Liverpool 800*, Liverpool University Press, 2006.

British and Irish origins

Belchem, John, *Irish, Catholic and Scouse: The history of the Liverpool Irish, 1800–1939*, Liverpool, 2007.

Gallman, Matthew J., *Receiving Erin's children: Philadelphia, Liverpool, and the Irish famine migration, 1845–1855*, Chapel Hill, 2000.

Jones, R.M. and Rees, Ben D., *The Liverpool Welsh and their religion: Two centuries of Welsh Calvinistic Methodism*, Liverpool, 1984.

Munro, Alasdair and Sim, Duncan, *The Merseyside Scots: A study of an expatriate community*, Birkenhead, 2001.

European origins

Kolosalakis, N., *Ethnic identity and religion: Tradition and change in Liverpool Jewry*, Washington, 1982.

MacGregor, Jan, 'In search of ethnicity: Jewish and Celtic identities in Liverpool and Glasgow 1850–1900', M.Phil. thesis, University of Liverpool, 2003. (This thesis, and the following one, can be consulted in the University Library.)

Goodman, Mervyn, 'From Toxteth to Tel Aviv: The contribution of Merseyside to the establishment of the state of Israel 1880–1948', M.Phil. thesis, University of Liverpool, 2000.

Cooke, Terry, *Little Italy: A history*.

Asian origins

Wong, Maria Lin, *Chinese Liverpudlians: A history of the Chinese community in Liverpool*, Birkenhead, 1989.

Lee, Gregory B., *Chinas unlimited: Making the imaginaries of China and Chineseness*, London, 2003.

Burman, Ashok and McCarthy, Jennifer (Ed.), *Indian presence in Liverpool*, Liverpool, 2002.

Education

Procter, Margaret (Ed.), *Education on Merseyside: A guide to the sources*, 1992.
Linnell, G., 'Education in Liverpool, 1515–1870: A bibliography' *THSLC*, 1958.
Midwinter, E., 'The early years of the Liverpool School Board' in *Old Liverpool*, 1971, pp.115–130.
Tiffin, Herbert, *A history of the Liverpool Institute Schools, 1825 to 1935*, Liverpool, 1935.
Jones, Ken, *Education in Britain: 1944 to the present*, Cambridge, 2003.
Digby, Anne and Searby, Peter, *Children, school and society in nineteenth century England*, London, 1981.
Education Department, *Yesterday's schools, 1880–1980*, Liverpool, 1980.
Sadler, Michael, *Report on secondary education in Liverpool*, Liverpool, 1904.
Mays, John Barron, *Education and the urban child*, Liverpool, 1962.
Education Department, *Liverpool: The city and its schools*, Liverpool, 1969.
Kelly, Thomas, *A history of adult education in Great Britain*, Liverpool, 1970.
Evans, B., *The Training Ships of Liverpool*, Countyvise, 2002.
Charles Wootton News, **produced by the Charles Wootton Centre (later College) in the 1980s and 1990s.**
Heery, Pat, *The history of St Francis Xavier's College, Liverpool 1842–2001*, Liverpool, 2002.
Wainwright, David, *Liverpool Gentlemen – A History of Liverpool College, an Independant Day School from 1840*, Faber, 1960.
Goodacre, Kathleen A., *St Edmund's College Liverpool – a history 1898–1981*.
Harrop, Sylvia, *The Merchant Taylor's School for Girls, Crosby: One hundred years of achievement, 1888–1988*, Liverpool, 1988.
Royden, Michael, W., *Pioneers and Perseverance: A History of the Royal School for the Blind, Liverpool, 1791-1991*, Countyvise, Birkenhead, 1991.

Higher education

Elford, R. John (Ed.), *The foundation of Hope: Turning dreams into reality*, Liverpool, 2003.
Kelly, Thomas, *For advancement of learning: The University of Liverpool, 1881–1981*, Liverpool, 1981.
Harrop, Sylvia A., *Decade of change: The University of Liverpool, 1981–1991*, Liverpool, 1994.
Jones, David R., *The origins of civic universities: Manchester, Leeds and Liverpool*, London, 1988.
The University of Liverpool, *A photographic portrait, yesterday and today*, Liverpool, 1989.

Sharples, Joseph, Powers, Alan and Shippobottom, Michael, *Charles Reilly and the Liverpool School of Architecture, 1904–1933,* Liverpool, 1996.

Crouch, Christopher, *Design culture in Liverpool 1888–1914: The origins of the Liverpool School of Architecture,* Liverpool, 2002.

Reilly, Charles, *Scaffolding in the sky: A semi-architectural autobiography,* London, 1938.

Hair, Paul E.H. (Ed.), *Arts, letters, society: A miscellany commemorating the centenary of the Faculty of Arts at the University of Liverpool,* Liverpool, 1996.

Morris, Colin, *A history of Liverpool Regional College of Art, 1825–1970,* M.Phil thesis, CNAA, Liverpool Polytechnic, 1985.

Rowlands, Peter, *Oliver Lodge and the Liverpool Physical Society,* Liverpool, 1990.

—— *120 years of excellence: The University of Liverpool Physics Department 1881 to 2001,* Liverpool, 2001.

Clough, Anne, *Ladies wore hats: A history of the University of Liverpool Women's Club,* University of Liverpool Women's Club, 2000.

Truscot, Bruce, *Redbrick University,* London, 1943.

Peers, Edgar Allison, *Redbrick University revisited: The autobiography of Bruce Truscot,* Liverpool, 1996.

Medicine

Gray, T. Cecil, *Dr Richard Formby, founder of the Liverpool Medical School,* Royal College of Physicians, London, 2003.

Gray, T. Cecil and Sheard, Sally, *A brief history of medical education in Liverpool,* Liverpool, 2001.

Power, Helen, *Tropical medicine in the twentieth century: A history of the Liverpool School of Tropical Medicine, 1898–1998,* London, 1999.

Shepherd, John A., *A history of the Liverpool Medical Institution,* Liverpool Medical Institution, 1979.

Ormerod, Henry, *The early history of the Liverpool Medical School from 1834 to 1877,* Liverpool, 1953.

Gemmell, Arthur A., *The Liverpool Medical School, 1834–1934: A brief record,* Liverpool, 1934.

The War Experience

First World War

Maddocks, Graham, *Liverpool Pals: 17th, 18th, 19th, 20th (Service) Battalions, The King's (Liverpool Regiment),* Pen & Sword Military.

Mileham, P., *Difficulties Be Damned – The King's Regiment 8th 63rd 96th, A History of the City Regiment of Manchester and Liverpool.*

Wyrall, E., *The History of the King's Regiment Liverpool 1914–19,* 3 volumes, 1935, reprinted 2002.

McCartney, Helen B., *Citizen Soldiers. The Liverpool Territorials in the First World War*, Cambridge University Press, 2005.

McGilchrist, Colonel A.M., *The Liverpool Scottish 1900–1919*.

Giblin, H., *Bravest of Hearts, The Biography of a Battalion, The Liverpool Scottish in the Great War*.

Clayton, Ann, *Chavasse: Double VC*.

Crookenden, A., *History of the Cheshire Regiment in the Great War*, Naval & Military Press, 2005.

Barr, Ronald, *The Cheshire Regiment*, Images of England, The History Press, 2003.

McGreal, Stephen, *The Cheshire Bantams: 15th, 16th and 17th Battalions of the Cheshire Regiment*, Pen & Sword Military, 2007.

—— *Moreton & Districts Patriots 1914–1919*, Countyvise, 1999.

Fowler, S., *Army Service Records of the First World War*, TNA, 1998.

Spencer, William, *Records of Service of the First World War*, TNA, 2000.
'Soldiers Died in the Great War 1914–19 Part 13 The King's (Liverpool Regiment)', HMSO, 1920.

Second World War

Boyce, Joan, *Pillowslips and gasmasks: Liverpool's Wartime Evacuation*, Liver Press, 1989.

Wallis, Jill, *A Welcome in the Hillsides? The Merseyside and North Wales Experience of Evacuation 1939–1945*, 2000.

Whittington-Egan, Richard, *The Great Liverpool Blitz*, The Gallery Press, 1987.

Hughes, John, *Port in a Storm – The air attacks on Liverpool and its shipping in the Second World War*, National Museums and Galleries on Merseyside, 1993.

Whitworth, Rodney, *Merseyside at War – A day-to-day diary of the 1940–41 Bombing*, Scouse Press, 1988.

Wade, Beryl, *Storm over the Mersey*, 1990.

Liverpool Daily Post & Echo, *Bombers Over Merseyside*, 1943.

Spiegl, Fritz (Ed.), *Bombers Over Merseyside: The Authoritative Record of the Blitz, 1940-1941*, Scouse Press, 1984.

Johnson, Arthur, *Merseyside's secret Blitz diary: A remarkable personal account of Liverpool at war*, Liverpool, 2005.

Ayers, Pat, *Liverpool Docklands*, Liver Press, 1999.

Collard, Ian, *Mersey Ports: Liverpool and Birkenhead*, Tempus Publishing, 2001.

Dunn, C.L. (Ed.), 'The Emergency Medical Services Vol II' from the series *A History of the Second World War – United Kingdom Medical Series*, 1953.

Kemp, Paul, *Liverpool and the Battle of the Atlantic 1939–1945*, 1993.

Horton, Max, *Liverpool and the Western Approaches*, 1954.

Mersey Docks and Harbour Board, *Port at War: The Story of the Port of Liverpool, its ordeals and achievements during the World War 1939–1945,* 1946.

Marsh, B.J. and Almond, S., *The Home Port: Bootle, the Blitz and the Battle of the Atlantic,* 1993.

Battle of the Atlantic: An anthology of personal memories from those involved with the Battle of the Atlantic, Birkenhead, 1993.

The battle of the Atlantic: The official account of the fight against the U-boats 1939–1945, London, 1946. (Also British coaster, 1939–1945: The official story, London, 1947.)

Liverpool Record Office, *Liverpool at war, 1939–45,* 2002.

INDEX